ADA Corporate Logos

1960–1963

▼ The logo for use on ADA publications and stationery was first adopted in 1947 and first revised in 1951. The design has since gone through many revisions.

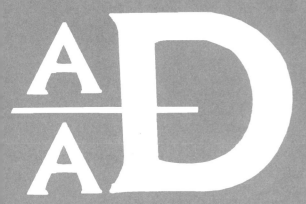

1964–1965

▲ Most of the early logos used lower case letters.

1966–1981

▶ This cursive lower case logo was incorporated into the design of the revolving door handles at the front entrance of the ADA Headquarters building in Chicago.

1982–2008

▲ This logo marks the adoption of the color green by the ADA for promotional purposes. Green was chosen because it engendered feelings of healthiness, freshness, and trust.

2009–

▶ Current logo. The logo was revised as part of a major corporate branding initiative. It uses both the letters and the name in the design.

ADA American Dental Association®

Great-West
LIFE & ANNUITY INSURANCE COMPANY

The American Dental Association gratefully
acknowledges the support of the Great-West Life
& Annuity Insurance Company, which underwrote
the production costs of this book. The gift from
Great-West was in commemoration not only of the
ADA's sesquicentennial year, but in recognition of
the seventy-five-year association between Great
West and the ADA. Great West began designing
insurance products to meet the unique needs of
ADA members in 1934.

Thanks to the generosity of Great-West, the ADA
is able to direct the proceeds from this volume to
support charitable programs of the ADA Foundation.

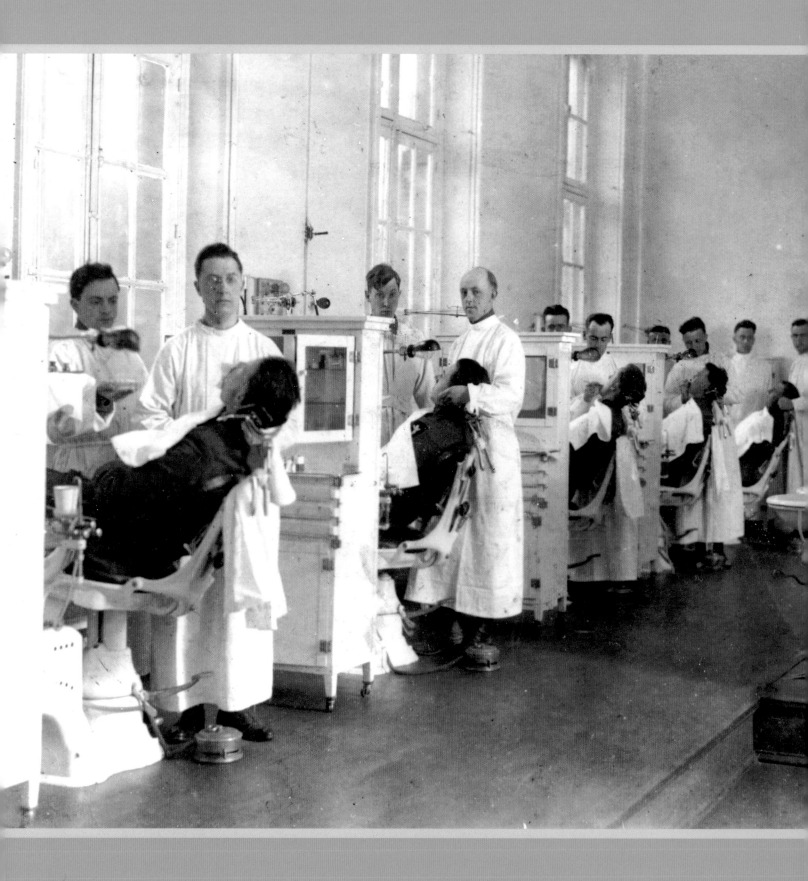

150 YEARS OF THE
American Dental Association
A PICTORIAL HISTORY, 1859–2009

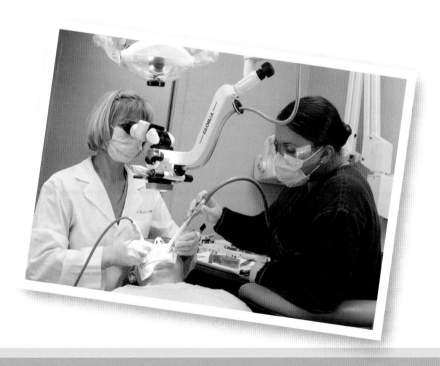

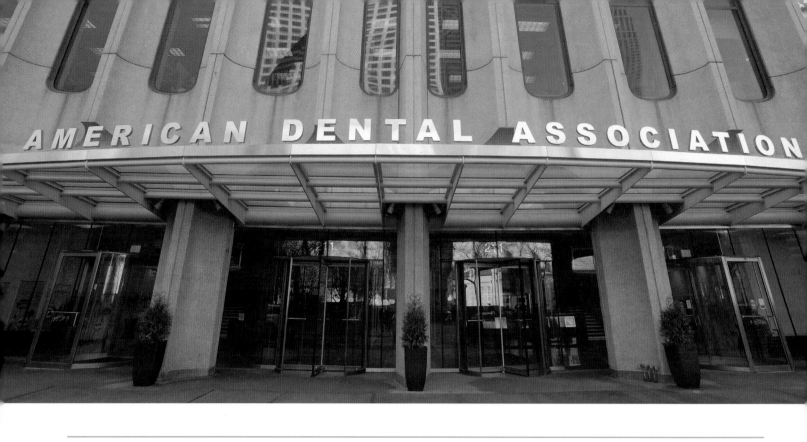

American Dental Association
211 East Chicago Avenue
Chicago, IL 60611-2678

Published by:
The Donning Company Publishers
184 Business Park Drive, Suite 206
Virginia Beach, VA 23462

Steve Mull, General Manager
Barbara Buchanan, Office Manager
Anne Cordray, Editor
Tonya Hannink, Graphic Designer
Derek Eley, Imaging Artist
Debby Dowell, Project Research Coordinator
Tonya Hannink, Marketing Specialist
Pamela Engelhard, Marketing Advisor

G. Bradley Martin, Project Director
Bill Beck, Author of Text, Lakeside Writer's Group

Library of Congress Cataloging-in-Publication Data

150 years of the American Dental Association : a pictorial history,
1859-2009.
    p. ; cm.
  Includes index.
  ISBN 978-1-57864-592-3
  1. American Dental Association--History. 2. Dentistry--United
States--History. I. American Dental Association. II. Title: One hundred
fifty years of the American Dental Association.
  [DNLM: 1. National Dental Association (1897-1922) 2. American Dental
Association. 3. Societies, Dental--history--United States. 4. History of
Dentistry--United States. 5. History, 19th Century--United States. 6.
History, 20th Century--United States. 7. History, 21st Century--United
States. WU 1 Z9 2009]
  RK34.U6A14 2009
  617.6006'073--dc22
                              2009037809

Printed in the United States of America at Walsworth Publishing Company

Table of Contents

Foreword

Few are the times that we as individuals have the opportunity to witness an event of historical significance; rarer still, when we realize in our own lifetime that we have played even a small part in an event that is of historical significance! Yet, most who will open this volume have had a very personal experience and even a significant part in what is chronicled within these pages: the birth and the evolution of a professional association; the establishment and the raison d'être of an organization dedicated and committed to caring for people. This is the story of the first century and a half of the American Dental Association.

The ADA had its beginning some eighty-three years after the Declaration of Independence, two years before the War Between the States, and one year before the Lincoln-Douglas debates; at a time when most people had lost all or most of their teeth by age forty, and life expectancy was only a few short years beyond that!

Since those early days of the ADA and the profession of dentistry, we have grown, prospered, and achieved remarkable heights in our efforts to provide care. With every advance in dental science, there has been a corresponding increase in the quality and availability of dental care. For the last 150 years, the Association and the profession have remained viable and relevant because we were founded on science, sustained by values, and justified by our works. Our Association's activities were and are predicated on the same values that placed service and care, the well-being of others, as our highest concerns.

As we celebrate this year, recognizing the heritage and significance of our past, let us make more important and more significant the path that lies ahead. Dentistry in the United States, and indeed this Association that represents the values of a great profession, stands to be more significant and more relevant to quality of life than our founding fathers could have ever imagined. We are poised to lead patient care in an environment that has proven: Dentistry is Health Care that Works!

John S. Findley, DDS
ADA President, 2008–2009

Acknowledgments

The American Dental Association would like to thank the members of the ADA Sesquicentennial Planning Committee and the Book Subcommittee for their work and dedication to make this 150th anniversary year a successful and memorable event.

The ADA Sesquicentennial Planning Committee

Dr. Walter Lamacki, Committee Chair; former ADA Trustee, Eighth District; Editor, *CDS Review* (Chicago Dental Society)

Dr. Jack Conley, former Editor, *Journal of the California Dental Association;* retired Associate Professor, University of Southern California School of Dentistry

Dr. Jack Gottschalk, Chair, Collections and Exhibitions Committee, Dr. Samuel D. Harris National Museum of Dentistry; Former President, American Academy of the History of Dentistry

Dr. Brandon Maddox, Chair, ADA Committee on the New Dentist

Ms. Martha Philips, Executive Director, Georgia Dental Association

Dr. Jeanne C. Sinkford, Associate Executive Director, American Dental Education Association; Dean Emeritus, Howard University College of Dentistry

Dr. Murray D. Sykes, Board of Trustees Liaison; ADA Trustee, Fourth District

ADA staff Committee members:

Barkley Payne, Executive Director, ADA Foundation

Michelle Kruse, Coordinator, Board and House Matters

Sesquicentennial Book Subcommittee
Dr. Lamacki
Dr. Conley
Dr. Gottschalk
Dr. Sinkford

Consultants to the Book Subcommittee:

Dr. Clifton Dummett, Distinguished Professor Emeritus, University of Southern California School of Dentistry; Author, *The Hillenbrand Era: Organized Dentistry's Glanzperiode* (1986).

Dr. Malvin Ring, Author, *Dentistry: An Illustrated History* (1985); Editor Emeritus, *Journal of the History of Dentistry*

ADA staff members of the Book Subcommittee:

Mary Kreinbring, Director, Department of Library Services

Andrea Matlak, Archivist/Reference Librarian, Department of Library Services

◄ Six members of the Sesquicentennial Committee pose at the June 2009 ADA Sesquicentennial Celebration (from left): Dr. Jack Conley; Dr. Brandon Maddox; Ms. Martha Philips; Dr. Walter Lamacki, committee chair; Dr. Jack Gottschalk; and Dr. Malvin Ring, committee consultant. Not pictured are Dr. Jeanne C. Sinkford, committee member; Dr. Clifton Dummett, committee consultant; and Dr. Murray D. Sykes, Board of Trustees liaison.

ADA Officers and Trustees 2008–2009

Charles L. Steffel
Seventh District

Dennis E. Manning
Eighth District

Raymond F. Gist
Ninth District

Edward J. Vigna
Tenth District

Mary Krempasky Smith
Eleventh District

R. Wayne Thompson
Twelfth District

Russell I. Webb
Thirteenth District

Kenneth J. Versman
Fourteenth District

S. Jerry Long
Fifteenth District

Charles H. Norman
Sixteenth District

Samuel B. Low
Seventeenth District

Kathleen T. O'Loughlin
Executive Director/Chief Operating Officer
Secretary of the House of Delegates

9

111th Congress

1st Session

H. RES. 204

In the House of Representatives
May 13, 2009

RESOLUTION

Whereas access to good oral health care is a vital element of overall health;

Whereas the American Dental Association works to improve access to oral health care services that are essential to help ensure the health of the American public;

Whereas the American Dental Association supports community prevention initiatives and promotion of good oral hygiene;

Whereas the American Dental Association continually works to improve dental technologies and therapies through research and adherence to sound scientific principles;

Whereas 'The Journal of the American Dental Association' is recognized internationally as a leader in peer-reviewed dental science;

Whereas the American Dental Association encourages its membership of more than 157,000 dentists to donate their time, resources, and services to providing charitable and uncompensated care;

Whereas dental practices provide over $2,000,000,000 in charitable and uncompensated care to specific underserved populations annually; and

Whereas the American Dental Association advocates sufficient funding for Federal dental research and military readiness programs: Now, therefore, be it

Resolved, That the House of Representatives—

(1) congratulates the American Dental Association for its 150th anniversary;

(2) commends the American Dental Association's work to improve the public's oral health as well as access to oral health care for all Americans, especially low-income children;

(3) recognizes the tens of thousands of dentists who volunteer their time and resources to provide charitable and uncompensated oral health care to millions of Americans; and

(4) commends the American Dental Association's efforts to keep American dentistry the best in the world.

The object of this Association shall be to encourage the improvement of the health of the public and to promote the art and science of dentistry.

ADA Constitution, Article II

Chapter One
Foundation and Formation, 1859–1909

When twenty-six dentists met in Niagara Falls, New York, on August 3 and 4, 1859, to form the American Dental Association, dentistry was already a profession with deep roots in the American Republic. The dentists who met that long-ago August at the resort community on the Niagara River were members of the existing national dental association—the American Dental Convention, founded in 1855—who were dissatisfied with the organization and how it managed its meetings. These dentists sought to form an association made up of representatives of all of the nation's dental organizations and based on high professional standards.

America was between eras in 1859. The young nation was searching for its own identity while moving away from its connections with Europe and moving toward industrialization and expansion. Dentistry was also moving away from its European identity while being embraced by those who came to this country searching for a better life. The twenty-six dentists who founded the ADA, born and educated in America, wanted to give dentistry a status that it was never able to obtain in Europe and to establish it as a learned profession based on high educational and scientific standards. Previous generations of dentists, who were born and educated in Europe and later immigrated to the American colonies, helped propel dentistry into the light and away from its sometimes dark past.

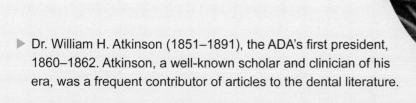

▶ Dr. William H. Atkinson (1851–1891), the ADA's first president, 1860–1862. Atkinson, a well-known scholar and clinician of his era, was a frequent contributor of articles to the dental literature.

Founding of the
American Dental Association

The American Dental Association was founded on August 3, 1859, in Niagara Falls, New York, by twenty-six dentists who were members of the American Dental Convention (ADC), the only national organization of dentists in America at the time. A number of the attendees were also former members of the American Society of Dental Surgeons, the world's first national dental association, which existed from 1840 to 1856.

The group of twenty-six dentists, dissatisfied with how the American Dental Convention managed its annual meetings, came together during the ADC's fifth meeting to start a national dental organization of their own, an association representing all of the country's dental organizations, dedicated to promoting the highest professional standards and scientific research.

The group represented eight dental societies and two dental colleges. Most were from Pennsylvania and Ohio, but some hailed from Indiana, Kentucky, Missouri, and Wisconsin. The attendees appointed a committee to draft a constitution for what was to become the ADA and agreed to meet in late July of the following year in Washington, D.C. They appointed a chair (Dr. Walter W. Allport) and someone to manage arrangements for the next meeting.

▲ Lithograph of the first meeting site of the American Dental Association: International Hotel, Niagara Falls, circa 1859. The building was destroyed by fire in 1918. *(Photo courtesy of the Buffalo Historical Society)*

The ADA's first president, Dr. W. H. Atkinson, was elected at the second meeting of the ADA, held in 1860 in Washington, D.C., from July 31 to August 2. Dr. Atkinson presided as president at the following meeting, which did not take place until 1862 because of the outbreak of the American Civil War.

These were the twenty-six dentists who attended the organizational meeting and are considered the founders of the ADA:

Walter W. Allport (Chicago, IL)

George T. Barker (Philadelphia, PA)

Thomas L. Buckingham (Philadelphia, PA)

William Calvert (Philadelphia, PA)

J. G. Cameron (Cincinnati, OH)

Isaiah Forbes (St. Louis, MO)

S. L. Hamlin (Cincinnati, OH)

Phineas G. C. Hunt (Indianapolis, IN)

Charles H. James (Cincinnati, OH)

John F. Johnston (Indianapolis, IN)

George W. Keely (Oxford, OH)

H. McCullum (Augusta, KY)

Henry J. McKellops (St. Louis, MO)

John H. McQuillen (Philadelphia, PA)

A. M. Moore (Lafayette, IN)

D. W. Perkins (Milwaukee, WI)

Joseph Richardson (Cincinnati, OH)

Henry A. Smith (Cincinnati, OH)

Jacob L. Suesserott (Chambersburg, PA)

Jonathan Taft (Cincinnati, OH)

Edward Taylor (Cincinnati, OH)

James Taylor (Cincinnati, OH)

John T. Toland (Cincinnati, OH)

Robert Vandervort (Pittsburgh, PA)

George Watt (Xenia, OH)

William M. Wright (Pittsburgh, PA)

Dr. Walter W. Allport (1824–1893), chair of the ADA's first meeting August 3, 1859. Allport maintained a successful practice in Chicago and is credited with inventing the tooth chart for keeping records of procedures.

Dr. Allport's chart was printed in large ledgers that were sold to dentists by the S. S. White Dental Manufacturing Company. Shown is a page of one of the ledgers Allport used in his own practice.

DENTISTRY IN COLONIAL AMERICA TO 1800

When America was first being colonized in the seventeenth century, dentistry had been known and practiced for centuries but had not progressed much in its ability to diagnose and treat problem teeth. Residents of the American colonies in the seventeenth and eighteenth centuries had an average life span of about thirty-five years. Most Americans had lost their teeth by their early twenties. Clove, mustard, cinnamon, and horseradish were the typical home remedies for toothache. In Colonial America, as was common in Europe during this era, so-called barber-surgeons took care of simple hygienic needs, which traditionally included bloodletting and tooth extraction. Bloodletting was considered a cure-all for many illnesses, and tooth extractions were performed with primitive instruments such as the toothkey, which resembled a hook with a handle.

Early dentists, like their American patients, were European immigrants. The first educated dentists came from Great Britain and began to arrive in the American colonies in the second half of the eighteenth century. The first trained and educated dentist known to arrive was Robert Woofendale, who advertised in a 1766 New York newspaper that he

ISAAC GREENWOOD,
DENTIST,

ACQUAINTS the publick, that he has REMOVED from Nᵒ. 49 to Nᵒ. 19, Marlborough Street, opposite Meſſrs. Amorys' Store, where he continues to perform the neceſſary branches of that art, carefully and faithfully. Removing every ſubſtance tending to deſtroy the Teeth and Gums. Cures the Scurvy in the Gums, makes the Teeth white, &c. Sells BRUSHES that are ſuitable for the Teeth, with a POWDER that never fails to recommend itſelf, at 1/4 per box. Fixes NATURAL TEETH on plates of gold or ſilver, with gold ſprings, if wanted. Alſo, ſubſtitutes ARTIFICIAL TEETH, of different ſubſtances, from 2ſ. to 6ſ. each—that give a youthful air to the countenance, and render pronunciation more agreeable and diſtinct—In a word, both natural and artificial are of ſuch real ſervice, as are worthy the attention of every one. He with pleaſure attends on thoſe who may incline to employ him, provided they cannot conveniently attend on him, at his HOUSE, where he has every accommodation neceſſary for their reception.

At the ſame place may be had;

Oil, Silk, and Ladies' UMBRELLAS, cheap. Old Umbrellas repaired, oiled, newly covered, &c. Oil Silk CAPS for bathing, German Flutes, Fifes, Violins, and Strings for ditto, Reeds for hautboys, Men, Boxes and Dice for back-gammon, Chesmen, Billiard Balls, Ivory Combs, variety of Canes, by wholeſale and retail, Catt Strings, Whips, electrical Machines with apparatus for experiments and medical uſe—artificial Magnets, &c. &c. &c.

N. B. Said GREENWOOD offers his ſervice electeriſe thoſe who ſtand in need of that almost univerſal remedy, at 1/6 each time, at his Hou ☞ *Adviſe with your phyſicians.* MAY 3, 1

◀ Advertisement placed in *The Massachusetts Centinel* of May 3, 1788, by Isaac Greenwood. He sold tooth powders and brushes and fixed natural teeth on plates of gold or silver with gold springs. Greenwood also ran a mercantile shop with his dental practice where he sold such sundries as ladies' umbrellas, dice, and billiard balls.

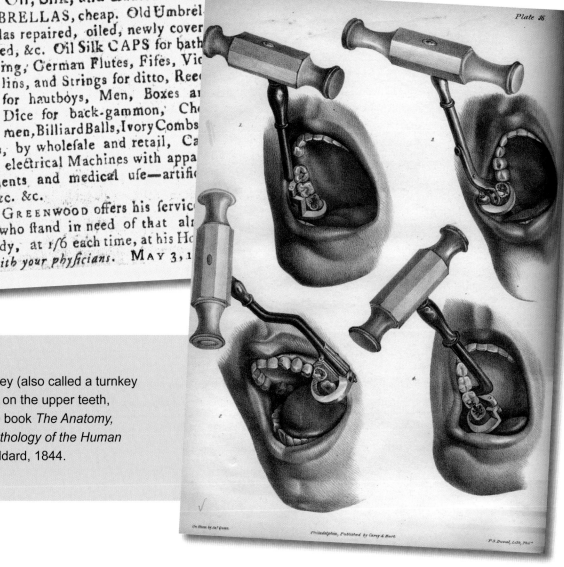

▶ Dental extracting key (also called a turnkey or toothkey) in use on the upper teeth, as illustrated in the book *The Anatomy, Physiology and Pathology of the Human Teeth*, Paul B. Goddard, 1844.

Dentures worn by George Washington, made by John Greenwood. The first U.S. president was plagued by bad teeth throughout his life and at least nine different dentists made dentures for him. Greenwood, one of his favorite dentists, made him four sets of teeth, including the set with which Washington was buried. The dentures used carved hippopotamus or elephant ivory for the teeth, gold and other metals for the base, and gold springs to hold the upper and lower teeth together.

performed "all operations on the teeth, sockets, gums and palate" as well as denture repair.

The great patriot Paul Revere, who made his living as a silversmith, also made false teeth of gold and silver for wealthy Bostonians. Revere became a pioneer of forensic dentistry when he identified the body of Dr. Joseph Warren, a local physician killed in combat at Bunker Hill, from a partial denture that he had made for Warren.

Two of Revere's contemporaries, John Baker of Philadelphia and Isaac Greenwood of Boston, were among the best-known colonial American dentists.

The first chair adapted for use in dental care. Prominent nineteenth-century dentist Josiah Flagg, Jr., attached a headrest to a common Windsor chair.

Baker, who set up practice here in 1760, was the earliest medically trained dentist to practice in America. Greenwood was the first native-born American dentist, and both of his sons became dentists. One of his sons, John Greenwood, counted George Washington among his patients.

Josiah Flagg, Jr., one of the most prominent early American dentists, is remembered as the first to use a dental chair, an ordinary Windsor chair that he adapted for dentistry by attaching a headrest.

DENTISTRY IN THE EARLY NINETEENTH CENTURY

The first half of the nineteenth century was a time of great advancement in American dentistry. In 1800, there were fewer than one hundred dentists practicing in the United States. Less than sixty years later, when delegates gathered at Niagara Falls for the inaugural meeting of the ADA, dentistry had become

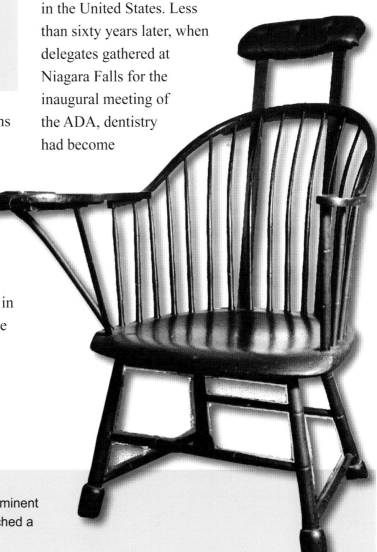

Lucy Hobbs Taylor
and Other Early Women Dentists

▲ Dr. Lucy Hobbs Taylor (1833–1910), the first woman to receive a dental degree.

Lucy Hobbs Taylor was the first woman in the world to receive a dental degree. In 1859, twenty-six-year-old Lucy Hobbs, after studying with a Michigan physician, moved to Cincinnati to enroll in medical school. When she was denied entry in the medical school on the basis of her sex, she was advised that she might try enrolling in a dental school.

In preparation for this, she apprenticed in dentistry with a sympathetic Cincinnati dentist, Dr. Sam Wardle, for two years. Then in 1861, she applied to the Ohio College of Dental Surgery and was denied entry, once again solely on the basis of her sex. That same year she started a practice in Cincinnati, but soon moved to Iowa, where she practiced dentistry during the Civil War.

In 1865, she was the first woman to become a member of a state dental organization when she was admitted to the Iowa State Dental Society (ISDS). Later that year, she accompanied the ISDS delegation to the ADA's Annual Session in Chicago. While there, the Iowa dentists lobbied the representatives of the various dental colleges for her admission as a student under the threat of withdrawing the support of the ISDS. Now with the backing of the school's dean, Dr. Jonathan Taft, Hobbs was admitted to the Ohio College of Dental Surgery. She closed her Iowa practice and entered the dental school in Cincinnati in November 1865. The school granted her a DDS in 1866, making her the first woman in the world to be awarded a dental degree.

In 1867, Dr. Hobbs moved to Chicago, where she met and married James M. Taylor. She convinced her husband to become a dentist, and he apprenticed with her. The couple moved to Lawrence, Kansas, at the end of 1867 where they practiced jointly until James's death in 1886. Afterwards she continued to practice dentistry part-time and was a woman's rights activist until her death in 1910.

There were other nineteenth-century pioneering women dentists, including Dr. Emmeline Roberts Jones, the first woman known to own and operate a dental practice in America (in 1859 in Connecticut); Dr. Henriette Hirschfeld Tiburtius, the second woman to receive a dental degree (in 1869 from the Pennsylvania College of Dental Surgery) and the first woman to open a dental practice in Germany; and Dr. Marie Grubert, the first woman to be elected an officer of a dental society (elected vice president of the Mississippi Valley Dental Society in 1872). By the turn of the twentieth century, there were more than one thousand women dentists. Today, women represent nearly half the dental students in some U.S. dental schools, and surveys predict that as many as 20 percent of U.S. dentists will be women by the year 2020.

In 1884, Dr. Lucy Hobbs Taylor marveled that people just twenty years before "were amazed when they learned that a young girl had so forgotten her womanhood as to want to study dentistry."

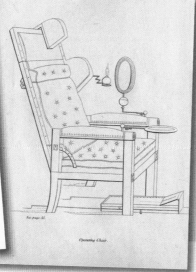

◀ The first substantive book on dentistry published in the United States, *A Treatise on the Management of the Teeth* by Benjamin James, was issued in 1814. The illustration on the title page, showing a person suffering from a toothache, is the first illustration of a dental subject to appear in an American book.

◀ The book *A Practical Guide to Operations on the Teeth* by James Snell, first published in 1832, features the earliest description and illustration of a fully functional dental chair. Snell is credited with inventing the first reclining dental chair, which he used in his practice. The chair also had an attached lamp and mirror.

a more respected profession, with its own dental college, dental journals, and a growing scientific body of knowledge.

In 1840, Drs. Solyman Brown, Chapin A. Harris, Horace A. Hayden, and Eleazar Parmly opened the Baltimore College of Dental Surgery, the world's first dental college. Harris was also the founding editor of the world's first dental journal, *The American Journal of Dental Science*, which began publication in 1839. Between 1840 and the end of the 1860s, a dozen new dental schools were founded, giving the profession educational respectability.

The world's first national dental organization, the American Society of Dental Surgeons (ASDS), was founded in 1840. The Society quickly became embroiled in a debate, known as the "amalgam war," over the use of silver amalgam as a filling material. The dispute, which pitted rank-and-file dentists against organized dentistry, would consume the profession for half a century.

The controversy began in 1833 with the arrival from France of a couple of charlatans known as the Crawcour

▶ Dr. Chapin A. Harris (1806–1860), the founding editor of *The American Journal of Dental Science*, the world's first dental journal, and co-founder of the Baltimore College of Dental Surgery, the world's first dental school. Harris published a well-known nineteenth-century textbook of operatory dentistry, which was widely used by most dental schools and practicing dentists. *(ADA file photo by Ashman)*

THE

AMERICAN JOURNAL

OF

DENTAL SCIENCE,

DEVOTED TO

ORIGINAL ARTICLES,

REVIEWS OF DENTAL PUBLICATIONS;

THE LATEST IMPROVEMENTS IN

SURGICAL AND MECHANICAL DENTISTRY,

AND BIOGRAPHICAL SKETCHES OF DISTINGUISHED

DENTISTS.

WITH PLATES.

NEW-YORK,

1839.

brothers. The brothers advertised their services as dentists and claimed that they had invented a new material for filling teeth, which they called Royal Mineral Succedaneum. The new material was an amalgam made of nothing but shavings from silver coins mixed with mercury to form a paste. Since the brothers were not educated as dentists, they did not have the expertise for filling cavities properly. They did not first remove the decay and did not insert the filling material correctly. Their patients often ended up with sore gums and toothaches and were soon seeking out competent dentists to relieve their pain. The Crawcours were quickly identified as hucksters; as the market for their services dried up, they left the scene.

Meanwhile some dentists began to experiment with the new material and realized that if it was mixed and inserted properly, it offered a viable and inexpensive filling material for the many who could not afford gold. Other dentists believed that the Crawcour brothers' misuse of amalgam proved that it was unsuitable as a filling material and should be banned outright. The ASDS took a strong stance against amalgam and began a campaign to label any dentist who used it as unethical. Anyone who joined the organization had to sign an oath decrying amalgam users as unethical, which many dentists would not sign. With its membership dwindling, the organization fell apart and ceased operations in 1850. By then, amalgam was already widely used. Its mixture was continually improved in the following years, so by the end of the nineteenth century it had become the filling material of choice for many dentists.

Drs. Horace Wells (1815–1848) (left) and William T. G. Morton (1819–1868) (right) remain at the center of the continuing debate concerning the discovery of anesthesia. In 1845, Wells performed a public tooth extraction using nitrous oxide, but observers considered it a failure. In 1846, Morton, an apprentice of Wells, conducted a successful public demonstration of ether as an anesthetic for surgery. Dr. Morton would take full credit for the discovery of anesthesia, going as far as repeatedly petitioning the U.S. Congress, without success, to officially recognize him as its true discoverer. Dr. Wells was so broken by Morton's repudiation of his role in the discovery that he eventually committed suicide in 1848.

The Collapsible Metal Tube
and the Rise of Commercial Toothpaste

In the mid-nineteenth century, Americans who wanted to clean their teeth each day used either tooth powder packed in tins and dissolved in water, or a thick paste that came in porcelain jars in which the toothbrush was dipped. These powders and pastes were often prepared by individual dentists who provided them directly to their patients. Either way, the concoctions were costly, messy, and easily contaminated.

Without the invention of the collapsible metal tube in 1841, the tube of toothpaste would not have become the bathroom staple that we know today. The metal tube was originally designed to hold artists' paints. Most of the early tubes were made in France and England. It was not until 1870 that an American manufacturer first used them for cosmetic preparations.

Dr. Washington Wentworth Sheffield, a dentist from New London, Connecticut, introduced what he called Crème Dentifrice, a creamier paste than what was standard for the period, which he packaged in metal tubes starting in the 1890s. The collapsible tube made it much easier to mass produce, package, and distribute toothpaste. It was a commercial hit and was quickly imitated by others. Within twenty years, toothpaste brands such as Pepsodent®, Ipana®, and Colgate® had become household names in America.

▶ A bookmark (front and back) advertising Sheffield's Crème Dentifrice claims that its tube is the "most convenient package on the market." Dental manufacturers distributed cards like these to dentists as advertisements for a variety of dental products.

It was also during this era that two U.S. dentists played a major role in introducing surgical anesthesia to the world. In 1845, Dr. Horace Wells, a Connecticut dentist, conducted the first public demonstration of the use of nitrous oxide as an anesthetic. The demonstration was largely considered a failure because the patient stirred and moaned during the operation (an effect later identified as typical of anesthesia). In 1846, Dr. William T. G. Morton, a former apprentice of Wells, took credit for the discovery when he conducted the first successful public demonstration of ether as an anesthetic for surgery. The patient remained quiet during the operation and those who gathered to watch the demonstration at Boston's Massachusetts General Hospital, many of whom were prominent

▶ Dr. Samuel S. White (1822–1880), founder of the S. S. White Dental Manufacturing Company, the leading dental supply company of the nineteenth century. A practicing dentist, he started the company to sell porcelain teeth after discovering a superior method for their manufacture. White soon abandoned his practice to manage the company as it quickly expanded its inventory of dental products to meet the demands of a growing profession.

surgeons, were so impressed that the use of anesthesia was quickly embraced by the dental and medical professions.

In Philadelphia, Dr. Samuel S. White founded the S. S. White Dental Manufacturing Company in 1844 to help develop equipment, instruments, and materials for dentistry. It soon became the premier dental manufacturer and supply company of the nineteenth century and remained so well into the twentieth century. White also began publishing *The Dental Cosmos* in 1859, which would become one of the most influential dental journals of the late nineteenth and early twentieth centuries.

DENTISTRY DURING THE CIVIL WAR

Twenty-three dentists gathered for the second meeting of the ADA at the Smithsonian Institution Building in Washington, D.C., in July 1860. The delegates adopted the ADA's first constitution and established a series of standing committees to investigate

▶ Dental mirrors advertised in the 1867 S. S. White's Dental Catalogue. The company grew to become the world's largest manufacturer of dental instruments, materials, and equipment by the end of the nineteenth century and remained in business well into the twentieth century.

dental science, physiology, chemistry, pathology, and surgery, as well as mechanical dentistry. They engaged in a spirited discussion about the state of dental education in the United States, which resulted in the creation of a committee on dental education, one of the Association's first working committees. The delegates also created a committee to review dental improvements and inventions and established a committee on prize essays to award two $50 prizes each year for the best essays in dentistry.

The outbreak of the Civil War in the spring of 1861 scuttled plans for the ADA's third Annual Session. Less than ten days before the scheduled opening of the meeting, Union forces suffered a devastating loss to the Confederate States Army (CS Army) at the First Battle of Bull Run, west of the nation's capital.

Dentistry in the armies of the Civil War was more of an afterthought than a profession. The Union Army did not establish a formal dental corps until after the war was over. Nevertheless, recruits were rejected for having bad or no teeth, because a soldier in combat had to be able to tear open with his teeth a paper wrapper containing ball, powder, and wadding for his muzzle-loading rifle.

Surgeons were attached to both armies during the war. Army surgeons typically extracted teeth and lanced boils on the gums of patients. Soldiers in need of having cavities treated, teeth extracted, or rudimentary oral surgery typically went to see a civilian dentist, either in a fixed base camp or in a large occupied community such as Chattanooga or Atlanta.

The CS Army was probably more progressive in its treatment of dentists and dentistry than was the Union Army. When the war broke out, there were only about one thousand dentists in the southern

▲ The Smithsonian Institution, Washington, D.C., site of the ADA's second Annual Session, in July 1860. At this meeting the ADA's first officers were elected, a constitution and by-laws were adopted, and the following scientific papers were read: *The Claims of Dentistry Upon Dentists, Extraction of Teeth, The Demands of the Age Upon Dental Science*, and *The Buccal Secretions. (Photo courtesy of the Smithsonian Institution)*

states, and only 10 percent had received a formal dental education. The CS Army conscripted dentists, who were assigned to base hospitals where they were called upon to perform oral surgery, a near necessity at a time when face and jaw wounds were among the most common wounds suffered by soldiers on the battlefield.

Military dentistry was the topic of the 1864 meeting of the ADA at Niagara Falls. Dr. Samuel S. White

Foundation and Formation
1839–1909

1839
The world's first dental journal, *The American Journal of Dental Science*, begins publication.

1840
Drs. Solyman Brown, Chapin Harris, Horace Hayden, and Eleazar Parmly open the world's first dental school, the Baltimore College of Dental Surgery. The school merged with the University of Maryland in 1923.

1845
Dr. Horace Wells, a Connecticut dentist, conducts the first public demonstration of the use of nitrous oxide as an anesthetic.

1846
Dr. William Morton, a Massachusetts dentist who studied under Dr. Horace Wells, takes credit for the discovery of anesthesia when he conducts the first successful public demonstration of the use of ether as an anesthetic.

1859
Twenty-six U.S. dentists meet in Niagara Falls to found the American Dental Association.

The S. S. White Dental Manufacturing Company begins publishing *The Dental Cosmos*, one of the most influential dental journals of the late nineteenth and early twentieth centuries.

1864
Dr. Sanford C. Barnum invents the rubber dam.

1866
The ADA adopts its first code of ethics.

1867
Harvard University Dental School, the first university-affiliated dental school, is founded.

1871
Dr. James B. Morrison patents the first commercially manufactured foot-treadle dental engine, which mechanizes the drilling of teeth.

1877
Dr. Basil M. Wilkerson introduces the Wilkerson Chair, the first pump-type hydraulic dental chair.

▲ Dr. Horace Hayden (1769–1844), co-founder of the world's first dental school.

▶ Dr. Sanford C. Barnum (1838–1885), inventor of the rubber dam, a simple device made of a piece of elastic rubber fitted over a tooth by means of weights. This solved the problem of isolating a tooth from the oral cavity, but Barnum never sought any profit from the invention.

1896

Dr. C. Edmond Kells is the first U.S. dentist to use X-rays in the practice of dentistry.

1903

Dr. Charles Land introduces the porcelain jacket crown.

1906

Dentists nationwide donate $15,000 to aid colleagues whose offices are destroyed in the 1906 San Francisco Earthquake.

1887

The Stowe & Eddy Dental Laboratory, the first successful commercial dental laboratory in the United States, opens for business in Boston.

1882

The American Dental Trade Association is founded.

1909

The ADA publishes its first patient dental education pamphlet, which recommends brushing teeth at least twice daily, flossing regularly, and twice-a-year dental visits.

1899

Dr. Edward Hartley Angle establishes the first specialty school, the Angle School of Orthodontia, in St. Louis.

1884

The National Association of Dental Faculties recommends a two-year curriculum for dental students.

1893

Dr. Greene Vardiman Black introduces a system of dental nomenclature.

1905

German chemist Alfred Einhorn introduces the anesthetic procaine, which is later marketed in the United States as Novocain.

1907

The ADA Relief Fund is established with unused funds collected for relief of dentists in the 1906 San Francisco Earthquake to assist all dentists in need due to natural or man-made disaster.

The American Orthodontist, the first specialty dental journal in the U.S., begins publishing.

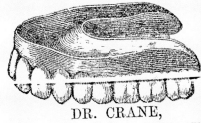

DR. CRANE,
SURGEON DENTIST,
WILL EXTRACT TEETH BY THE USE OF
CHLOROFORM!
BY the application of the Chloroform, (from which no injury results,) the system is put in such a state that teeth may be REMOVED WITHOUT THE LEAST
PAIN OR RISK TO THE PATIENT!
In administering it, he uses a small piece of cloth saturated with the Chloroform, or by putting a little of it upon a cambric handkerchief, just in the manner cologne is used. Five or six inspirations will produce insensibility, and a few more will put the system in such a state that any operation may be performed, by knife, cautery, or any other instrument, without causing pain.
I received the Chloroform from the manufacturers in Boston three days since, and have given it fifteen times with perfect success.
☞ A few ounces of Chloroform for sale.
Geneva, Jan. 26, 1847.

91

◄ This advertisement promoting painless dentistry with the use of anesthesia was published in a newspaper in 1847, only a year after Dr. William Morton's first successful demonstration of the use of anesthesia in surgery at Boston's Massachusetts General Hospital.

Robert Tanner Freeman
and Early African American Dentists

It is estimated that by 1840 there may have been over one hundred African Americans involved in dentistry either as apprentices or as laboratory assistants. When Dr. Robert Tanner Freeman graduated with the first class of the Harvard Dental School in 1869, he became the nation's first African American to receive a dental degree. Born in Washington, D.C., in 1846, the son of slaves who had purchased their freedom in 1830, Dr. Freeman went to work as a young man for Dr. Henry Bliss Noble, a white dentist in the District of Columbia who tutored his young charge and encouraged Freeman to follow a career in dentistry.

Freeman's career hopes were initially dashed when two dental schools rejected his application on the basis of race. However, Dr. Noble stepped in, and with the support of Dr. Nathan C. Keep, the first dean of the Harvard University School of Dental Medicine, Freeman was one of sixteen students admitted to the first class of Harvard's dental school. Dr. Keep wrote to trustees that Harvard would "know no distinction of nativity or color in admitting students."

After receiving his dental degree, Dr. Freeman returned to Washington, D.C., and practiced in the same building that had housed Dr. Noble's offices. Just four years after earning his DMD, Dr. Freeman died at the age of twenty-seven.

Dr. Robert Tanner Freeman was followed by other African American dentists. Dr. George Franklin Grant, who enrolled in the Harvard Dental School the same year as Dr. Freeman, received his dental degree in 1870. He went on to join the school's faculty, becoming the first African American faculty member at Harvard University. Dr. Ida Gray Nelson was the first African American woman to receive a dental degree (from the University of Michigan Dental School in 1890). Dr. Rufus Beshears, the first African American to graduate from the University of Iowa College of Dentistry (in 1906), has been identified as the first African American member of the American Dental Association.

Both Howard University and Meharry Medical College (schools founded to educate African Americans) opened dental schools in the 1880s. By 1885, there were about twenty-five known licensed black dentists in the United States, and by 1900, there were an estimated 125 licensed black dentists.

▲ Dr. Robert Tanner Freeman (1846–1873), the first African American to earn a dental degree.

◄ Dr. Ida Gray Nelson (1867–1953), the first female African American dental school graduate, Class of 1890, University of Michigan School of Dentistry. *(Courtesy of Sindecuse Museum of Dentistry, School of Dentistry, University of Michigan, Ann Arbor)*

Earliest known photograph of Annual Session delegates taken in 1864 at Niagara Falls, New York. During the nineteenth century, it was customary to take a group photograph of the delegates at each Annual Session.

reported that he had discussed military dentistry in a meeting with President Abraham Lincoln earlier in the year. White later spoke to the acting surgeon general, who said that nothing could be done while the armies were in active operation, but perhaps something could be accomplished when the armies went into winter quarters.

However, nothing was done until the Spanish-American War, more than thirty years later, when the sad shape of dental health of most American recruits was revealed. It was not until 1901 that President William McKinley signed legislation establishing a dental corps of thirty contract dentists within the United States Army.

The first constitution adopted at the ADA's second meeting had no restrictions on membership but this would change by the end of the 1860s. As the dental profession grew throughout the decade and more dental organizations and schools were established, it became necessary for the Association to limit the number of delegates allowed for each so that all

of them were being fairly represented. At the 1869 Annual Session in Sarasota Springs, New York, the constitution was completely revised to include restrictions on membership that would keep the number of members in the Association to a small body throughout the nineteenth and into the twentieth century.

The 1869 constitution provided for two types of members, delegates and permanent members, which ensured that the organization would be representative of the whole profession. The delegates were appointed by dental societies and dental colleges. Dental societies were allowed to send one delegate to each meeting for every five of its active members, and dental schools could send one faculty member per year as a delegate. After serving one year, delegates could become permanent members by declaring their membership prior to the annual meeting and by signing the constitution. The permanent members were considered equal with the delegates, but in fact, they controlled much of the affairs of the ADA in its formative years.

ARTICLE II.

MAINTAINING PROFESSIONAL CHARACTER.

SECTION 1. A member of the dental profession is bound to maintain its honor, and to labor earnestly to extend its sphere of usefulness. He should avoid everything in language and conduct calculated to discredit or dishonor his profession, and should ever manifest a due respect for his brethren. The young should show special respect to their seniors; the aged special encouragement to their juniors.

SECT. 2. The person and office arrangements of the dentist should indicate that he is a gentleman; and he should sustain a high-toned moral character.

SECT. 3. It is unprofessional to resort to public advertisements, cards, handbills, posters, or signs calling attention to peculiar styles of work, lowness of prices, special modes of operating, or to claim superiority over neighboring practitioners, to publish reports of cases, or certificates in the public prints, to go from house to house to solicit or perform operations, to circulate or recommend nostrums, or to perform any other similar acts.

SECT. 4. When consulted by the patient of another practitioner, the dentist should guard against inquiries or hints disparaging to the family dentist, or calculated to weaken the patient's confidence in him, and if the interests of the patient will not be endangered thereby, the case should be temporarily treated, and referred back to the family dentist.

SECT. 5. When general rules shall have been adopted by members of the profession practising in the same localities, in relation to fees, it is unprofessional and dishonorable to depart from these rules, except when variation of circumstances requires it. And it is ever to be regarded as unprofessional to warrant operations or work as an inducement to patronage.

◄ A page from the ADA's first code of ethics, adopted at the 1866 Annual Session, which remained unchanged until 1899 when it was amended to include a recommendation for consultations on difficult or protracted cases.

A "GOLDEN" ERA FOR DENTISTRY

The end of the Civil War in 1865 ushered in a golden era for dentistry in the U.S. Dentistry by the late 1860s was so well established in the United States that American dentists increasingly were in demand to treat wealthy patients abroad. Dentistry achieved a growing reputation for professionalism, thanks in part to an explosion in dental education. In the post-Civil War era, more and more dentists were graduates of the nation's growing number of dental schools. Between the end of the Civil War in 1865 and 1902, more than ninety dental colleges—most of them proprietary, i.e. privately owned and operated for profit—were founded in the United States. This same period also saw the establishment of more than fifty state and local dental organizations. Moreover, the ADA's adoption of a code of

▶ Delegates to the 1866 Annual Session in Boston stand on the steps of the Massachusetts state house. During the six-day meeting, the ADA's first code of ethics was adopted and the governor of Massachusetts addressed the delegates. Topics of the papers read and discussed at the meeting included dental hygiene, dental physiology, dental pathology and surgery, reproduction of the alveolar processes, operative dentistry, mechanical dentistry, interglobular spaces in dentin, dental education, dentifrice formulations, dental literature, appliances for cleft palate, and amputation of exposed pulps. A hot issue at the meeting was the Goodyear Dental Vulcanite Company's vigorous pursuit of licensing fees on rubber used in dentistry; many dentists considered it unjust. Entertainment at the meeting included an organ concert and a steamboat excursion around Boston Harbor. *(Photo courtesy of the National Library of Medicine)*

Dr. James Beall Morrison invented the foot-treadle dental engine in 1871. Foot power transmitted to a movable arm through a belt and pulley activated a handpiece. This simple device revolutionized restorative dentistry; it made drilling easier, more accurate, and quicker to accomplish. This model, manufactured by the London firm of Claudius Ash & Son, was one of the first on the market.

ethics in 1866 established a basis for dentistry's reputation as an ethical profession.

The late nineteenth century is known as the "Gilded Age" because of the extreme wealth and opulence that characterized the era. The period was also a "gilded" age for dentistry. The invention of the dental foot engine by Dr. James B. Morrison in 1871 literally transformed dentistry. Dentists were now freed of the awkward machinations of powering a drill by hand. The engine, operated by a foot pedal, could achieve drill speeds of up to one thousand revolutions per minute. This allowed the drill to cut faster and smoother, facilitating the work of the dentist and adding to the comfort of the patient. Postwar discoveries of gold and silver in the mountains of the Colorado, Nevada, and Dakota territories proved serendipitous, as these metals became inexpensive commodities for much of the Gilded Age. Coupled with the introduction of the foot engine, silver amalgam and gold fillings became standard restorative materials for most

Delegates pose for a group photograph at the 1886 Annual Session. Niagara Falls was a popular site for nineteenth-century Annual Sessions due to its reputation as a resort town and because it was accessible by rail. The ADA met there thirteen times from 1859 to 1902, more times than any other city in the ADA's first 150 years.

The Vulcanite Litigations
and the Murder of Josiah Bacon

One would not normally associate dentures with anything criminal, but in the late nineteenth century, a struggle over who owned the patent rights to vulcanized rubber (also known as vulcanite), a key material used in the manufacture of dentures, resulted in a notorious murder by a dentist driven to the edge. Surrounding the murder was a story of greed and litigious behavior that characterized the emergence of capitalism in Industrial Age America.

In 1844, Charles Goodyear patented the rubber vulcanization process in which natural rubber was mixed with sulfur and heated to a high temperature to create a permanently hardened but elastic and easily molded substance. The use of vulcanite in the manufacture of various products was soon being patented. Dentists discovered that it was the perfect material for use as a denture base, and it quickly became the standard for dentures in the United States.

▲ Dentures made of various materials including vulcanite (left), plastic (middle two), acrylic (right), and gold (top).

By 1866, Josiah Bacon, a Boston businessman, was able to obtain the sole patent rights for the use of the vulcanite process in denture construction, as well as the controlling interest in the Goodyear Dental Vulcanite Company, which was established to administer licensing of the process. Bacon immediately instituted large fees for the rights to use the process, charging dentists $25.00 to $50.00 for an annual license, plus a royalty fee of $1.00 to $2.50 per denture. Those who did not pay were liable for large fines or even imprisonment. Most dentists refused to pay, arguing that they should only be charged for the vulcanite itself. However, the financial stakes were immense for Bacon. After he embarked on a nationwide campaign suing dentists for non-payment, an estimated five thousand dentists paid the fees to avoid legal action, and Bacon's company took in more than $3 million in license fees and royalties.

The ADA and state dental societies openly questioned the legality of the vulcanite patent process. In numerous court cases, some funded by state and local dental societies, it was argued that Bacon could not hold rights to a process that had long been used for molding denture bases of other materials. Most dentists believed that this superior and inexpensive method for making dentures should be free to use for the good of the public and that Bacon was preventing the progress of dental science. Finally, in 1872, Bacon was able to get the U.S. Supreme Court to rule in his favor on the legality of the patent. However, afterwards it was proven that Bacon had paid off the defendant's lawyer in the appeals case. As a result, the Supreme Court, for the first time in its history, reversed itself and vacated its decision saying that the entire appeal suit was collusive.

The Supreme Court's reversal did not end Bacon's pursuit of dentists for licensing fees and royalties, however, as he still held the patent rights. It was on one of his trips to hound dentists that he met his end. Bacon was in San Francisco in the spring of 1879, in pursuit of Dr. Samuel P. Chalfant, a Pennsylvania native who had moved his practice from several cities to avoid paying Bacon's fees. In court, on April 12, 1879, Bacon cross-examined the San Francisco dentist mercilessly.

The next morning, Chalfant visited Bacon in his room at the city's Baldwin Hotel in order to arrange a compromise. Bacon refused to compromise and threatened to ruin Chalfant, who then pulled a pistol from his frock coat. Bacon lunged for the weapon. The pistol went off in the ensuing struggle and Bacon sank to the floor with a fatal gunshot wound to the abdomen.

Chalfant fled the scene but turned himself in to San Francisco police three days later and was charged with murder. The trial was followed closely by the dental profession. Many believed that Bacon had only gotten what he deserved. Dentists in New York City even established a defense fund for the San Francisco dentist. A jury convicted Chalfant of second-degree murder, and he was sentenced to ten years in prison. When he was released in 1889, he returned to San Francisco to practice dentistry with his nephew.

The vulcanite denture patents expired in 1881 while Chalfant was in prison. With Bacon's demise, the fortunes of the Goodyear Dental Vulcanite Company declined, and rights to the patents were not extended. Dentists could now use the vulcanite denture process freely. Vulcanite, which today we call rubber, remained an important part of denture construction for years to come, but never again would dentists have to pay a royalty to use it.

Americans visiting the dentist in the latter nineteenth century. Equally important was the invention of hard rubber and improved porcelain that allowed for superior construction of dentures.

The growth of dental education and the increase in the number of dental societies helped advance the state of knowledge exponentially during the quarter-century following the Civil War. The growth of associations created a major opportunity, and an equally difficult problem for the ADA. The Association early on established a cordial relationship with the American Dental Convention (ADC), a predecessor to the ADA that existed until 1883. The ADA was founded by members of the ADC who were dissatisfied with its open membership policy and the conduct of its meetings. One did not have to be a licensed dentist to join the ADC, and the meetings tended to be more socially oriented. The ADA had a rockier relationship with the Southern Dental Association (SDA). Founded in 1869 as an outgrowth of informal organizations of Confederate dentists during the Civil War, SDA had an on-again, off-again relationship with the ADA over much of the late nineteenth century. As early as 1878, the ADA, ADC, and SDA met jointly at Niagara Falls to discuss ways in which the three organizations could unite. A committee appointed at the 1878 meeting took two years to report its findings, which were pessimistic. The committee reported to the ADA's 1880 Annual Session in Boston that unification would not happen until members of the profession throughout the United States

"come to this Association with proper authenticated credentials from their state or local societies."

Agitation for consolidation between the ADA and SDA picked up steam again in the early 1890s when the two organizations jointly sponsored the Columbian Dental Congress in conjunction with the Chicago Columbian Exposition in 1893. The Congress brought visiting dentists to Chicago from around the world and afforded the nation's dentists from the north and south the opportunity to get together, socialize, and discuss issues of mutual concern.

Attendees at the World's Columbian Dental Congress in Chicago in 1893, which the ADA helped to organize and manage. It was the largest dental conference ever held at the time and the first held on an international scale. The congress was part of the World's Columbian Exposition, known as the "White City," a world's fair commemorating the four hundredth anniversary of Christopher Columbus's arrival in the new world. *(ADA file photo by Bolton & Co.)*

The merger with the Southern Dental Association did not take place until 1897, when a joint meeting of the two groups at Old Point Comfort, Virginia, resulted in consolidation and the renaming of the merged organizations as the National Dental Association (NDA). During the 1880s and 1890s, the SDA had become a formidable rival of the ADA, boasting membership across the south, in many of the western states and even some in the north. The renaming of the ADA to the NDA was the price that the SDA exacted for joining the national organization, and former members of the SDA called

The Mouth and The Teeth

Published by

The National Dental Association

Copyrighted, 1909, by The National Dental Association.

◄ The ADA's first patient education brochure, *The Mouth and The Teeth*, first published in 1909, recommended brushing teeth twice a day, flossing regularly, and visiting the dentist twice a year.

Presidents of the American
Dental Association

1878-1896

H. J. McKELLOPS
1878

L. D. SHEPARD
1879

C. N. PIERCE
1880

H. A. SMITH
1881

W. H. GODDARD
1882

E. T. DARBY
1883

J. N. CROUSE
1884

W. C. BARRETT
1885

FRANK ABBOTT
1887

C. R. BUTLER
1888

M. W. FOSTER
1889

A. W. HARLAN
1890

W. W. WALKER
1891

J. D. PATTERSON
1892-1893

J. Y. CRAWFORD
1894-1895

JAMES TRUMAN
1896

for the dental profession. The Association had achieved what it set out to do in 1859. After forty years of existence, it had helped establish dentistry as a profession with a basis in science and education by its promotion of credentialed dentists and its solicitation of scientific papers at its annual meetings. It had also helped establish dentistry as an ethical profession by its adoption of a meaningful code of ethics.

DENTISTRY PROGRESSES

Dental education came into its own during the last quarter of the nineteenth century. By the mid-1870s, students at dental schools around the country were taking a rigorous course of studies that led to a degree in dental science. For example, at Harvard Dental School, students in 1874 took courses in chemistry, anatomy, and physiology and were in the dental laboratory four mornings a week.

Research and science led to dozens of new discoveries and innovations. In 1891, Dr. Willoughby Dayton Miller linked dental caries to bacterial origins in his monumental book, *Micro-Organisms of the Human Mouth*.

themselves the Southern Branch of the National Dental Association even into the second decade of the twentieth century.

When the merged organization met in Niagara Falls in 1899, the fortieth anniversary of the Association's founding, 194 delegates attended the meeting, and membership had grown to 334 regular members. Attendance had grown more than sevenfold over the twenty-six who met at the first meeting. The newly named National Dental Association was now truly national in scope and had become the nation's most important advocate

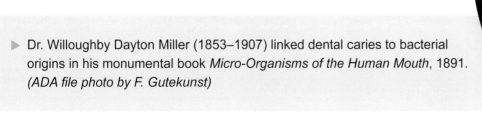

▶ Dr. Willoughby Dayton Miller (1853–1907) linked dental caries to bacterial origins in his monumental book *Micro-Organisms of the Human Mouth*, 1891. (ADA file photo by F. Gutekunst)

Dr. Greene Vardiman Black
1836–1915

Dr. G. V. Black is considered one of the great men in the history of dentistry. He was an influential writer, educator, scholar, and inventor whose contributions included work on the theory of plaque, amalgam formulation, the physical character of teeth, dental calculus, dental caries, a system of cavity preparation, and dental nomenclature. His non-dental pursuits included a lifetime interest in histology, nature, and music. His longtime deanship of the Northwestern University Dental School helped to make Chicago a center for dentistry.

Dr. Greene Vardiman Black
(1836–1915)

Greene Vardiman Black was born in 1836 on a farm near Winchester, Illinois. He grew up on the Illinois frontier, apprenticed in dentistry under a mentor in a nearby community, and opened a practice in his hometown. After being wounded in combat fighting for the Union Army during the Civil War, he was mustered out of service in 1863 and set up a dental office in Jacksonville, Illinois, where he practiced for the next thirty-three years.

Black was considered one of the greatest dental educators of his time, and he influenced generations of dentists as a professor of both operative dentistry and dental pathology at

Missouri Dental College in St. Louis, the University of Iowa in Iowa City, and Northwestern University in Chicago. He served as the second dean of the Northwestern University Dental School from 1897 until his death in 1915.

Black is best known for his principles and classification of cavity preparation that is still taught in dental schools today. The principles were the major focus of his popular textbook, *Operative Dentistry,* first published in 1908. The book had several editions (edited by his son, Dr. A. D. Black, after his father's death) and was widely used in American dental schools until the mid-twentieth century. G. V. Black is also remembered for his standardization of dental instruments and for his development of the amalgam mix used for filling teeth.

He was an early researcher into the effectiveness of fluoride for cavity prevention. Dr. Frederick McKay, of Colorado, sought Black's assistance in determining what caused staining of some of his patients' teeth, which were also remarkably caries free. The collaborative efforts of Black and McKay led to the

G. V. Black at his workbench.

ADA past presidents gather for the dedication of the G. V. Black Memorial in Chicago's Lincoln Park, during the 1918 Annual Session. The sculpture was funded through the contributions of ADA members, and Dr. Black's four granddaughters were on hand for the unveiling. As part of the dedication, Annual Session attendees could visit a replica of Black's dental office and view a display of his memorabilia. The memorial still stands at the south end of Lincoln Park. *(ADA file photo by Kaufmann & Fabry Co.)*

discovery that the high level of natural fluoride in the water supply inhibited caries in certain populations. This research was the basis for studies leading to modern-day fluoridation.

Black was a major force in the evolution of modern dentistry. He always maintained that the practice of dentistry should be grounded in research and science. However, he often told associates that his research and teaching would have been meaningless without the decades of clinical experience gained in his small-town practice in Jacksonville.

Black served as president of the ADA, 1900–1901, and died in 1915. In 1918, members of the ADA erected a statue in his honor in Chicago's Lincoln Park, where it remains today as a monument to his contribution to the science and practice of dentistry.

Inventors tinkered with applying electric power to dental engines and other equipment in the typical dentist's office. The discovery of X-rays by Wilhelm Roentgen, a German physicist, at the University of Wurzburg in 1895 led to the development of the X-ray machine, an important new diagnostic tool for dentists.

As the century moved forward, dentists took an increasing role in educating the public about dental health. In 1887, an ADA resolution called for the introduction of a dental health course in public schools. In 1909, the Association took the first steps in becoming a strong advocate for improving America's health through preventive dental care by publishing its first patient education brochure, *The Mouth and The Teeth*, which instructed patients to brush twice a day, floss regularly, and see the dentist twice a year.

Dentistry made huge strides in the half-century between the initial meeting of the ADA and 1909. In the wake of the Civil War, dentistry began its emergence from the barber-surgeon tradition that had prevailed since the late eighteenth century. Dental education and accreditation would mark the passage to a respected profession, and by the early twentieth century, American dentists had established preeminence in two specialties, oral surgery and orthodontics.

The next quarter-century would bring even more advancements, both in the evolution of dentistry as a recognized profession and in better care for the nation's oral health.

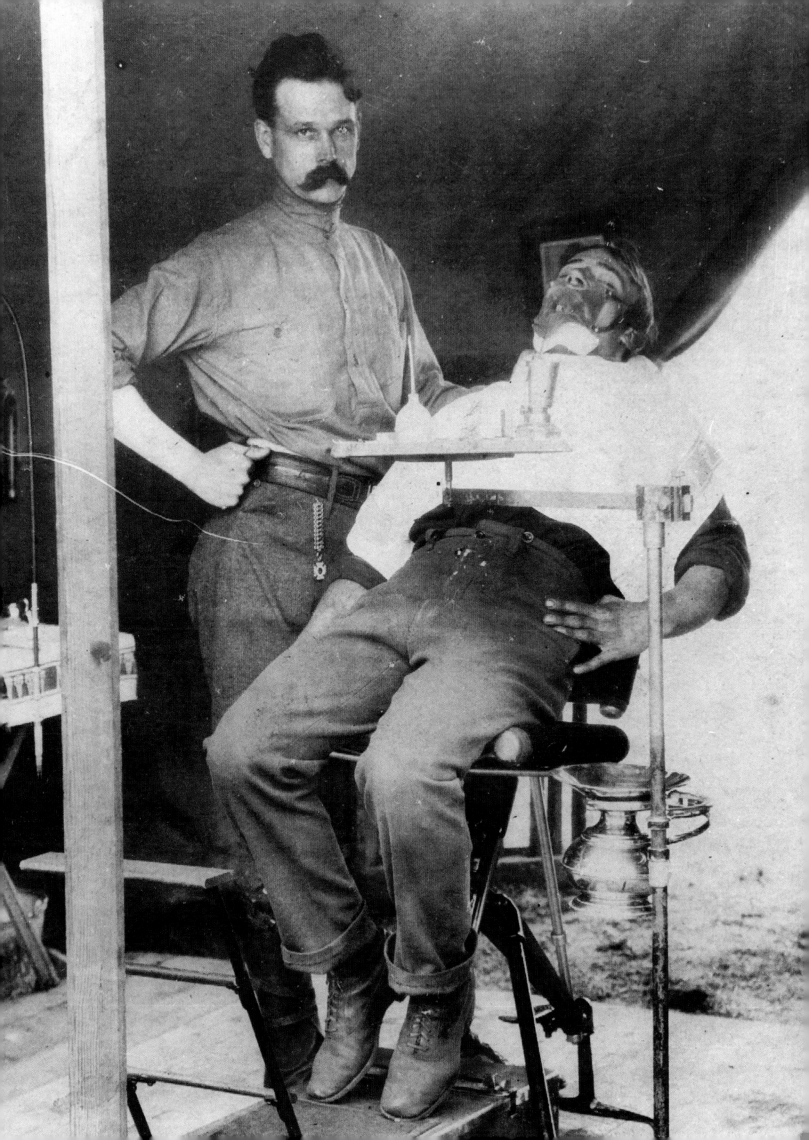

Chapter Two
Growth and Development, 1910–1935

During the first third of the twentieth century, the American Dental Association made steady strides toward expanding membership and establishing itself as the premier organization for dentistry. The profession's progress was marked by a blossoming of dental education, the formal emergence of a number of dental specialties, and the beginnings of dentistry's long and fruitful collaboration with federal and state governments. Dentistry and the ADA began the transition from looking inward to looking outward.

TRIPARTITE ESTABLISHED

In 1912, the Association reorganized and adopted a new constitution and bylaws establishing the tripartite membership structure that has characterized the Association ever since. The Association's leadership understood that restrictive membership rules had precluded the organization from taking its rightful place as the nation's advocate for the dental profession. Membership in 1899 was just 362 at a time when there were about 30,000 dentists in the United States.

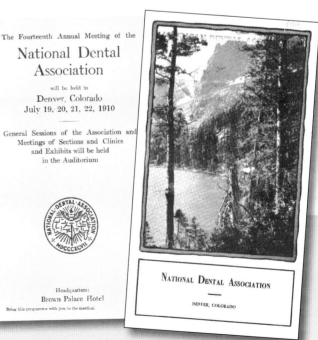

▲ Top: The first issue of *Official Bulletin of the National Dental Association*, November 1913. The publication continues today as *The Journal of the American Dental Association*.

▶ Bottom: Program for the 1910 Annual Session. Held in Denver's Brown Palace Hotel, it was the first Annual Session held west of the Mississippi River and the largest up until that time.

Delegates pose for a group photograph at the 1910 Annual Session in Denver. Although the identities of most of the delegates have been lost to history, the man with the long, white beard (front row, tenth from right) is known to be Dr. William Smedley (1836–1926). A prominent Denver dentist and lifelong ADA member, Smedley was a regular attendee of the ADA's Annual Sessions. His conspicuous beard makes him easy to spot in photographs of delegate groups. *(ADA file photo by Mile High Photo Co.)*

By the turn of the twentieth century, the membership structure had become cumbersome and overly restrictive. Any permanently organized dental society could send one delegate for every six of its active members to the national convention. Delegates could become permanent members after one year. Only permanent members were allowed to hold office in the Association so they, and not the delegates, held the real power in the organization.

Dr. G. V. Black, the Association's president, 1900–1901, called for a "rigorous revision" of the Association's constitution. Black wanted to curb the power of the permanent members and make the Association a voice for scientific dentistry. Although one of the most respected figures in American dentistry, Black was unable to sway the membership to his point of view.

Support for reform continued to build through the early 1900s. In 1904, the reform movement was given a boost when a committee chaired by Dr. A. D. Black (the son of G. V. Black) reorganized the Illinois State Dental Society along the lines of the Illinois State Medical Society (ISMS). The ISMS had greatly increased its numbers by granting membership to those who had joined any local or specialist society.

At the Association's 1907 Annual Session, a report on the positive effects of the restructuring of the Illinois

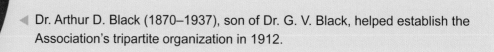

Dr. Arthur D. Black (1870–1937), son of Dr. G. V. Black, helped establish the Association's tripartite organization in 1912.

State Dental Society was presented and discussed. At the 1908 Annual Session, President William Carr proposed that the Association's bylaws be revised to open membership to every member of a state dental society or an affiliated local society. Carr's suggestion stirred debate, but no immediate action was taken.

Talk of reorganization dominated the 1909 Annual Session, and a committee spent the next two years revising the constitution and bylaws. At the 1911 Annual Session, a reorganization plan based on the structure of the American Medical Association found support among the delegates from the twenty-four state dental societies in attendance. This model took policy-making authority from the permanent members and gave it to a house of delegates elected by affiliated state societies.

Reorganization finally became a reality at the Association's 1912 Annual Session, when the delegates adopted a plan setting up not only an elected House of Delegates with the legislative authority for the organization, but also a Board of Trustees to oversee its

financial matters. The tripartite membership structure of national organization, constituent (state), and component (local) societies that characterizes the Association's membership to this day was established. The 1913 meeting in Kansas City ratified those changes, and the organization was instantly transformed. Membership increased from eight hundred in 1912 to almost twelve thousand in 1913. In addition, proportional representation for the House of Delegates was instituted, giving the Association broad-based support from the dental community.

PUBLISHING A JOURNAL

Besides the more than tenfold increase in membership, the most visible manifestation of the 1913 reorganization was the decision to begin publishing an official Association

▶ ADA President William Carr (1842–1925) proposed at the 1908 Annual Session that the Association's bylaws be revised to open up membership to every member of a state dental society or an affiliated local society.

The Rise of
Dental Specialties

Although the American Dental Association traces its roots to 1859 and American dentistry goes back to colonial times, specialized practice did not become a formal part of the dental profession until the early years of the twentieth century. Beginning in the late nineteenth century, areas of specialization evolved with the establishment of their own organizations, journals, and boards, and the word "specialty" was used to describe these areas of specialized practice. However, a dispute soon arose within the profession over what constituted a specialty. The issue was resolved in the 1940s when the ADA established requirements and a process for specialty recognition. As of 2009, the ADA recognizes these nine specialties: dental public health, endodontics, oral and maxillofacial pathology, oral and maxillofacial radiology, oral and maxillofacial surgery, orthodontics and dentofacial orthopedics, pediatric dentistry, periodontics, and prosthodontics.

Orthodontics was the first area of dental specialization to become organized and the second specialization in the entire health field to do so, following only ophthalmology. Dr. Edward H. Angle promoted the idea of using appliances to straighten teeth as early as the 1880s. Angle and his students founded the American Society of Orthodontists, which held its first scientific meeting in St. Louis in 1901. *The American Orthodontist*, the first dental specialty journal, began publication in 1907. The American Board of Orthodontics became the first dental specialty board when it was established in 1929. In 1938, the Society became the American Association of Orthodontists, which now publishes *American Journal of Orthodontics and Dentofacial Orthopedics*. Orthodontics was officially recognized as a specialty in 1950.

(Left) Drs. Gillette Hayden (1880–1919) and (below) Grace Rogers Spalding (1881–1953) together organized the Academy of Periodontology in 1914 (now the American Academy of Periodontology). *(Photo on left, ADA file photo by Ye Portrait Shoppe)*

The American Academy of Periodontology held its first annual meeting with seventeen of its eighteen members in attendance in Washington, D.C., in November 1914. Founded by two women, Dr. Gillette Hayden and Dr. Grace Rogers Spalding, the Academy brought together dental practitioners interested in the prevention and treatment of diseases affecting the gums and the supporting structures of the mouth. The Academy began publication of *Journal of Periodontology* in 1930 and established the American Board of Periodontology in 1939. Recognition of the specialty was gained in 1947.

The American Society of Exodontists was founded in the summer of 1918 by twenty-eight dentists from fifteen states who were in Chicago for an ADA meeting. For much of the latter half of the nineteenth century, oral surgery had been affiliated with medicine rather than dentistry. It was only after the turn of the

Dr. Edward H. Angle (1855–1930) is considered the father of orthodontics. Known for his classification of various forms of malocclusion, Angle is also credited with making orthodontics a dental specialty. He founded the first school of orthodontics (Angle School of Orthodontia, St. Louis, 1900) and was instrumental in establishing the first orthodontic society (American Society of Orthodontists, which became the American Association of Orthodontists) and the first dental speciality journal (*The American Orthodontist*).

◀ Dr. George B. W. Winter (1878–1940), founding member of the American Society of Exodontists (now the American Association of Oral and Maxillofacial Surgeons) and ADA president, 1935–1936. He developed and taught advanced methods for tooth extraction, particularly impacted third molar extraction. He is credited with coining the term "exodontia" to describe the operation of tooth extraction.

◀ Dr. William A. Giffen (1866–1929), first president of the National Society of Denture Prosthetists, which later became the Academy of Prosthodontics. He also served as ADA president, 1923–1924, and was considered an expert in denture construction.

twentieth century that those who practiced oral surgery realized that their affinity was with dentistry. In the first three years following the establishment of the organization, the Society grew nearly tenfold, to 230 members. In 1975, after a series of name changes, the organization adopted its current name, the American Association of Oral and Maxillofacial Surgeons. The organization gained new recognition with the establishment of the American Board of Oral Surgery in 1946. The organization's *Journal of Oral Surgery* (currently *Journal of Oral and Maxillofacial Surgery*) was first published in 1943. Recognized in 1947, the specialty was the first to gain formal recognition.

The National Society of Denture Prosthetists held its organizational meeting in August 1918. Forty-nine members were invited to join, and thirty-one charter members attended the Academy's first meeting in Chicago. The organization changed its name to the American Academy of Denture Prosthetics in 1941 and again in 1991 to its current name, the Academy of Prosthodontics. In 1946, the Academy helped establish the American Board of Prosthodontics and sponsored it for its first twenty-five years. (The Board is currently sponsored by the American College of Prosthodontists.) In 1950, the American Academy of Denture Prosthetics joined with the American Denture Society and the Pacific Coast Society of Prosthodontists in launching *The Journal of Prosthetic Dentistry*. The specialty gained recognition in 1948.

The American Academy of Pedodontics was founded in 1947 to promote research and education in children's dentistry. It changed its name to the American Academy of Pediatric Dentistry (AAPD) in 1995. For years, it coexisted with the American Society of Dentistry for Children (ASDC), which was founded in 1927 to provide better dental care for children. The ASDC merged with the AAPD in 2002. In 1940, the ASDC organized the American Board of Pedodontics (changed to the American Board of Pediatric Dentistry in 1995) sponsorship of the Board was transferred to the American Academy of Pedodontics in 1964. The official journals of the AAPD are *Pediatric Dentistry*, published since 1979, and *Journal of Dentistry for Children*, started by the ASDC in 1934. The specialty gained recognition in 1948.

The American Registry of Dental and Oral Pathology was organized in 1933. This led to the establishment in 1948 of the American Academy of Oral Pathology (renamed the American Academy of Oral and Maxillofacial Pathology in 1995) in Washington, D.C. The Board of Oral Pathology (currently the American Board of Oral and Maxillofacial Pathology) was

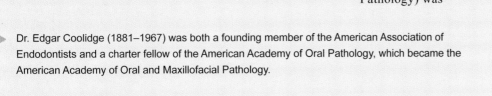

▶ Dr. Edgar Coolidge (1881–1967) was both a founding member of the American Association of Endodontists and a charter fellow of the American Academy of Oral Pathology, which became the American Academy of Oral and Maxillofacial Pathology.

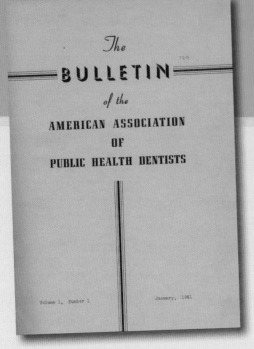

founded in 1948. The journal *Oral Surgery, Oral Medicine and Oral Pathology* became the official journal of the Academy in 1948 and was renamed *Oral Surgery, Oral Medicine, Oral Pathology, Oral Radiology, and Endodontics* in 1995. The specialty was recognized in 1950.

Another specialty that became increasingly prominent during the Great Depression was public health dentistry. The American Association of Public Health Dentistry (AAPHD) was formed in 1937 in Atlantic City, New Jersey. In 1941, the Association began publishing *The Bulletin of the American Association of Public Health Dentists,* currently *Journal of Public Health Dentistry.* In 1949, the AAPHD helped establish the American Board of Dental Public Health. The specialty gained recognition in 1951.

The growing number of root canals performed during the 1930s led to an increasing specialization in endodontics. A small group of dentists gathered in Chicago in 1943 to form the American Association of Endodontists (AAE). Even though travel was sharply restricted during World War II, more than two hundred members of the new organization attended the AAE's 1944 annual meeting in Chicago. The AAE began publishing *Journal of Endodontia* (now called *Journal of Endodontics*) in 1946. The American Board of Endodontists was founded in 1956. The specialty was recognized in 1963.

The American Academy of Oral Roentgenologists was founded in October 1949 in San Francisco. In 1988, after a

▶ Dr. Samuel D. Harris (1903–2003) helped to establish the American Society of Dentistry for Children in 1927 and in 1947, the American Academy of Pedodontics, now called the American Academy of Pediatric Dentistry. He practiced dentistry for fifty-four years and generously supported children's oral health initiatives over his lifetime. His financial contributions resulted in The Samuel D. Harris National Museum of Dental History in Baltimore and the ADA Foundation's Samuel D. Harris Fund for Children's Dental Health. Dr. Harris received the ADA Distinguished Service Award in 1998 and died in 2003, just two weeks short of his one hundredth birthday.

series of name changes, the organization adopted its current name, the American Academy of Oral and Maxillofacial Radiology. In 1959, the Academy chose an existing publication, *Oral Surgery, Oral Medicine, Oral Pathology,* to become its official journal and to which the publishers then added a regular section on oral radiology. It was renamed *Oral Surgery, Oral Medicine, Oral Pathology, Oral Radiology and Endodontics* in 1995. The Academy established the American Board of Oral and Maxillofacial Radiology in 1979. The specialty gained recognition in 2001.

▶ Dr. H. Cline Fixott (1879–1959) was a founding member of the American Academy of Oral Roentgenologists in 1949 and served as its first president. The society is now known as the American Academy of Oral and Maxillofacial Radiology.

journal. Now known as *The Journal of the American Dental Association* (*JADA*), it was first issued in November 1913. It was published under several other titles before the current title was adopted in 1922. The first issue went to more than fifteen thousand names on the Association's mailing list. Dr. Otto U. King, *The Journal*'s first editor, noted that a two-horse dray wagon hauled the fifty-four mail sacks and several boxes of the publication to the post office.

Publishing a journal gave impetus to another ADA goal: to increase the focus on dental research. The Association had created a committee on scientific research in 1908. By 1914, the Association's Scientific Foundation and Research Commission had secured $17,000 in pledges, enough to begin funding three research projects. However, the outbreak of WWI in the summer of 1914 and American involvement in the war less than three years later turned the Association's attention to more pressing defense issues for the remainder of the decade.

Research Institute in Cleveland, Ohio, where the Association's sponsored research was conducted from 1915–1925.

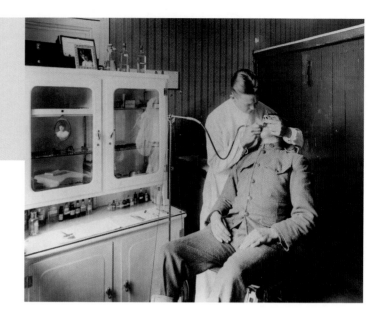

Lieutenant Jack W. Scherer treats a patient in a base hospital in Contrexeville, France, during World War I. Dr. Scherer was a member of the dental staff at Base Hospital No. 32 in 1917–1918. *(Photo courtesy of the National Library of Medicine)*

DENTISTRY IN WWI

The federal government accorded a long-delayed recognition to the profession in 1911 and 1912 when the U.S. Army and U.S. Navy both established dental corps. Army and navy dentists performed valuable service when the military ballooned to meet the manpower needs of World War I in 1917 and 1918.

As far back as the Civil War, the Association had lobbied unsuccessfully for the appointment of dentists to serve in the U.S. Army and U.S. Navy. The government maintained that members of the military should be responsible for their own dental care until 1900, when Congress passed a law providing for contract dental surgeons to serve with the U.S. Army. The Association continued to lobby for the establishment of a separate dental corps for the military, staffed with dentists of officer rank.

Instrumental in that effort was Dr. Williams Donnally. During his more than thirty years of practice in Washington, D.C., Donnally became skilled in lobbying Congress and government officials. He worked closely with the Association's Legislative Committee to lobby Congress for passage of a bill establishing a military dental corps. These efforts bore fruit in 1911 when President William Howard Taft signed legislation establishing the Army Dental Corps. President Taft signed similar legislation establishing the Navy Dental Corps in 1912 and the Navy Dental Reserve Corps in 1913. Each of the three newly established military dental corps provided for the recruiting of commissioned officers, equal in pay and grade to officers in the Army and Navy Medical Corps. Donnally, at the age of sixty-two, capped his two-decade-long quest to have the army and navy officially recognize the value of dentistry as a profession by obtaining a commission in the Navy Dental Reserve Corps. In 1913, Donnally was appointed as the first Navy Reserve officer.

When Congress declared war against Germany in April 1917, there were eighty-six Army Dental Corps officers on active duty and thirty-five in the Navy Dental Corps. By the end of the War, in 1918, the

Dr. Williams Donnally (1851–1929), a prominent Washington, D.C., dentist, worked closely with the Association's Legislative Committee to lobby Congress for passage of a bill establishing a military dental corps.

Uncommon Valor

Although military dentists are not normally expected to engage in combat during the nation's wars, two members of the United States Navy Dental Corps committed acts of bravery in World War I that earned them the Congressional Medal of Honor, the nation's highest military award.

Dr. Weedon E. Osborne, a 1915 graduate of Northwestern University Dental School, was commissioned as a surgeon in the U.S. Navy Dental Corps in 1917 and arrived in France in 1918. He was unable to set up his dental unit because his equipment had been delayed enroute. Instead, Lieutenant Osborne volunteered as a stretcher-bearer and spent weeks crawling under heavy enemy fire to retrieve seriously wounded comrades.

On June 6, 1918, near Bouresches, France, a U.S. advance patrol was caught under heavy fire. Its commanding officer was seriously wounded. Osborne went to the officer's aid and was carrying him to safety when an artillery shell exploded in front of them, killing both men instantly. Osborne was posthumously awarded the Congressional Medal of Honor for this extraordinary act of heroism, becoming the first naval officer killed in land combat during World War I and the first dental corps officer ever killed in combat. He was also awarded the Distinguished Service Cross by General John J. Pershing. His remains are interred in the National Cemetery at Belleau Aisne, France, along with many other Americans who died in WWI.

▶ Lieutenant Weedon E. Osborne (1892–1918) died under fire saving a comrade in World War I and was awarded the Congressional Medal of Honor posthumously in 1918. He was the first Navy Dental Corps officer killed in combat and the first naval officer killed in land combat during World War I.

America's other World War I Medal of Honor dentist was a career naval officer, Dr. Alexander G. Lyle. After graduating from the Baltimore College of Dentistry in 1912, he joined the U.S. Navy Dental Corps. When the United States entered World War I, he was sent to France. While under heavy shellfire on the western front on April 23, 1918, Lieutenant Commander Lyle rushed to the assistance of a seriously wounded soldier and administered medical aid, saving his life. Lyle was awarded both the Congressional Medal of Honor and the Army's Silver Star for his gallantry in action.

He remained in the U.S. Navy between the two world wars, serving in several capacities at various naval installations. In March 1943, he was promoted to dental surgeon with the rank of rear admiral, the first elevation of a Navy Dental Corps officer to flag rank.

Admiral Lyle and Lieutenant Osborne exemplified the best of a generation of Americans who answered the call to serve their country. It was immaterial to the record of their heroism that they were dentists, but their sacrifice reaffirmed the wisdom of the ADA's longstanding support of military dentistry.

◀ Rear Admiral Alexander G. Lyle (1889–1955), the first Navy Dental Corps officer to obtain flag rank. During WWI, while serving as a lieutenant commander, Lyle saved the life of a soldier while under fire. He was awarded both the Congressional Medal of Honor and the Army's Silver Star for his gallantry in action. *(Official U.S. Navy Photograph)*

Growth and Development
1910–1935

1910
At the Ohio College of Dental Surgery, Dr. Cyrus M. Wright establishes the first formal training program for dental nurses (similar to today's dental assistants).

The Dental Educational Council of America is founded to unify standards for the educational requirements of dentists and the accreditation of dental schools.

1912
The U.S. Navy establishes a dental corps.

1917
Irene Newman receives the world's first dental hygiene license.

1919
William J. Gies, PhD, publishes the first issue of *The Journal of Dental Research*.

1921
Students entering dental school are required to have four years of high school and one year of college.

1911
The U.S. Government establishes the U.S. Army Dental Corps, the nation's first armed services dental corps.

1918
The Association opens its first permanent central office in Chicago.

1913
Dr. Alfred C. Fones opens the world's first dental hygiene school in Bridgeport, Connecticut.

The first issue of *The Journal of the American Dental Association* is published under the title *Official Bulletin of the National Dental Association*.

1922
The National Dental Association changes its name back to the American Dental Association and is incorporated in the state of Illinois.

1920
The International Association for Dental Research is founded.

The American College of Dentists is founded.

◄ Dr. Alfred C. Fones (1869–1938), founder of the Fones Clinic for Dental Hygienists in Bridgeport, Connecticut, the first dental hygiene school, established in 1913. Fones was also the first dentist to use an auxiliary in his practice solely for oral prophylaxis, and he coined the term "dental hygienist" to describe the position. *(ADA file photo by J. P. Haley Photo)*

► ADA corporate seal, 1922. The design of a torch over a map of the United States was first used in 1897. The winged torch symbolizes knowledge.

1926

The Carnegie Foundation-sponsored Gies Report on the state of dental education in America is published, leading to changes in dental school curricula and accreditation.

1935

The ADA reports thirty-six thousand members, a strong recovery from the membership low of the early 1930s.

1930

The ADA establishes the Council on Dental Therapeutics to oversee the evaluation of dental products.

1929

The ADA Annual Session is held in Washington, D.C., just twenty days before the stock market crash that ushers in the Great Depression. President Herbert Hoover meets attendees on the White House lawn.

1923

The American Association of Dental Schools is established.

1931

The ADA Council on Dental Therapeutics awards the first ADA Seal of Acceptance to a cod liver oil product.

1928

The National Board of Dental Examiners is founded with representation from the ADA, state dental examining boards, and dental school faculty.

The ADA establishes a cooperative research program at the National Bureau of Standards.

1933

The Chicago Centennial Dental Congress is held in conjunction with the 1933 Century of Progress World's Fair.

The first National Board Dental Examinations are conducted.

1924

Juliette Southard and several colleagues found the American Dental Assistants Association.

1932

The Interstate Dental Association, the official organization of African American dentists, adopts the name National Dental Association.

▲ The ADA's first Seal of Acceptance, used in the 1930s. The seal appeared on products reviewed and accepted by the ADA Council on Dental Therapeutics.

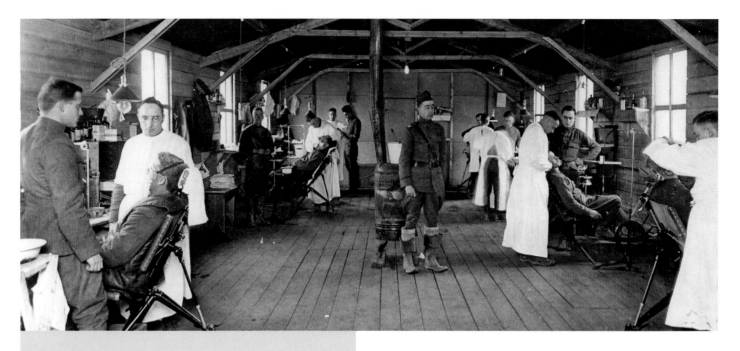

Army Dental Corps counted more than forty-five hundred officers on active duty, with more than five hundred in the Navy Dental Corps.

During the war, army dentists treated nearly 1.4 million soldiers, in every kind of camp and condition, from modern post dental clinics in the United States, to primitive facilities in the trenches of France. Military dentists helped reconstruct the faces and jaws of thousands of wounded soldiers,

sailors, and marines. Moreover, seven army dentists and seven army dental assistants were killed in combat.

World War I proved beyond a doubt that dentistry was critical to the health and well-being of the recruits in the modern army and navy. Military dentists had proven their worth. The War Department integrated dentistry into the regular army during the early 1920s. In 1920, the army created the Dental Reserve Officer Training Corps, and in 1922 opened the Army Dental School in Washington, D.C.

A RETURN TO NORMALCY

The 1920s were a time of solid achievement for both the dental profession and organized dentistry. In 1917, the Association became more of a formal organization when it hired Dr. Otto U. King as its first full-time chief administrative officer, a position then known as secretary. A practicing dentist from

The ADA Central Office
1918–1956

Although America was in the throes of the Great Depression in 1931, the American Dental Association was financially secure enough to buy a building to house its central office.

The ADA had made its home in the Windy City since early in the Association's history. In the nineteenth century, tradition dictated that the ADA central office reside in the city of the Association's general secretary, and for much of that time, the secretary lived in Chicago. The Association first rented space for a central office in 1918 at 127 North Dearborn Street in Chicago, then moved in 1922 to rented rooms at 5 North Wabash Avenue and leased an office building at 58 East Washington Boulevard in Chicago from 1925 to 1931. The decision to buy and not lease in 1931 was driven by the Association's need for more and more space for its growing activities. By the end of the 1920s, the ADA's central office employed ten people, including a general secretary (equivalent to today's executive director), an editor, an assistant editor, a cashier, an advertising manager, a director of dental health education, a librarian, and several clerical personnel. The Association's library, established in 1927, already occupied one large room in the central office by 1929.

The 1931 purchase of a converted residence building at 212 East Superior Street just off North Michigan Avenue provided the ADA with 15,000 square feet of office space. The

This converted residence building at 212 East Superior Street on Chicago's North Side served as ADA's central office from 1931–1943. (ADA file photo by Photo Ideas, Inc.)

Association expected that the attractive four-story greystone building would meet its space needs for decades to come. Although membership dropped precipitously during the early 1930s, the ADA rebounded sharply during the latter half of the decade. By 1940, the Association's central office was already bursting at the seams, and so in 1941, a decision was made to buy another building with four times the usable space down the street at 222 East Superior Street. The commodious five-story office building was entirely remodeled to suit the organization's needs, and in February 1943, Association staff moved into the building that would serve as the ADA's central office until 1956.

Huntington, Indiana, King had long been active in Association affairs and had served as secretary of the Indiana State Dental Association, 1907–1913. King's partner for much of the growth achieved by the organization in the 1920s was Dr. Homer C. Brown, the Association's president, 1913–1914, and a longtime power on the Legislative Committee. Together, Brown and King reorganized the Association in 1922 and presided over

the change of name from the National Dental Association back to the American Dental Association, a move that was strongly supported by the organization's more than thirty thousand members.

With a more formal structure established, the ADA continued to expand during the 1920s. As it grew, the Association moved to larger offices in Chicago,

Dr. Homer C. Brown, ADA president, 1913–1914, oversaw the establishment of the tripartite membership structure and the Board of Trustees.

to 5 North Wabash Avenue in 1922, and then to 58 East Washington in 1925. By 1931, Association activities had increased to the point that the ADA purchased a building to house the central office at 212 East Superior Street.

The steady growth of the ADA during the 1920s reflected the concurrent growth and development of the dental profession. Dental education came under increasing scrutiny and regulation during the decade. The Dental Educational Council of America, made up of representatives from the ADA, the National Association of Dental Faculties, and the National Association of Dental Examiners, was founded in 1910 to improve dental education and to accredit dental schools. The group had problems from the start in coming to a consensus about the accreditation process and the continuing recognition of privately owned, for-profit schools. This situation came to a head in the 1920s.

In 1922, the Carnegie Foundation selected biochemist William J. Gies to head a blue-ribbon committee to investigate the future of dental education in America. This major survey of the state of dental education and resulting report marked a turning point for how dentists were trained and educated. Four years in the making, the Gies Report was critical of the state of dental school curricula and the continuing existence of proprietary dental schools. The report argued that dentistry "should be made the full equivalent of an oral specialty of the practice of medicine." One of its first recommendations was the formation of an umbrella advocacy organization to oversee the development of dental schools. The result was the 1923 establishment of the American Association of Dental Schools (AADS), currently called the American Dental Education Association, which gave a newfound impetus to the increasing importance of curriculum and faculty in dental education. The AADS quickly became the voice for reform and professionalization of America's dental schools. The Gies Report also recommended that dental education be based on what it called the "two-three year plan" requiring dental students to take two years of college followed by a three-year dental curriculum. Five dental schools immediately initiated the Gies Report recommendations, and the report sounded the death

Exhibition Hall at the 1922 Annual Session in Los Angeles, the largest Annual Session held up to that time. That year, the House of Delegates adopted a resolution changing the Association's name from the National Dental Association back to its original name, the American Dental Association.

DENTAL EDUCATION
IN THE UNITED STATES AND CANADA

A REPORT TO THE CARNEGIE FOUNDATION
FOR THE ADVANCEMENT OF TEACHING

By
WILLIAM J. GIES

WITH A PREFACE BY HENRY S. PRITCHETT
PRESIDENT OF THE FOUNDATION

BULLETIN NUMBER NINETEEN

NEW YORK
THE CARNEGIE FOUNDATION
FOR THE ADVANCEMENT OF TEACHING
522 FIFTH AVENUE
1926

◄ The Gies Report reported on the state of dental education in the United States and Canada in 1926.

THE GREAT DEPRESSION

The ADA was an increasingly influential force in American dentistry during the 1920s. By the end of the decade, it represented nearly thirty-six thousand U.S. dentists. Its relationships with state and community dental societies gave the Association entry into every facet of dentistry. With the ADA's growth in membership came a corresponding growth in revenues.

Growth, unfortunately, came to a halt with the stock market crash in late October 1929. Overnight, the superheated American economy, on an ever-upward trajectory since the end of World War I more than a decade before, ran out of steam. Banks failed, unemployment skyrocketed to as much as 25 percent of the workforce, and soup kitchens became fixtures on the streets of major American cities.

knell for the last of the proprietary dental schools in the United States.

The 1928 establishment of the National Board of Dental Examiners gave foundation to a consistent system of credentialing based on examination. By 1935, the AADS had suggested even stricter curriculum requirements than the Gies Report—two years of college and four years of dental school. In 1940, the ADA Council on Dental Education, founded in 1937, also embraced the concept of a four-year dental school.

The Great Depression was just getting under way in 1929, but the ADA was already studying how its members were affected by the worsening economic conditions. In 1929, the ADA appointed

► William J. Gies, PhD (1872–1956), conducted the first comprehensive survey and study of U.S. dental education. Funded by the Carnegie Foundation, the report was released in 1926 and had a profound effect on dental education. Dr. Gies also helped establish the International Association for Dental Research and founded *The Journal of Dental Research*.

1929 Annual Session Washington, D.C.

A sign of the influence that the American Dental Association wielded early in the twentieth century came in 1929 when President Herbert Hoover met with attendees and guests during the 1929 Annual Session. Earlier that week, Vice President Charles Curtis addressed the House of Delegates in their meeting at the Mayflower Hotel in Washington, D.C. The October 9, 1929, reception for the ADA on the White House lawn illustrated the federal government's growing approval of working with professional associations. Though he was hosting British Prime Minister Ramsay McDonald on an official state visit, President Hoover took time out from his busy schedule to welcome the ADA delegates and to pose for a panoramic souvenir photograph.

For the ADA, the 1929 Washington Annual Session was evidence that the Association would take on a wider role in socio-economic issues in the future. For Hoover and the nation, that meeting on the White House lawn was the end of an era. Three weeks later, Wall Street would be rocked by a massive market loss on Black Tuesday, the first of a number of financial shocks that would jolt America in the years ahead. Widely blamed for the onset of the ensuing Great Depression, Hoover would suffer a landslide defeat at the hands of New York Governor Franklin D. Roosevelt in the 1932 presidential election.

▼ Annual Session delegates and guests meet with U.S. President Herbert Hoover on the White House lawn in 1929, less than a month before the stock market crash and the onset of the Great Depression. *(ADA file photo by Rideout)*

the Committee on the Study of Dental Practice to cooperate with the Cost of Medical Care Committee, a national coalition established two years before to analyze health care costs in the United States. The Committee on the Study of Dental Practice established baseline data on a number of economic issues important to the membership, including dental income, the cost of outfitting a dental office, the cost of a dental education, and the development of health insurance networks and their relation to the practice of dentistry. In 1930, the ADA appointed a Committee on Dental Economics to continue monitoring economic issues during the 1930s.

▲ A motor-driven toothbrush booth, part of a popular health sciences exhibit at the 1933 Century of Progress in Chicago, the first world's fair to feature exhibits on the health sciences and dentistry. About eight million people visited the fair's dental health exhibits. *(Official Century of Progress photo by Kaufmann-Fabry)*

The election of President Franklin Delano Roosevelt in 1932 brought about a new activism to the nation's political arena. On the medical front, the Roosevelt administration was a strong proponent of public health programs designed

▶ The preliminary program for the Chicago Centennial Dental Congress. The Congress was a joint meeting of the American Dental Association and the Chicago Dental Society held in conjunction with Chicago's Century of Progress World's Fair in 1933. The Congress also marked the seventy-fifth anniversary of the ADA's founding.

to improve the health of citizens long denied the most basic dental and medical care. The ADA, through its Legislative, Economic, and Public Health Committees, worked closely with state and local societies to provide dental public health programs for underserved populations. In 1935, the Association entered into a joint venture with the U.S. Public Health Service to survey the oral health of U.S. schoolchildren. As part of the project, dental examinations were provided to 1.5 million children in twenty-six states particularly hard hit by the Great Depression. The ADA had first worked with the U.S. Public Health Service in the early 1930s to select five dentists to serve with the newly created National Institutes of Health, a Public Health Service division at the time.

The quarter-century between 1910 and 1935 saw the ADA come of age, especially in its relationships with government and society. Those relationships would be brought into sharper focus during the quarter-century to come.

Chapter Three
Coming of Age, 1936–1959

Bunting of lavender and white, the traditional colors of dentistry, bedecked San Francisco when the ADA convened its Annual Session there in July 1936. One of the Association's tasks at that meeting was to install a new president, and it was little wonder that, from a membership of 40,073, the dentists had selected Dr. Leroy "Roy" Miner.

Even among his professional colleagues, Miner had exceptional credentials. Both a dentist and a physician, Miner was a role model for the dentist of the future and for what Miner himself challenged all his colleagues to be—"a learned professional in an important branch of the great art and science of healing."

At its 1936 Annual Session, according to *TIME* Magazine, which featured Miner on its cover, the ADA "signaled to the world that henceforth any man or woman licensed to practice dentistry in the U.S. will be well-educated, well-trained. Beginning next September no student will be admitted to any one of the 38 first-class U.S. dental schools unless he has had at least two years of college education. He will not get his Doctorate of Dental Surgery until he has passed four more years of grounding himself in such medical fundamentals as anatomy, pathology, diagnosis, hygiene, as well as special dental problems of the jaws, gums, and teeth." In that regard, Miner was way ahead of the learning curve; he was both dean and professor of clinical oral surgery at Harvard Dental School and he lectured on oral disease at the Boston University School of Medicine.

Dr. Leroy Miner, ADA president, 1936–1937, is the only dentist ever featured on the cover of *TIME* Magazine. *(Reprinted by permission of Wright's Reprints)*

TIME wrote glowingly,

> Dr. Miner's life is a dentist's dream....By 8 o'clock he is driving his 1933 Franklin to one of six Boston hospitals, where he operates for an hour or so. Thence he goes to his private office on Marlboro Street, a 14-room suite where go the big Boston names who make up his clientele, keeps two associates, three nurses, two secretaries and a receptionist busy....Two mornings and two afternoons a week he attends to his duties as Dean of Harvard Dental School....Among his operations, consulting and school schedules he squeezes in one class a week to Harvard dental students...one class a week to juniors...[and] one dental clinic. At Boston University School of Medicine he gives four formal lectures a year on stomatology. He also gives three lectures a year to dental hygienists studying at Boston University. Dental and medical societies get another dozen or so lectures from him each year.

At the 1936 Annual Session, he pledged that he would keep in touch with the forty-eight state dental societies and keep the members' noses glued to dental ideals.

▲ Attendees crowd the presenters to get a better view of table clinics at the 1938 Annual Session in St. Louis. *(ADA file by Taylor Photographers)*

DENTAL SCHOOL ACCREDITATION

The 1936 ADA Annual Session was not devoted just to a celebration of its new president. The members and their leadership also turned their attention to what *Time* called "vigorous criticism" of the Dental

◄ Students in Oklahoma City display posters submitted for the ADA National Dental Health Poster Contest in 1938. The contest was part of the ADA Dental Health for American Youth initiative, which was launched in 1937. The winners received awards at the Annual Session in St. Louis in 1938, and their photos were published in *The Journal of the American Dental Association. (ADA file photo courtesy of Oklahoma County Dental Society)*

▲ The commercial exhibits at the 1941 Annual Session in Houston. *(ADA file photo by Bob Bailey)*

Educational Council of America (DECA), which the ADA charged had "proved incompetent in promoting good educational standards in the dental schools." DECA, made up of representatives from the ADA, the National Association of Dental Schools, and the National Association of Dental Examiners, was formed in 1910 to improve dental education and to accredit and classify dental schools. DECA was dissolved in 1936. The ADA Council on Dental Education was established in 1937 to oversee the accreditation of dental schools and the professional certification of dentists, with representation from the three original DECA organizations.

In 1941, the Council began accreditation work with the promulgation of its Requirements for the Approval of Dental Schools. There was a delay in the inspection of schools due to wartime restrictions on travel, but the Council was finally able to publish its first list of accredited schools in 1945.

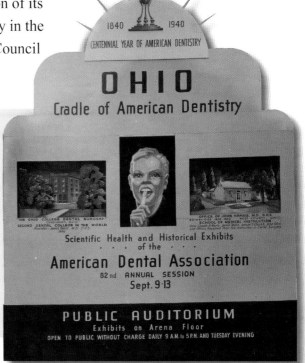

▶ A sign directs attendees to exhibits at the 1940 Annual Session in Cleveland. The centennial year of American dentistry was celebrated in 1940, commemorating the establishment of the Baltimore College of Dental Surgery, the world's first dental school, which merged into the University of Maryland in 1929. The sign cites Ohio as the cradle of American dentistry because it was home to the Ohio College of Dental Surgery, the world's second dental school, and many early nineteenth-century dentists were trained by Dr. John Harris, a Bainbridge, Ohio, physician who ran a school out of his medical office prior to 1840.

Dr. George Paffenbarger
and the Rise of Dental Research

The ADA and the then National Bureau of Standards laid a solid foundation for dental research in 1928 when the two organizations began a unique collaboration that has paid dividends for the past eighty years.

The National Bureau of Standards (NBS), the federal government's agency for determining measurements, began a dental materials research group in 1919. During the 1920s, the NBS group developed the first comprehensive set of amalgam standards. In 1928, NBS and the ADA signed a cooperative research agreement that was the first public-private research pact in the field of dentistry.

Named to head the joint research effort in 1929 was an unassuming Ohio dentist who would put his stamp on dental research for the next half-century. Dr. George C. Paffenbarger was born and raised in McArthur, Ohio, and was a graduate of the College of Dentistry of Ohio State University. Paffenbarger had been a member of the NBS dental group staff for only two years when he was asked to serve as its director. However, the director never referred to himself as anything other than senior research associate. His only time away from the Maryland research laboratory that housed the ADA-NBS team involved service with the Navy Dental Corps during World War II.

Paffenbarger and his research team helped revolutionize dentistry during the middle years of the twentieth century. What was

Dr. George C. Paffenbarger, longtime director of the ADA-sponsored Dental Research Unit at the National Bureau of Standards. The Research Unit was renamed the Paffenbarger Research Center in 1985 in honor of his dedicated leadership and commitment to research. NBS is now the National Institute of Standards and Technology. *(ADA file photo by the National Bureau of Standards)*

called simply "the Research Unit" was responsible for a host of dental breakthroughs including panoramic X-rays, the turbine contra-angle handpiece, front-surface dental mirrors, and new dental composites and fillers. In a retrospective of his career that appeared in *The New York Journal of Dentistry,* Paffenbarger said that "the turbine handpiece and the composites, which replaced silicate cements, are the two discoveries, in the author's opinion, that had the greatest impact on chairside practice."

Paffenbarger retired in 1974 after forty-five years of heading the Research Unit. In 1985, the Research Unit was renamed the Paffenbarger Research Center (PRC) to honor its longtime director. Dr. Paffenbarger died in December 1985. The National Bureau of Standards became the National Institute of Standards and Technology in 1988. In April 2008, the PRC celebrated its eightieth anniversary.

SPECIALTIES WORTHY OF RECOGNITION

In 1936, there were five established dental specialties: oral surgery, orthodontia, pedodontia, periodontia, and prosthodontia, but the ADA had not formally recognized any of them or authorized the certification of specialists. There was not yet even consensus on the definition of a specialty.

The ADA Council on Dental Education appointed a Committee on Dental Specialties in December 1940 to conduct "a comprehensive study of the specialties in dentistry with a view to determining (1) what constitutes a specialty, (2) what specialties are warranted, (3) what the additional training of the specialist should be beyond graduation from a dental school, and (4) how the specialist would be recognized by the public."

◀ Dr. Harry B. Pinney, ADA secretary, shows a chart at the ADA's central office in 1940 illustrating the effect that the establishment of the tripartite in 1913 had on membership growth. Looking on are visitors Dr. Irma Eilerts de Haan, a dentist from the Dutch East Indies, and Dr. Elsie Gerlach, a trustee of the American Association of Woman Dentists. *(ADA file photo by Len Arnold & Julian J. Jackson)*

and prosthodontia; (3) that the limits of the practice of a specialty should be determined by each specialty group; (4) and that certification by an approved specialty examining board is the most desirable method of giving public recognition to the specialist."

The ADA formally recognized the certification of specialists in oral surgery and periodontics in 1947, pedodontics and prosthodontics in 1948, orthodontics and oral pathology in 1950, dental public health in 1951, and endodontics in 1963. The last specialty to be recognized by the ADA was oral and maxillofacial radiology in 2001.

The specialty committee's work was interrupted by WWII, when restrictions on travel in 1942 caused the Council on Dental Education to suspend its work for the duration. It was not until 1947 that the committee could prepare a full report. The findings and recommendations were "(1) that a specialty is a field of practice which calls for intensive study and experience beyond graduation from a dental school; (2) that the specialties now worthy of recognition are: oral surgery, orthodontics, pedodontia, periodontia,

DENTISTS IN WORLD WAR II

More than twenty-two thousand dentists served their country in WWII and many lost their lives. They served in all branches of the armed forces and on far-flung war fronts around the world. Dentists also served on the home front. Dental offices back home were crowded because of the great number of dentists serving their country. Dentists coped with wartime shortages of silver, gold, and other materials. Dentists and their staffs wrapped bandages for Red Cross packages, participated in scrap metal drives, and invested part of their paychecks in bonds to help finance the war.

◀ A 1941 chart showing that before the U.S. entered World War II, dental defects were the number one reason men failed the Selective Service's physical examination.

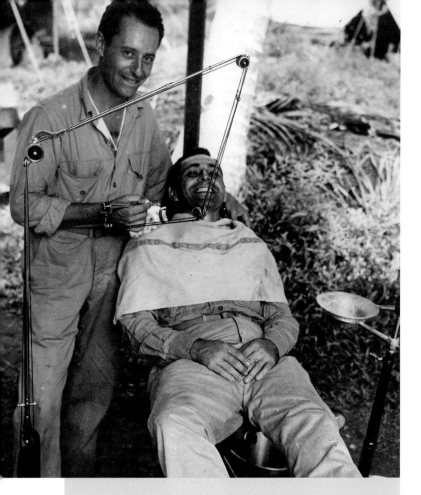

Lieutenant Louis N. Heller, a dentist from San Francisco, provides dental treatment at his military post on Guadalcanal. Dentists performed under all kinds of conditions at the battlefront in World War II. *(Official US Marine Corps Photo)*

Young American men, it turned out, were not an especially fit bunch as our country entered the war. In June 1941, even before the U.S. entered the war, the Selective Service reported that three hundred eighty thousand men out of the one million registrants who took the Selective Service physical exam failed to qualify physically for military service. The leading deficiency: 17 percent of those who failed their physicals did so on the basis of their teeth. Indeed, failure to meet the minimum standard of having six opposing teeth was a leading cause of rejection from military service in both world wars.

Dentists served all over the globe and many faced the same discomforts and dangers as the frontline troops. U.S. military dentists practiced their profession at places like Guadalcanal, the Kasserine Pass, Anzio, and the Huertgen Forest, often under difficult conditions. They restored teeth and did complex oral surgery in mobile dental units or makeshift operatories in tents that were often the targets of enemy shelling or aircraft attacks. At Pearl Harbor, on December 7, 1941, two Navy Dental Corps officers were killed, and four others were wounded. In the Pacific Theater, fifty-three American military dentists were captured by the Japanese and held as prisoners of war. A total of twenty-two dentists died as Japanese POWs, a 40 percent mortality rate.

The ADA could not hold an Annual Session during 1945 due to wartime travel and resource restrictions, but it remained active throughout the war years. The Association worked closely with the U.S. military to assess wartime dental needs and successfully lobbied Congress and wartime regulatory agencies for the same extra gasoline rations that the nation's physicians enjoyed. In addition, the ADA and state dental organizations were instrumental in outfitting mobile dental units for the use of the troops in combat zones.

Dental officer's field kit used during World War II.

Sailors at the U.S. Naval Magazine in Montauk, New York, wait in line at a mobile dental unit for treatment in 1945. Dentists used mobile dental units to provide dental care near battlefronts, at army camps, and on navy vessels underserved by the dental corps during World War II. Because they were expensive to manufacture, organizations, civic groups, and businesses often donated the units. *(Official U.S. Navy Photo)*

A number of military dentists earned the nation's highest awards for bravery in battle. In the African and European Theaters, Dr. Robert Moyers became one the most decorated dental officers in U.S. history. His exploits included ten months behind enemy lines as an agent for the Office of Strategic Services, the predecessor of the Central Intelligence Agency. Among his many honors was the Legion of Merit—presented in person by the legendary Major General William "Wild Bill" Donovan. In civilian life, Moyers went on to an exemplary career in Michigan in orthodontics. In 1988, he received the Albert H. Ketcham Memorial Award, the highest national honor in orthodontics. He retired as a professor emeritus at the University of Michigan.

The dentist most highly honored for his service in World War II was Dr. Ben Salomon, a native of Milwaukee, Wisconsin. Captain Salomon was inducted as an infantryman with the rank of private, but later joined the Army Dental Corps as an officer. He proved to be both an outstanding soldier and an inspirational leader of men. On the morning of July 7, 1944, on Saipan in the Marianas Island, Salomon's frontline aid station, where he was lending a hand as a surgeon's aide, was attacked during a surge in fighting. He grabbed a machine gun and fought back, killing ninety-eight enemy soldiers before he too perished. Because he was wearing a Red Cross brassard at the

◄ U.S. President George W. Bush presents Dr. Robert L. West with the Medal of Honor for Captain Ben L. Salomon during a White House ceremony in May 2002. Dr. Salomon was the first U.S. Army dental officer to receive the Medal of Honor, which was awarded to him posthumously for heroism in World War II. West was instrumental in securing recognition for Salomon.

Origins of National Children's Dental Health Month

One of the most popular programs in ADA history is National Children's Dental Health Month, celebrated each year in February. The celebration, which brings oral hygiene tips and reminders to millions of American children and parents each year, traces its roots to a program initiated by the Cleveland Dental Society (CDS) in February 1941. Dr. Norman H. Denner, president of the local society at the time, suggested that CDS sponsor a one-day event to educate Clevelanders about dental disease and proper oral hygiene methods for children. Members of the local society enthusiastically supported the proposal, and Cleveland celebrated the first Children's Dental Health Day on February 3, 1941.

After a couple of years, the CDS made Children's Dental Health Day an annual observance and, in 1946, approached the ADA about sponsoring the event on a national scale. In 1949, the Association began to promote the observance of a National Children's Dental Health Day to its constituent societies by distributing a planning kit for the observance. In 1950, President Harry S. Truman signed a presidential proclamation formally establishing a National Children's Dental Health Day. By the early 1950s, the event was increasingly celebrated in cities and communities across America on the first Monday in February each year. The ADA House of Delegates formally extended the observance to a week in 1955 and then made it a month-long event in 1981.

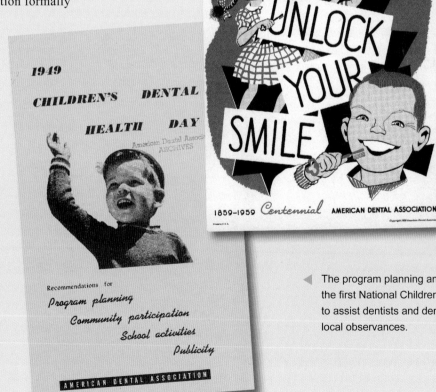

Posters used to promote National Children's Dental Health observances in 1958 and 1959. Planning organizers have always used slogans as an effective way to focus the observance on a particular theme.

The program planning and publicity kit developed for the first National Children's Dental Health Day in 1949 to assist dentists and dental organizations in planning local observances.

▼ ADA leaders gather with others in an NBC studio to tape a discussion of international dental problems. The broadcast was featured during the 1947 Annual Session in Boston, which was held in conjunction with the Tenth International Dental Congress.

▲ ADA President-elect Harvey B. Washburn, incoming ADA President Sterling V. Mead, and Dr. Harold Hillenbrand (left to right) at the 1946 Annual Session in Miami, where Dr. Hillenbrand was installed as ADA secretary. Hillenbrand served as the ADA's chief administrative officer from 1946 until his retirement in 1969, a period in which the ADA grew in membership, prestige, and influence. *(ADA file photo by Walter Davis Photo Service)*

▲ U.S. President Harry S. Truman, surrounded by dental and legislative leaders, signs the congressional bill to formally establish the National Institute of Dental Research (NIDR) on June 24, 1948. The passage of this legislation concluded an eight-year campaign by the ADA, assisted by U.S. Senator James Murray of Montana, to secure the first federal legislation in support of dental research. The federal agency is now known as the National Institute of Dental and Craniofacial Research. *(ADA file photo by National Institutes of Health, Public Health Service)*

Coming of Age

1936–1959

1936

ADA President Leroy Miner appears on the cover of *TIME* Magazine featuring a report on the Association's 1936 Annual Session in San Francisco.

1937

The ADA's newly established Council on Dental Education takes responsibility for the accreditation of the nation's dental schools and the standardization of dental school curricula.

ADA member Dr. Alvin Strock inserts a dental screw implant made of Vitallium, the first successful biocompatible implant metal.

1938

The S. S. White Dental Manufacturing Company signs over all rights to *The Dental Cosmos* to the ADA, which merges the nearly eighty-year-old publication with *The Journal of the American Dental Association.*

The first toothbrush made with nylon bristles goes into commercial production.

1940

The ADA adopts an official emblem for professional dentistry, incorporating the staff of Asclepius, the traditional symbol for medicine.

1941

The Cleveland Dental Society establishes Children's Dental Health Day.

1944

As American forces push toward victory in the European and Pacific Theatres of World War II, more than twenty-two thousand U.S. dentists are serving their country in uniform.

1945

Grand Rapids, Michigan, and Newburgh, New York, become the first two U.S. communities to fluoridate their water supplies.

1947

The ADA formally recognizes the specialties of oral surgery and periodontics.

1948

President Harry S. Truman signs legislation establishing the National Institute of Dental Research (now the National Institute of Dental and Craniofacial Research) and initiating federal funding for dental research.

The ADA formally recognizes the specialties of pedodontics and prosthodontics.

APRIL

THE JOURNAL OF THE AMERICAN DENTAL ASSOCIATION AND THE DENTAL COSMOS

Reactions to Anesthetic Solutions—*Miller*
Mandible and Postnatal Development—*Dunn*
Management of Soft Tissues—*Sorensen*
Edentulous Mouth and Infection—*Sweet*
Immediate Restorations—*Frahm*
Orthodontic Treatment—*Atkinson*
Pulpless Tooth Problem—*Huff*
Platinum-Centered Gold Foil—*Rule*
Gold and Gold-Platinum Foils—*Shell*
Master Mandibular Impression—*Ostrem*
Sterility of Anesthetic Solutions—*Grossman & Appleton*
Hemorrhage—*Fitzgerald*
Empyema—*Lucas*
Occlusal Forms—*Sears*
EDITORIALS
Does Our Code of Ethics Mean Anything?
Changing Concept of Oral Focal Infection
ASSOCIATION ACTIVITIES
BUREAU OF PUBLIC RELATIONS
DENTAL ECONOMICS
COUNCIL ON DENTAL THERAPEUTICS

FIFTY CENTS

◀ A cover of *The Journal of the American Dental Association* (*JADA*) that includes both *The Dental Cosmos* and *JADA* in the title, circa 1938.

1951

The ADA establishes an accreditation program for dental laboratory technicians.

The ADA formally recognizes the specialty of dental public health.

1949

The first National Children's Dental Health Day under the auspices of the ADA is observed.

Swiss chemist Oskar Haggar develops the world's first system for bonding acrylic resin to dentin.

1953

A research team headed by Dr. Robert J. Nelsen, and composed of staff members from the ADA and the National Bureau of Standards develops the first workable turbine contra-angle handpiece.

1957

Dr. John Borden introduces the Airotor, the first commercially successful air-driven high-speed handpiece.

Congress amends the Social Security Act to include dentists who were formerly covered under a federal insurance program.

1950

The ADA endorses community water fluoridation.

The ADA formally recognizes the specialties of orthodontics and oral pathology.

1952

The ADA establishes an accreditation program for dental hygienists.

1955

Dr. Michael Buonocore first describes the acid etch technique, which is used to increase the adhesion of composite fillings to enamel, thus paving the way for modern esthetic dentistry.

Joint ADA-National Bureau of Standards research teams develop panoramic dental X-ray equipment.

1959

In the midst of the cold war, the ADA makes national headlines when it refuses to move its centennial celebration from the ballroom of the Waldorf-Astoria Hotel for a luncheon in honor of visiting Soviet Premier Nikita Khrushchev.

1958

John Naughton develops the first fully reclining, upholstered dental chair.

The official emblem of dentistry, sometimes referred to as a caduceus, was adopted in 1940.

Mission to Japan
1950

Only five years after Japan surrendered to the United States at the end of WWII, the ADA answered a call from the U.S. Occupation Force in Tokyo to provide a dental mission to the Japanese Dental Association to assist in Japan's reconstruction. The invitation, from General Douglas MacArthur, Supreme Commander Allied Powers, arrived at the ADA's Chicago central office in the spring of 1950. In June 1950, the Board of Trustees officially accepted the invitation and selected a group of five representatives including Dr. Harold Oppice, the Association's president at the time, to compose the mission to Japan.

Geopolitics had changed dramatically in East Asia since the end of WWII in 1945. China had fallen to Mao Tse Tung and the Communists, and Russian troops were poised on the borders of Manchuria and North Korea. Between the time that the mission to Japan was appointed in mid-June 1950 and the day the

group left for Tokyo on June 30, the North Korean Army had invaded South Korea and taken its capital city of Seoul, setting off the conflict known as the Korean War. America was once again at war, and former enemies such as Japan were now U.S. allies.

The mission to Japan arrived in Tokyo on July 2 and began a whirlwind, thirty-day visit that took the group to the country's seven dental schools, as well as the dental departments of several hospitals and health service centers. At every stop, the American dentists met with their Japanese counterparts for lectures and social gatherings. On July 27, the mission met with officers of the Japanese Dental Association and officials of the U.S. General Headquarters in Tokyo to report on the state of Japanese dentistry and make suggestions for its improvement. Though recognizing the impossibility of analyzing an entire nation's dental infrastructure in a thirty-day visit, the mission felt that it had accomplished its main objectives and made valuable recommendations.

Japan's dentists echoed those sentiments. Dr. Kazuo Sato, the president of the Japanese Dental Association, wrote to thank the mission members for their "valuable advice and guidance...[that] will greatly contribute to the future development of dental science and practice in this country."

◀ Members of the ADA dental mission to Japan and their Japanese hosts sightsee in Nikko, Japan, in 1950. The thirty-day trip to Japan included visits to dental schools and hospital dental departments, conferences, and social gatherings.

time, he was technically ineligible for a Medal of Honor because medical personnel were not eligible. That misunderstanding was corrected years later and on May 1, 2002, in a White House Rose Garden ceremony, President George W. Bush announced that Captain Benjamin Lewis Salomon had been given a posthumous Medal of Honor.

Thousands of young men who served combat tours of duty with fighting units—armor, infantry, artillery, fighter planes, and battleships—were future ADA members. They returned to the United States following the war to earn college degrees on the GI Bill, went to dental school, and opened practices in the late 1940s and 1950s.

▲ Attendees at the first State Secretaries Management Conference in 1948 (now known as the Managment Conference).

▼ The ADA Board of Trustees during the 1949 Annual Session in San Francisco. *(ADA file photo by Melgar Studios)*

A NEW ERA BRINGS FLUORIDATION

During the mid-twentieth century, dentistry was marked by one advance after another in science, technology, and equipment. One significant advancement was community water fluoridation.

On January 25, 1945, Grand Rapids, Michigan, became the first city in the world to add fluoride to its drinking water. Grand Rapids added the fluoride, at one part per million parts, to its municipal water supply as part of a National Institute of Dental Research (NIDR) study on fluoride's effectiveness in preventing tooth decay. Previous studies had identified this amount to be the safest while still being effective. The decrease in tooth decay was so striking that the control city in the study, Muskegon, Michigan, started fluoridating its water before the study was even concluded.

Although the first citywide fluoridation was in Michigan, in 1945, the trail to Grand Rapids actually began in Colorado several decades prior. Dr. Frederick McKay, a graduate of the University of Pennsylvania, was practicing in Colorado Springs when he became curious about something he called the "Colorado Stain." In a scientific paper, he described a staining of the teeth (now called fluorosis) among Colorado Springs children. He suggested that it could be related to the water supply. McKay requested the assistance of Dr. G. V. Black to investigate the stain. Together they wrote the paper "Mottled Teeth—an Endemic

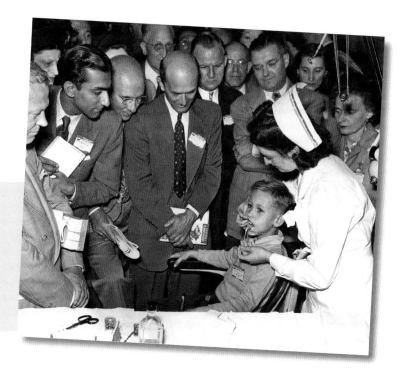

► A nurse from the Illinois State Department of Public Health draws a crowd at the 1948 Annual Session in Chicago by demonstrating a topical application of sodium fluoride. Clinical tests at the time indicated that topical fluoride therapy reduced the incidence of dental decay among children by 40 to 50 percent.

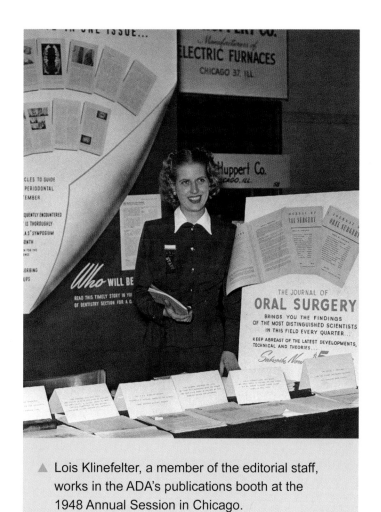

Lois Klinefelter, a member of the editorial staff, works in the ADA's publications booth at the 1948 Annual Session in Chicago.

Developmental Imperfection of the Teeth, Heretofore Unknown in the Literature of Dentistry" (1918). Later, in the 1930s, McKay suggested that "caries were inhibited by the same water which produced mottled enamel." Further studies led to the breakthrough conclusion that adding fluoride to a city's water supply would inhibit tooth decay among its residents.

Dr. James L. Wieland, who along with Dr. Kim Erickson co-chaired the original NIDR study committee, would comment nearly fifty years later, "The story of fluoridation is so significant. Fluoridation is safe, effective and its impact on dental health is overwhelming." Wieland further noted, "Today water fluoridation has spread throughout the nation and the world. It is currently estimated that over 130 million people in the United States and 270 million people in 30 countries enjoy the benefits of water fluoridation." According to Erickson, "Fluoridation is like the Salk vaccine of dentistry." In a ringing endorsement of the effectiveness of water fluoridation, the U.S. Centers for Disease

A commercial exhibit booth at the 1949 Annual Session in San Francisco features advertisements for dental chairs claiming that they relieve the back and feet, alleviate tension, and preserve good posture. *(ADA file photo by Melgar Studios)*

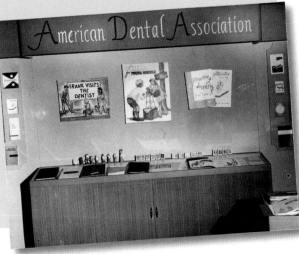

An ADA exhibit booth at the 1949 Annual Session in San Francisco displays some of the children's merchandise, including posters and toys, available in the ADA product catalog. *(ADA file photo by Elbee's)*

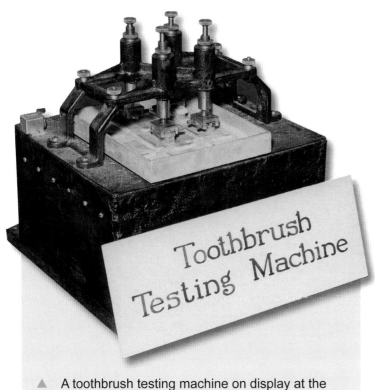

A toothbrush testing machine on display at the scientific and health exhibit hall at the 1949 Annual Session in San Francisco. *(ADA file photo by Melgar Studios)*

Dr. Henry C. Lineberger congratulates the first women to earn fellowship degrees in the American College of Dentists. They were (from left) Dr. Dorothea Radusch, assistant professor, University of Minnesota Dental School; Dr. Dorothy Hard, assistant professor, University of Michigan Dental School; and Dr. Ruth Martin, professor of pedodontics, Washington University Dental School. The degrees were conferred at the college's convocation at the 1950 Annual Session in Atlantic City. The fourth woman to earn the degree at this time, Dr. Grace Rogers Spalding, well-known for her part in establishing the American Academy of Periodontology, was absent due to illness. *(ADA file photo by Fred Hess & Son)*

Control named it one of the ten great public health achievements of the twentieth century.

Fluoridation was not limited just to city water supplies. The work of Indiana University School of Dentistry researchers Drs. Joseph Muhler, Harry

The ADA House of Delegates in session during the 1950 Annual Session in Atlantic City. The ADA met at Atlantic City five times between 1937 and 1971. *(ADA file photo by Fred Hess & Son)*

ADA President Harold W. Oppice (second from left) pays homage to dentists who died while serving in the armed forces at the tomb of the Unknown Soldier at Arlington National Cemetery during the 1951 Annual Session in Washington, D.C. *(Official U.S. Navy Photo)*

▲ A health exhibit at the 1954 Annual Session in Miami promotes dental care as an important part of overall health. *(ADA file photo by Moser & Son)*

▲ A somber display at the 1952 Annual Session in St. Louis, created by the Dental Division of the U.S. Navy Bureau of Medicine and Surgery, shows the role of the dentist in an atomic disaster. *(ADA file photo by Ferman Photographers)*

▲ Guests admire one of the gowns featured at the fashion show at the 1952 ADA Annual Session in St. Louis. The fashion show was a popular Annual Session event for many years.

Frank Taylor (center), director of the Smithsonian's Museum of History and Technology, admires the original prototype of the contra-angle turbine handpiece designed in 1953 by Dr. Robert J. Nelsen (right). Also pictured is John W. Kumpula, who assisted in the mechanical development of the instrument. The prototype was developed at the ADA Research Unit at the National Bureau of Standards and donated to the Smithsonian during this 1963 ceremony at the museum. The Research Unit is now the Paffenbarger Research Center and remains on site with the same federal agency, now known as the National Institute of Standards and Technology. *(ADA file photo courtesy of the Smithsonian Institution)*

Day, and William Nebergall led to the introduction of the world's first stannous fluoride toothpaste, which debuted in 1955 as Procter & Gamble's Crest®, an effective caries fighter and a commercial blockbuster. Crest also spawned an advertising legend: "Look, Mom — no cavities!" In 1960, the ADA Council on Dental Therapeutics recognized that Crest with fluoride was effective against caries and awarded it the ADA's coveted Seal of Acceptance.

IMPORTANT TECHNICAL ADVANCES

The development of the high-speed dental handpiece during the 1950s revolutionized the work of the dentist. There were a number of designs and modifications introduced during the 1940s and 1950s that continually increased the speed and usability of the handpiece. In 1953, Dr. Robert J. Nelsen, working with associates at the ADA-sponsored research unit at the National Bureau of Standards in Washington,

Crowds surround table clinics at the 1954 Annual Session in Miami.

Members of a seventy-five-woman delegation of dentists from Finland are assisted by ADA staff at the 1959 Annual Session in New York City. Many international guests attended the ADA's one hundredth anniversary meeting. *(ADA file photo by Standard Flashlight Co.)*

The ADA Centennial
and the War for the Ballroom, 1959

One hundred years after its founding in 1859 at Niagara Falls, the ADA met again in the state of New York to commemorate its centennial anniversary. More than thirty-two thousand members and guests attended the centennial Annual Session at the Waldorf-Astoria Hotel in New York City, September 14–18, 1959. However, the gala celebration almost did not happen when the ADA became embroiled in a cold war international incident that threatened to derail the Association's centennial fete.

The flap began in early September when the ADA's president, Dr. Percy T. Phillips, received two letters, both dated September 9. One of the letters was from Robert F. Wagner, mayor of the city of New York. Mayor Wagner explained that the city was hosting Soviet Premier Nikita Khrushchev on an official state visit to the United States and needed to use the Grand Ballroom of the Waldorf-Astoria Hotel on September 17 to hold a luncheon in honor of the premier. The ADA had a longstanding reservation for the ballroom on the same day. The hotel management had referred Wagner to the ADA since it was legally obligated to honor the ADA's reservation. The letter politely described the necessity for the use of the ballroom as a matter of security and asked the ADA to voluntarily relinquish its use on that day and time.

ADA leaders welcome Vice President Richard Nixon to the 1959 Annual Session in New York commemorating the ADA's one hundredth anniversary. Nixon (third from left) and Senator Frank Carlson (second from right) spoke at the ADA meeting's opening session.

The other letter, from Wiley T. Buchanan, Jr., U.S. State Department chief of protocol, notified the ADA, "Our security people have returned from a visit to the Waldorf and have advised us that they feel it absolutely imperative for security reasons that the official luncheon of the Mayor of New York be held in the Grand Ballroom of the Hotel." Buchanan continued that he was sorry to inform Dr. Phillips that this was a change "in the national interest [and]…most urgently recommended."

The ADA, however, had a rock-solid contract with the Waldorf-Astoria for the room and was adamant in its right to use it. Since the event that was scheduled for the Grand Ballroom on September 17 was the ADA's centennial meeting of the House of Delegates, moving the event elsewhere with less than a week's notice would be impossible. President Phillips replied to Mayor Wagner by letter, with a copy to Buchanan, on September 11. The letter said the ADA, "respectfully declines your request and… will use all possible means to enforce its contract with the Waldorf-Astoria Hotel."

First-day cover with an ADA centennial anniversary stamp. A first-day cover is an envelope to which has been affixed a newly issued U.S. postage stamp that has been postmarked on the first day of issue for the stamp.

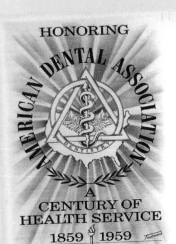

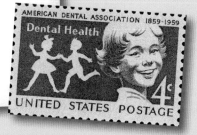

Stamp issued by the U.S. Postal Service in commemoration of the ADA centennial in 1959.

By then, the ballroom controversy was on the front pages of nation's newspapers. The ADA's refusal to give up the room was broadly supported by the general public and the media. The State Department had to advise the mayor to find another ballroom and so the soviet premier's luncheon was held at the Commodore Hotel, nine blocks away. The ADA celebrated its centennial meeting in the Waldorf-Astoria's Grand Ballroom as planned. Vice President Richard M. Nixon, addressing the opening session of the Annual Session, weighed in on the side of the denists. Referring to the Soviets' Luna 2 unmanned spacecraft which had crash-landed on the moon just days earlier, Nixon noted to great applause that "the Russians got to the moon first, but the American Dental Association got to this ballroom first."

Public opinion came down squarely on the side of the ADA, in standing up for its rights in a free and democratic society. Although there were a handful of critics who assailed the Association for not rolling over in the "interests of world peace," most Americans applauded the ADA's uncompromising stand. "Bully for you," one Maryland writer paraphrased Teddy Roosevelt. The media, of course, had a field day with the story, with one reporter noting that getting the dentists to give up the ballroom was like pulling teeth. An editorial writer for the *Los Angeles Examiner* noted that the ADA victory should drill into the Soviets "the fact that our democracy has teeth."

In the end, the centennial Annual Session went off flawlessly, and the ADA came away with a sense of renewal and optimism for the challenges ahead in the Association's second century.

► One of the many telegraphs, postcards, and letters sent to the ADA by members, dentists, and the general public in support of the Association's refusal to give up the Waldorf-Astoria ballroom for the visiting Russian premier Nikita Khrushchev in 1959. The media widely supported the ADA's stance.

D.C., developed the first operable high-speed contra-angle handpiece driven by a turbine to be put on the market. Nelsen's handpiece used a hydraulic (water-driven) turbine and succeeded where previous attempts failed because it did not overheat and seize up. It was marketed under the name Turbo-Jet but was not commercially successful due to its size and cumbersome nature. In 1957, Dr. John Borden introduced the Borden Airotor, a handpiece powered by an air turbine that reached higher speeds, without undue noise or vibration, than any previous equipment. When the Airotor went on the market, it made such an impact that by the end of the 1960s, almost all dentists were using high-speed handpieces in their practices.

A list of advancements in dentistry of the first half of the twentieth century, published by the ADA Bureau of Public Information in 1958, included improvements in local anesthetics; the use of antibiotics; improvements in artificial dentures and retention techniques; acrylics for dentures, crowns, and bridgework; improvements in drugs; new chemical and mechanical techniques in endodontics; chemical germicides for instrument disinfection; and new surgical methods of treating orofacial injuries.

The election of John F. Kennedy to the White House in 1960 brought a New Frontier to American society. The ADA's successful penetration of that frontier during the 1960s would elevate the Association and the profession to heights unimagined at the end of the Second World War.

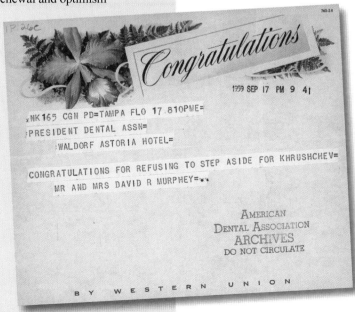

765-58

Congratulations

1959 SEP 17 PM 9 41

NK165 CGN PD=TAMPA FLO 17 810PME=
PRESIDENT DENTAL ASSN=
WALDORF ASTORIA HOTEL=

CONGRATULATIONS FOR REFUSING TO STEP ASIDE FOR KHRUSHCHEV=
MR AND MRS DAVID R MURPHEY=

AMERICAN
DENTAL ASSOCIATION
ARCHIVES
DO NOT CIRCULATE

BY WESTERN UNION

Chapter Four
A Voice in National Affairs, 1960–1969

The 1960s were a tumultuous decade in the United States. America waged an unpopular war in Vietnam, racial and political tensions led to unrest in cities, and a stunned citizenry coped with the political assassinations of President John F. Kennedy, his brother Robert Kennedy, and the nation's most dynamic civil rights leader, Martin Luther King, Jr.

The upheavals of the decade spilled over into the nation's dental and medical professions. In 1960, the ADA called on its constituent and component societies to eliminate any existing discriminatory membership practices. The passage of the landmark Civil Rights Act of 1964 gave impetus to this goal, which was finally achieved by the Association in 1966.

Among other significant legislation passed during the 1960s were Medicare and Medicaid, signed into law by President Lyndon B. Johnson in 1965. The federal government addressed health care workforce planning in 1963 when Congress passed the Health Professions Educational Assistance Act that provided funding for dental and medical schools. For the ADA and other

President John F. Kennedy passes out pens after the signing of the Health Professions Educational Assistance Act in 1963. The signing of H.R. 12, which provided federal aid for dental and medical education, was an occasion for a major gathering of congressional and other governmental leaders in the Oval Office. The only person present at the signing who was not connected with government was Hal M. Christensen, director of the ADA Washington Office (fourth from left). *(ADA file photo by Cecil W. Stoughton)*

Establishment of the
ADA Foundation

When the ADA established its charitable foundation in 1964, it was a time of unprecedented change in American society. President Lyndon Johnson's Great Society was pushing a program of health insurance for seniors through Congress, while young Americans were being sent to fight a war in Vietnam.

Originally named the ADA Research and Educational Foundation, the Foundation had a broad charter. It was established to "operate exclusively for charitable, scientific, literary, or educational purposes, including making gifts and contributions to non-profit organizations."

In 1964, the same year as its founding, the Foundation launched the popular health evaluation program, now called the Health Screening Program (HSP), at ADA Annual Sessions, which has since provided complimentary state-of-the art screenings for a variety of occupational health risks to over sixty thousand dental team professionals. Dentists' participation in the HSP has not only helped to monitor their personal health but the overall health of the dental profession. The information gathered by the HSP has created the largest national database on the health of dental professionals. Since 1975, investigators have published over fifty articles in peer-reviewed journals based upon data obtained from the HSP. In 2008, the HSP took a brief hiatus to be retooled and modernized for return at the 2009 Annual Session.

The Foundation changed its name in 1971 to the ADA Health Foundation (ADAHF). During the 1970s and most of the 1980s, the Foundation concentrated on dental research. In 1973, the ADAHF asked researchers it employed at the ADA Research Unit to sign an agreement covering patents as a condition of employment or funding. Two years later, in 1975, the U.S. Department of Health, Education, and Welfare (HEW) approved an institutional patent agreement with the Foundation that allowed it to retain patent rights arising from Foundation-supported research, as well as awards sponsored with HEW funding. Previously, scientific discoveries that led to patents reverted to the federal government.

In 1980, the Foundation received its first royalty payment on a patent. It was for an improved composite resin material developed by ADA scientist Dr. Rafael L. Bowen, whose

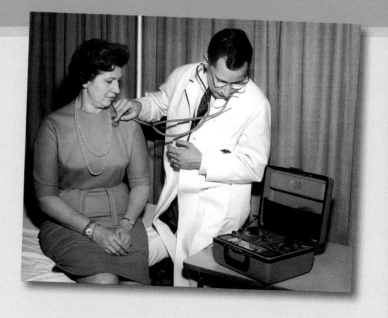

▲ A participant is examined at the first Health Screening Program, which took place at the 1964 Annual Session in San Francisco. *(ADA file photo by Cristof Studio)*

research had been supported by the Foundation. Under the agreement with HEW, the Foundation was able to license its patents to manufacturers and use the resulting royalty payments to fund further research, as well as educational programs. By 1984, the Foundation held thirty patents developed by Bowen and his colleagues at the National Bureau of Standards Research Unit/Paffenbarger Research Center (NBS/PRC).

Although the NBS/PRC remained a pillar of Foundation funding and support, in later years the ADAHF broadened its scope of giving. In 1994, the ADA Board of Trustees designated the Foundation as the Association's principal charitable agency. In 2003, the Foundation took over management of the ADA's long-established Relief, Disaster, and Emergency Assistance Funds, which had been administered separately by other ADA entities. The Relief Fund assisted dentists in need due to accident, illness, or misfortune. The Disaster and Emergency Assistance Funds helped dentists to rebuild after natural disasters and provided dental services to areas hard hit by disaster.

The ADA Health Foundation was renamed the ADA Foundation to reflect its broader mission of "uniting people and organizations to make a difference through better oral health." In addition to research and charitable assistance, the Foundation also provides support for dental education and access to care for children and older adults.

U.S. dental and medical associations, it was apparent that Washington was becoming an ever more active participant in health care issues.

The ADA became more outward looking during the decade. The Association signaled its emergence as the nation's most prominent dental organization when it moved into its new high-rise general office building just off Michigan Avenue in Chicago in 1965. The Association established the ADA Research and Educational Foundation in 1964 as the charitable branch of the organization. The establishment of the Council on Dental Materials and Devices in 1966 positioned the ADA as the nation's authority on evaluating dental materials and devices.

Even the Association's improvements in member benefits had connotations for issues of national significance. The enhancement of member insurance programs during the decade was an outgrowth of increased societal interest in seeing that Americans were fully covered in the event of illness or accident.

▲ In 1961, the U.S. Dental Exchange Mission to the U.S.S.R. and officials from the Soviet Ministry of Health arrive at Tbilisi, Georgia, where the group toured the Tbilisi Institute of Stomatology and did some sightseeing. Tbilisi was just one of many stops for the group consisting of Dr. Harold Hillenbrand, ADA secretary; Dr. Charles H. Patton, ADA president; Dr. John R. Abel, ADA president-elect; Dr. Gerald D. Timmons, speaker of the ADA House of Delegates; Dr. Francis A. Arnold, Jr., director of the National Institute of Dental Research; and Dr. John W. Knutson, chief dental officer, U.S. Public Health Service.

EYEBALL TO EYEBALL WITH THE RUSSIANS

The decade started with an ADA outreach program that resulted in the first U.S. Dental Exchange Mission to the U.S.S.R. The election of President John F. Kennedy in 1960 and the de-Stalinization of the Soviet Union by Premier Nikita S. Khrushchev created a short-lived opportunity for a cold war thaw in 1961.

A New Headquarters
1965

The growth of the ADA in the postwar era put constant pressure on the organization to find adequate space to house its growing operations. During World War II, the Association had purchased a building at 222 East Superior Street, in a mixed-use Chicago residential and commercial neighborhood, one mile north of the Loop and just east of North Michigan Avenue. Neighbors included the Chicago campus of Northwestern University.

Dr. Harold Hillenbrand, who in 1946 became ADA secretary (the chief administrative officer), began planning to expand the facilities during the late 1940s and early 1950s. In 1957, the ADA completely remodeled the existing structure, adding frontage and an addition that doubled the space. By 1961, the central office building had more than 45,000 square feet of office space and housed 160 ADA employees.

In 1961, Hillenbrand was out of the country when he received a call from a longtime friend, a Chicago banker. The friend informed him that the Chicago Red Cross was interested in selling a one-story garage at 211 East Chicago Avenue that had been used to house emergency vehicles and was on a lot with a 200-foot frontage. The Board of Trustees had previously tasked Hillenbrand with finding potential property in the area for a proposed new central office building. Hillenbrand

Dr. Harold Hillenbrand (left), ADA secretary, shows off the architect's painting of the ADA Headquarters building that was under construction when Dr. D. Greer Walker (right), president of the British Dental Association, visited Chicago in 1964.

immediately began negotiations for purchase of the property, and the Association bought the garage and lot for $740,000 in the summer of 1962.

The ADA selected the Chicago architectural firm of Graham, Anderson, Probst and White to draw up plans for a building on the 26,000 square foot site. The architects presented plans for construction of a twenty-three story bronzed glass, concrete, and steel tower with about 12,000 square feet

The ADA's headquarters was housed in this building with a gothic revival façade at 222 East Superior, Chicago, Illinois, 1943–1956. In 1956 the adjacent property was acquired and the ADA added on to the building, modernized the existing space, and added a new façade.

The ADA's headquarters building at 222 East Superior, Chicago, Illinois, as it looked 1957–1965.

The ADA Chicago headquarters building in an early stage of its construction in 1964. The service core of the building that houses the elevators and stairwells was erected first and the steel girders for the walls and floors were built around it. The Chicago landmark Water Tower building is seen in the foreground.

of usable space on each floor. Costs were estimated at $12–15 million; the ADA would use $6 million of its own funds with the balance coming from a mortgage. The Association also planned to help pay for the new building by leasing space to other health organizations.

The site had its fair share of critics, who dubbed the building "Hillenbrand's Folly." In the 1960s, before North Michigan Avenue was redeveloped, the area had deteriorated from the 1920s when it was one of Chicago's more upscale neighborhoods. Critics of the new building thought the money would have been better spent on a site closer to the Loop. But Hillenbrand held his ground, and the later construction of Water Tower Place and the John Hancock Building assured the renaissance of North Michigan Avenue. Real estate values in the neighborhood skyrocketed, and Hillenbrand and the ADA proved to have made one of the wisest decisions in the Association's history.

ADA leaders break ground for the construction of the ADA Headquarters building in Chicago, November 11, 1963. Building construction continued until 1965.

The ADA began work on the new building on November 11, 1963, and crews broke ground as soon as the frost lifted in the spring of 1964. Construction went relatively smoothly, and the framework rose into the Chicago skyline in 1964 and 1965. The general contractor handed over the keys to the ADA just before Thanksgiving in 1965—almost two years to the day after the groundbreaking. Final costs came in at $14.6 million.

There was still a great deal of work to do before the building could be fully functional. Employees gave up much of their long Thanksgiving weekend to help moving crews work around the clock, shuttling furniture and files. On Monday, November 28, 1965, more than two hundred ADA employees reported to their new home at 211 East Chicago Avenue.

The ADA Headquarters building at 211 East Chicago Avenue, Chicago, Illinois, as it looked when it opened in 1965.

The governments of the United States and the U.S.S.R. had begun negotiating agreements for the exchange of medical, technical, educational, and cultural missions as early as 1957. The ADA, which had participated in a very successful dental mission to Japan in 1950, quickly expressed an interest in a dental exchange program.

Government negotiators did not achieve consensus on the program with the Soviets until early 1958, at which time the ADA wrote the Soviet Ministry of Health to hammer out the details of an exchange agreement. A somewhat frustrating correspondence ensued, and it was not until early 1961 that the Ministry of Health and the U.S. State Department informed the ADA that it would host a Soviet Dental Mission to the United States in April and May, followed by an ADA mission to the Soviet Union in June 1961.

The Soviet Dental Mission consisted of four dentists, a dental engineer, and an industrial designer who worked with dental laboratories in the Soviet Union. They visited ADA Headquarters in Chicago and dental offices, laboratories, and research institutions in New York, Washington, D.C., Philadelphia, and Bethesda, Maryland. The senior member of the Soviet mission, Dr. Anatoli Ivanovich Rybakov, wrote

▼ ADA officials meet on August 23, 1963, with the Secretary of Health, Education and Welfare, Anthony J. Celebrezze (seated). After the meeting a joint statement was issued urging the passage of H.R. 4999, a bill to provide a ten-year grant program for expansion of existing dental schools and construction of new ones.

Publication of a Spanish translation of the ADA publication *Accepted Dental Remedies* was announced at a ceremony on May 3, 1963, attended by (left to right) Senator Lister Hill; Dr. Abraham Horowitz, director of the Pan American Health Organization; Dr. Gerald Timmons, ADA president 1962–1963; Vice President Lyndon B. Johnson; Senator Hubert Humphrey; and Dr. Willard Camalier, ADA assistant secretary. Vice President Johnson complimented the ADA on the translation project, adding that the dental health of our Latin American neighbors would be immeasurably enhanced by the use of this book.

later in a Soviet dental journal, "The meeting of Soviet and American dentists has enabled a neutral, mutual comparison of standards of dental service in the U.S.S.R. and the U.S.A., and will serve in further development of mutual understanding in communication of citizens of both countries."

No sooner had the Soviet dentists returned to Russia than a delegation of eight U.S. dentists prepared to leave New York for Moscow. Appointed by the ADA Board of Trustees, most of the members of the delegation had longtime ties to the Association and included ADA Executive Director Harold Hillenbrand and ADA President Charles H. Patton.

The group flew to Moscow from Paris in June 1961 and visited dental facilities in Moscow, Leningrad, Kiev, Tbilisi, and Sochi. The

Scientific exhibit at the 1963 Annual Session in Atlantic City describing the affiliated dental teaching program of the Veteran's Administration Hospital and New York University College of Dentistry which were located across the street from each other in New York City. *(ADA file by Fred Hess & Son)*

A crowd gathers around a table clinic on the use of rubber dam in modern dentistry given by Dr. David Marmer at the 1963 Annual Session in Atlantic City. *(ADA file photo by Fred Hess & Son)*

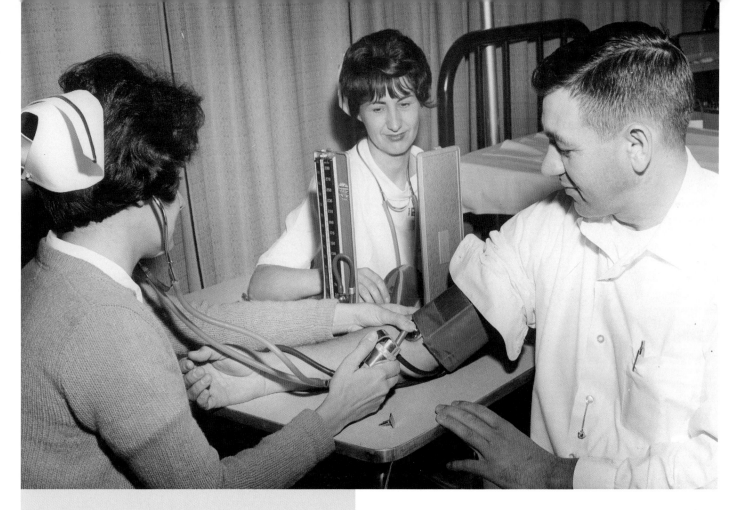

Dr. R. H. Heath of Concord, California, is examined at the first Health Screening Program at the 1964 Annual Session in San Francisco. He was one of the first of the thirteen hundred dentists who participated in the program that year. *(ADA file photo by Cristof Studio)*

mission spent its last three days in Moscow before heading home to the United States on June 25.

The mission noted that the personal and official hospitality extended by their hosts was "overwhelming" and that "the Mission had free access to most of the facilities it wanted to see." However, the eight members unanimously agreed that Soviet dentistry was at least a quarter-century behind dentistry practiced in the United States. "Whatever lead the Soviet Union may claim in the scientific activities in which it competes with the

Watch
"THE DICK VAN DYKE SHOW"
On CBS-TV · Wednesday, February 10th · 9:00 to 9:30 P.M. E.S.T.
Check your newspaper for local time and channel

Presented by the American Dental Association and your Dental Society as part of
NATIONAL CHILDREN'S DENTAL HEALTH WEEK

Marketing brochure for the *Dick Van Dyke Show* promotion of the 1965 National Children's Dental Health Week. The ADA co-sponsored an episode of the Emmy®-winning, top-rated television show in observance of National Children's Dental Health Week in both 1964 and 1965. Procter & Gamble, the show's regular sponsor, donated all of the commercial time to the ADA to present dental health messages. The 1965 episode was seen in over fourteen million homes, almost 27 percent of the total TV audience, and it was the fifteenth most watched show during that week.

United States," mission members reported to the ADA, "it has no lead in the provision of dental health care for its citizens."

The ADA's Dr. Hillenbrand considered the mission a huge success and further evidence that the ADA's social outreach was bearing fruit. Shortly after returning from the Soviet Union, Hillenbrand helped relocate the new ADA Washington Office to 808 Seventeenth Street NW, just down the street from the offices of the American Medical Association and the American Hospital Association. Later in 1961, President Kennedy received ADA leadership at the White House to brief him on current dental affairs.

CUBAN MISSILE CRISIS JARS ANNUAL SESSION

The thaw in the cold war was back in the deep freeze by the time the ADA held its 1962 Annual Session in Miami Beach, October 29–November 1. During the two weeks prior to the opening session, the U.S. had accused the Soviet Union of installing nuclear missiles in Cuba, just ninety miles south of the Florida Keys. On Monday, October 22, as preparations for the ADA Annual Session began in Miami, President John F. Kennedy announced to the nation that the U.S. was implementing a naval blockade of Cuba to cut off the flow of arms and equipment from the Soviet Union in order to prevent the establishment of Soviet missile bases in Cuba. The meetings of both the Board of Trustees and the House of Delegates were held during the tense week that followed while the world seemed on the verge of nuclear war as the leaders of the United States and the Soviet Union engaged in a test of wills. Miami quickly took on the appearance of a military outpost as troops and equipment poured through the area. ADA staff, delegates, and board members in attendance endured the discomfort of being miles from loved ones during a crisis that seemed to be leading the country into a war on U.S. soil.

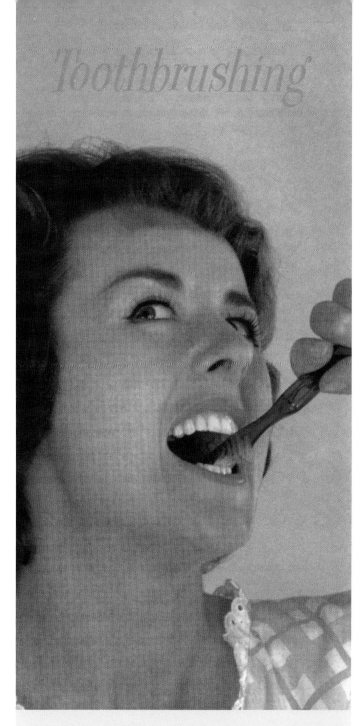

▲ The first ADA patient education brochure to use color photographs was published in 1963. It provides information on the proper care of the teeth and toothbrushing instruction.

On Monday, October 29, the opening day of the Annual Session, President Kennedy announced that the Soviets had agreed to dismantle the missile bases under construction in Cuba, and the whole world breathed a sigh of relief. The crisis would leave its mark. Although the scientific session and commercial exhibits took place as planned, only twelve thousand attendees of the anticipated fifteen thousand showed

A Voice in National Affairs
1960–1969

1961

The ADA helps coordinate a U.S. dental mission to the Soviet Union and the visit of a Russian dental delegation to the United States.

1963

The ADA formally recognizes the specialty of endodontics.

U.S. Congress passes the Health Professions Educational Assistance Act, which provides capital funding for dental schools.

The ADA breaks ground for a new headquarters building off Chicago's North Michigan Avenue.

1962

The ADA opens its Annual Session in Miami, Florida, during the week of the Cuban Missile Crisis, prompting some members to wonder if Premier Khrushchev is still mad about the Waldorf-Astoria ballroom incident three years before.

The Association goes on record supporting seat belt use in automobiles to help cut down on a rash of craniofacial injuries.

Dr. Rafael Bowen, of the ADA-sponsored dental research unit at the National Bureau of Standards, develops Bis-GMA, a thermoset resin complex used in many modern composite resin restorative materials.

1964

The ADA Research and Educational Foundation is established as the Association's agency to raise and distribute funding for scientific, educational, and charitable purposes.

The Association produces the first color television public service announcement by a non-profit health agency.

ADA participants in the 1961 U.S. Dental Exchange Mission to the U.S.S.R. are briefed by Soviet officials at the Tbilisi Institute of Stomatology.

1965

President Lyndon B. Johnson signs Medicare and Medicaid legislation, vastly increasing the government's role in health care.

The ADA moves into its new twenty-three-story headquarters building in Chicago.

The ADA mandates constituent and component societies to eliminate discriminatory membership restrictions.

1967

The ADA Bureau of Dental Health Education is awarded a U.S. Public Health Service contract to develop anti-smoking materials for members to use in their private practices.

1966

The ADA formally dedicates the new headquarters building with a banquet and the installation of a time capsule.

1969

The Family sculpture is installed in the west courtyard of the Association's Chicago headquarters building.

Dr. Harold Hillenbrand wraps up a remarkable career when he retires as the ADA's executive director after twenty-seven years of service to the ADA.

ADA membership reaches more than 112,000 to end the decade of the 1960s, an increase of 22,000 members since 1959.

▶ *The Family* sculpture is installed in front of the ADA's Chicago headquarters building in May 1969. The sculpture has since become a neighborhood landmark and an ADA icon. It epitomizes the family of man and reflects the dental profession's concern for humanity.

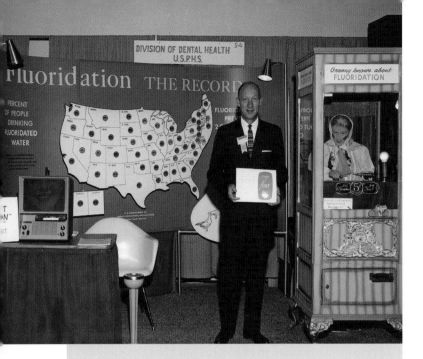

A scientific exhibit on fluoridation presented by the U.S. Public Health Service at the 1965 Annual Session in Las Vegas. *(ADA file photo by Edward J. Allen Associates)*

up. Furthermore, the scheduled keynote speaker at the opening ceremony, Assistant Secretary of State Harlan Cleveland, had to cancel his appearance abruptly because his presence was needed at the United Nations.

Ironically, the Annual Session that year had a Pan-American theme "Better Dental Health in the Americas" and many of its activities concerned relations with Latin America. Among the 125 resolutions submitted to the House, several pertained to Cuban refugee dentists. The House conferred affiliate membership to all Cuban dentists in exile and passed a resolution requesting the U.S. Public Health Service to employ Cuban refugee dentists to provide dental services to Cuban refugees. A significant indication that the Cuban Missile Crisis had cooled off was the telegram that ADA President John Abel received from President Kennedy on Wednesday, October 31, only two days after its peaceful resolution. In the aftermath of the intense week, the White House took time to salute the Association for its "work to improve the dental health of other peoples—including those in Latin America."

MEDICARE AND MEDICAID

The ADA once again found itself on the national stage in 1965 when Congress passed, and President Lyndon B. Johnson signed, the Social Security Act of 1965, establishing Medicare and Medicaid. Each of these programs separately addressed the health care needs of two groups of people: Medicare for senior citizens and Medicaid for children of low-income families.

The establishment of these two programs initiated sweeping changes in the health care industry. Senior citizens and children who heretofore had little or no medical insurance coverage would now be able to avail themselves of diagnoses and treatments that had been financially out of reach. The legislation would be the largest expansion of the social "safety net" for the elderly since the original passage of the Social Security Act in 1935 and would serve as the capstone of President Johnson's "Great Society," his program of social reforms to eliminate poverty and racial injustice.

Initially, the ADA opposed the establishment of Medicare, fearing that an ever-expanding federal role in health care would lead to a decrease in the quality of care, less control for health care providers over their patients' needs, workforce shortages, and excessive bureaucracy. The ADA joined other health care organizations such as the American Medical Association and the American Hospital Association in opposition to Medicare. However, once Medicare was established, the ADA used its influence to effect changes in policies that would benefit dental professionals and their patients. In the late 1960s, the Association's growing stature in Washington political circles did allow the ADA to negotiate successfully for amendments in Medicare payment plans providing parity for dentists with physicians who performed similar services.

On another front, the ADA's endorsement resulted in the inclusion of dental care in another Great Society program, Medicaid, with the goal of achieving better dental health for the nation's children. The ADA had been a champion of children's dentistry since the late nineteenth century and since the 1930s had urged the U.S. government to provide federal support for a national children's dental health program. In the 1960s, incessant lobbying for children's dentistry paid dividends and led to the establishment of dental care under Medicaid. In 1967, Congress added an Early Periodic Screening, Diagnosis, and Treatment program to Medicaid.

As the decade progressed, the ADA worked ever more closely with federal regulators on a host of government programs, including federal poverty initiatives, health care education funding, comprehensive health planning, and regulation of dental X-ray machines. The 1960s were one of the most socially explosive decades in American history. Despite the tumult, the ADA took strides in cooperating with government for the benefit of the American people in delivering dental care to all segments of the public.

TAKING CARE OF THE MEMBERS

The 1960s were also a time in which the ADA paid increasing attention to the needs of its growing membership, which topped 100,000 early in the decade and reached a record of 112,000 in 1969. By the 1960s, the ADA was particularly strong in providing its members benefits in the fields of legislation, public information, dental health education, therapeutics, dental education, and dental materials.

The ADA Bureau of Dental Health Education produced posters and pamphlets used in dentists' offices around the U.S., as well as health education movies that component societies frequently used to promote oral health in their communities. The Bureau of Public Information issued six hundred news releases on dental topics to newspapers and radio and television stations across the country. The Bureau also promoted National Children's Dental Health Week.

The ADA Council on Dental Therapeutics was the primary agency responsible for evaluating dental pharmaceuticals. Since 1934, the Council's report on tested products, *Accepted Dental Therapeutics* (published since 2006 under the title of *ADA/PDR Guide to Dental Therapeutics*), has been considered an authoritative guide. The ADA Council on Dental Research provided funding to the National Bureau of Standards, the National Institute of Dental Research, and selected university research projects. Another body, the ADA Council on Dental Materials and Devices, evaluated dental equipment, instruments, and materials.

The ADA Council on Dental Education accredited dental schools and schools for dental hygienists and technicians. The Council's budget included funding for the Division of Career Guidance, as well as administration of the Dental Aptitude Test.

The ADA Council on Legislation and Washington Office staffers often appeared before congressional committees and sub-committees, and the Association held frequent briefings for congressional staffers on items of interest to the profession. The ADA told its members that the Council on Legislation and the Washington Office would continue to "assure that the quality of care is maintained on its present high level and that the character of private practice of dentistry is not changed."

Among the benefits available to members was the ADA's comprehensive member insurance coverage. In 1966, the Association offered members a health and accident package, along with inexpensive life insurance policies to protect their families. With more than one hundred thousand members, the ADA

▲ Dr. Edith Straus (left), immediate past president of the American Association of Women Dentists, passes the gavel of office to her successor, Dr. Marilyn Stone (right), the group's new president, while Dr. Fae Ahlstrom (center), the group's secretary, looks on during the 1965 ADA Annual Session in Las Vegas. *(ADA file photo by Edward J. Allen Associates)*

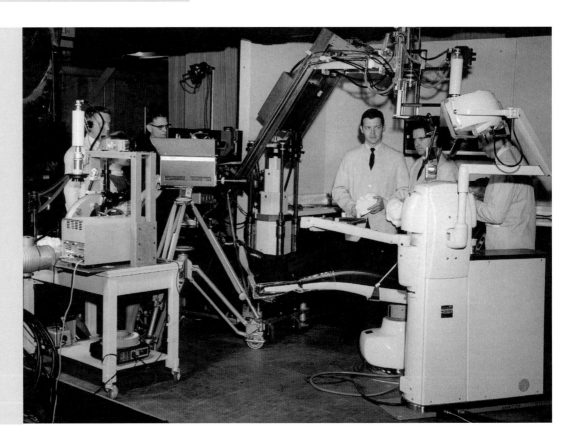

▶ The 1966 Annual Session in Dallas featured live operative and surgical procedures that were televised on a 20-foot closed-circuit TV screen in the exhibit hall. *(ADA file photo by Squire Haskins)*

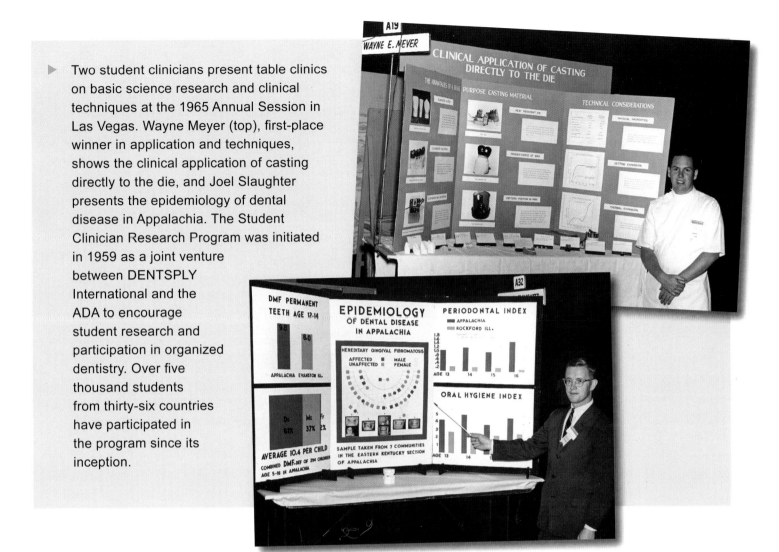

Two student clinicians present table clinics on basic science research and clinical techniques at the 1965 Annual Session in Las Vegas. Wayne Meyer (top), first-place winner in application and techniques, shows the clinical application of casting directly to the die, and Joel Slaughter presents the epidemiology of dental disease in Appalachia. The Student Clinician Research Program was initiated in 1959 as a joint venture between DENTSPLY International and the ADA to encourage student research and participation in organized dentistry. Over five thousand students from thirty-six countries have participated in the program since its inception.

could offer excellent health insurance policies at a low cost. The ADA Council on Insurance monitored the program and negotiated better coverage and less expensive rates whenever possible.

As part of its focus on the health of members, the ADA in 1964 began a health evaluation program for members attending the Annual Session. Members were provided access to a battery of free tests, including blood pressure screening, electrocardiograms, panoramic X-rays, and visual acuity tests.

The ADA's member insurance programs were expanded, beginning in 1969, to include professional liability insurance for members on a state-by-state basis. The insurance also included some casualty and property coverage for the payment of a nominal fee.

GENERAL DENTISTRY IN THE 1960S

General dentistry in the United States underwent a profound change in the 1960s. A younger generation of dentists, who attended dental school during the post-World War II boom in dental education, was introduced to new materials, technologies, and concepts, which transformed the way dentistry was practiced in the United States. These advances affected all aspects of the dental operatory.

The dental office of the 1960s was typically equipped with high-speed handpieces, which first came on the commercial market in the 1950s. The new handpieces revolutionized dentistry because the extreme speeds allowed for smoother and more efficient cutting. This facilitated the work of the dentist and made dental

Civil Rights
The Movement and the ADA

If the early 1960s were characterized by the ADA's foray into international affairs, the middle years of the decade saw the Association embroiled in domestic issues that transformed American society. Civil rights came to the forefront during the era, thanks to actions of African Americans unwilling to accept second-class citizenship. Inspired to participate in acts of civil disobedience by the charismatic Dr. Martin Luther King, Jr., African Americans were blasted by fire hoses in Birmingham and clubbed on the approaches to the highway bridge at Selma. Young black and white Freedom Riders risked jail and beatings to desegregate bus stations and lunch counters across the South.

In 1963, President John F. Kennedy introduced legislation banning discrimination in public facilities; this would later become the 1964 Civil Rights Act. Kennedy was struck down by an assassin's bullet in Dallas in November 1963 before Congress could pass the bill, but President Lyndon B. Johnson used the legacy of his martyred predecessor to pressure Congress to enact the legislation.

The ADA, like many other national organizations, was wrestling with equal rights issues at the same time that Congress and the president were negotiating the passage of landmark civil rights legislation. The ADA's national constitution and bylaws allowed membership to any ethical dentist practicing in the United States without any other conditions. But since 1912, the ADA's bylaws required that dentists join the ADA by way of a constituent and component dental society. As a result, many black dentists were unable to join the ADA because some constituent and component societies refused membership to dentists solely on the basis of race. Because the Association allowed its tripartite societies to self-govern, it had never closely examined their membership policies. However, by the time the ADA celebrated its centennial anniversary in 1959, Association leaders were aware of these limitations on membership and felt the situation needed to be addressed.

Dr. Clifton O. Dummett's call to action prompted the National Dental Association to approach the ADA concerning membership policies. A longtime active member of both dental associations, he was also made an honorary member of the ADA in 1969.

Officials of the National Dental Association and the ADA at the 1962 Annual Session in Miami: (sitting, left to right) Dr. Richard Layne, NDA president; Dr. Gerald D. Timmons, ADA president-elect; Dr. Russell A. Dixon, NDA past president and dean of the Howard University College of Dentistry; and Dr. Harold Hillenbrand, ADA secretary; (standing, left to right) Dr. Matthew Mitchell, NDA president-elect; Dr. James Wallace, Jr., secretary of the NDA executive board; Dr. John R. Abel, ADA president; Dr. Clifton O. Dummett, editor of the NDA journal; and Dr. G. W. Hawkins, member of the NDA Executive Board. The ADA and NDA met to discuss landmark action by the ADA House of Delegates concerning membership policies.

The National Dental Association (NDA), the national organization of African American dentists, brought the matter to the attention of the ADA in 1958. A 1957 editorial by Dr. Clifton O. Dummett, the young editor of the NDA's journal, called for the NDA to promote "the full and unhampered participation of all its members in American dentistry" and advocated for "the ultimate elimination of segregation within the professions." In 1958, the NDA adopted a resolution requesting that the ADA urge its constituent and component societies to eliminate racially restrictive membership provisions.

At the same time, the American Dental Hygienists Association (ADHA) asked the ADA for guidance in a dispute with a state dental society over race-based membership restrictions. At the national level, the ADHA bylaws, like those of the ADA's, had no race-based restrictions to membership. Unlike the ADA, the ADHA prohibited any of its constituent societies to include such restrictions. However, one state dental society refused to recognize the ADHA's state chapter unless its bylaws conformed verbatim to those of the state dental society's, which included a race qualification for membership. In a letter of inquiry to the ADA, the ADHA challenged the Association's acceptance of this state dental society's bylaws. The ADHA argued that the constituent society's race-restricted membership rules were clearly in non-compliance with the ADA's bylaws.

In 1960, the ADA Board of Trustees met with the NDA leadership about the issue. The ADA formally asked the constituent and component societies to study their bylaws to ensure that there were no restrictions on membership involving race, creed, or color. The ADA then conducted its own study of component and constituent society bylaws and found that fifteen societies included race-based

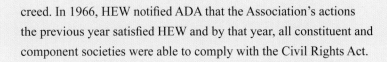

The first African Americans to serve as officers of the ADA were Dr. William B. Trice (left), who served as first vice president, 1991–1992, and Dr. Richard Simms (right), who served as first vice president, 2001–2002. Both also served on ADA councils and in the House of Delegates.

membership restrictions unlike the national bylaws. It became apparent that the ADA would have to take a more forceful position on the issue with those in non-compliance. By the early 1960s, African American dentists in three states had gone to court to force state dental societies to accept their applications for membership, which would make them *de facto* members of the ADA. In 1962, the House of Delegates amended the Association bylaws to give the ADA the right to refuse to seat the delegation of any constituent society whose bylaws were in conflict with those of the national organization. In 1964, the ADA and the NDA formed mutual Liaison Committees, which met regularly to foster communication and cooperation between the two national organizations. The two groups first met at the 1964 Annual Session and continued to meet throughout the 1960s.

The passage of the Civil Rights Act of 1964 brought the issue to a head. In 1965, four state dental societies petitioned the House of Delegates to enforce the 1962 resolution. At the same time, the U.S. Department of Health, Education, and Welfare (HEW) informed the ADA that a complaint had been lodged with HEW about the ADA's compliance with Title VI of the 1964 Civil Rights Act. The ADA House of Delegates moved quickly to respond to the situation, and in 1965 passed two resolutions that effectively eliminated all discriminatory membership practices of its component and constituent societies and assured membership for any ethical American dentist, regardless of race, color, or

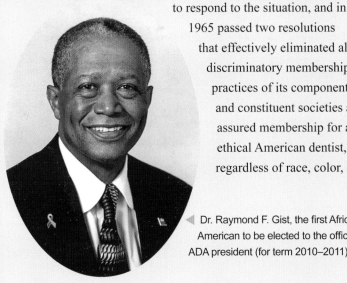

Dr. Raymond F. Gist, the first African American to be elected to the office of ADA president (for term 2010–2011).

creed. In 1966, HEW notified ADA that the Association's actions the previous year satisfied HEW and by that year, all constituent and component societies were able to comply with the Civil Rights Act.

African American dentists have been a part of the ADA throughout the twentieth century. In 1963, a comparative study of the membership rolls of the ADA with those of the NDA found that 632 out of the 1,719 members of the NDA were ADA members. The presence of these individuals added momentum in the struggle to eliminate lingering discrimination in organized dentistry.

Many notable African American members helped pave the way for those who followed. The earliest known African American member, Dr. Rufus Beshears, is believed to have joined the ADA as early as 1909. Dr. Eugene T. Reed joined the ADA in 1947 and was a fifty-five-year member when he died in 2002. He was active in the civil rights movement and participated in many of its key events. Dr. Clifton O. Dummett, a member of the first ADA-NDA Liaison Committee that met in 1964, joined the ADA in 1949. He has written extensively on the history of African Americans in dentistry, and he is a distinguished professor emeritus of the University of Southern California School of Dentistry. In 1968, Dr. Thomas H. Walters, of New York, became the first African American to be elected to the ADA House of Delegates. At the time of his election, he had been a member of the ADA for more than twenty years. Dr. Roy C. Bell first joined the ADA in 1968. He led picket lines at state dental society meetings in the early 1960s protesting discriminatory membership restrictions.

The first African Americans to serve as officers of the ADA were Dr. William B. Trice, who served as first vice president, 1991–1992, and Dr. Richard Simms, who also served as first vice president, 2001–2002. Dr. Trice also served as chair of the Council on Government Relations and Federal Dental Services and as a delegate from the Third Trustee District. Dr. Simms served as a member of the ADA Council on Government Affairs and a delegate from the ADA Thirteenth Trustee District. He is currently a member of the ADA Foundation Board of Directors. Dr. Raymond F. Gist was the first African American to serve as a trustee of the ADA (Ninth Trustee District, 2005–2009) as well as the first to be elected to the office of ADA president. He is president-elect 2009–2010, and will serve his term as president 2010–2011.

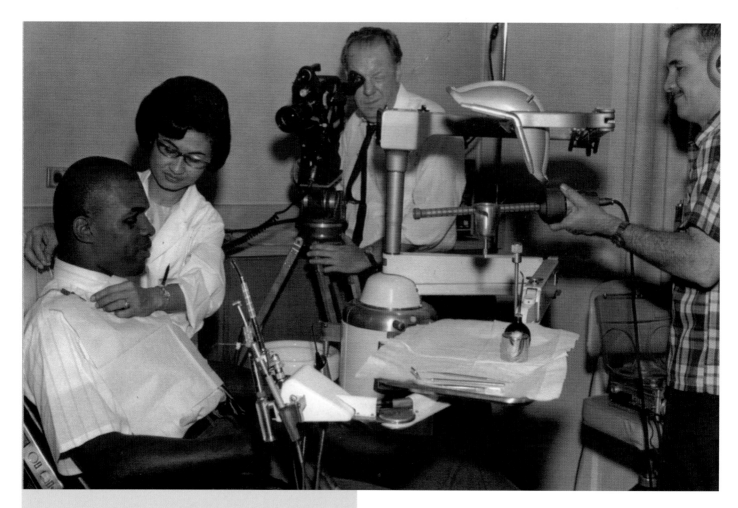

Gale Sayers (left), the famous Chicago Bears halfback, has a dental napkin placed around his neck by ADA staff member Dr. Luella Cosca as he prepares to take part in the production of a health education film at the ADA Headquarters building in 1967. *(Photo courtesy of UPI Telephoto)*

operations easier on the patient. The reclinable, contour couch-like dental chair, introduced in 1958, was another innovation that began to show up in dental offices during the following decade.

Radiology made great strides during World War II and the two decades following the war. By the mid-1960s, most U.S. dental offices were equipped with a new generation of X-ray equipment and faster X-ray film. Also new was the sterile disposable dental cartridge needle. Introduced in 1959, it became common in dentists' offices by the end of the 1960s.

Dentists were also gradually beginning to adopt four-handed dentistry, an operatory technique in which the dentist and dental assistant work efficiently together as a team. The technique evolved out of a series of efficiency, time, and motion studies conducted in the 1960s at the University of Alabama School of Dentistry, which included analysis of equipment used by the dentist and dental assistant.

By the end of the 1960s, dental specialization had become an important aspect of American dentistry. General dentists typically referred patients to periodontists, oral surgeons, and other specialists.

THE RISE OF DENTAL INSURANCE

While technology began to make its presence felt in the dental office, dental insurance became a growing staple of health care coverage during the 1960s. The era coincided with the peak of industrial unionism in the United States. Labor bargaining sessions at such manufacturing powerhouses as General Motors, Westinghouse, and Caterpillar increasingly included dental insurance packages for local union members.

Dental insurance was first negotiated as a benefit for members of the West Coast longshoremen's union in 1955. State dental associations in California, Washington, and Oregon established dental service corporations to monitor and administer the fledgling dental insurance programs. By 1957, even though the concept was in its infancy, the ADA House of Delegates endorsed prepaid dental care.

During the 1960s, a growing number of American companies began offering dental insurance plans to its employees through payroll deduction. A number of states established dental service corporations, and in 1965, the ADA created the National Association of Dental Service Plans to help coordinate the activities of the state organizations.

The growth and success of the state dental service corporations in the late 1960s demonstrated the need for a national underwriting agency to keep the various plans financially solvent. In 1968, the ADA House of Delegates approved the creation of the Dental Service Plans Insurance Company (DSPIC). Funded by appropriations from the ADA, state societies, and state dental service corporations, DSPIC in 1970 was first licensed in Illinois. At about the same time, the company changed its named to Delta Service Plans Insurance Company. Known thereafter as Delta Dental, the insurance company would bring prepaid dental coverage to millions of Americans in the 1970s and 1980s.

THE VIETNAM EXPERIENCE

One place that high-speed dentistry proved useful during the 1960s was in Vietnam. For the fourth time in the twentieth century, U.S. dentists found themselves serving in a combat zone halfway around the world. In 1961, President John F. Kennedy had begun to send U.S. troops to assist the government of South Vietnam against aggression from its neighbor, North Vietnam. The number of troops increased during the administration of President Lyndon B. Johnson; by 1966, a half-million U.S. troops were fighting in Vietnam.

ADA Executive Director Dr. Harold Hillenbrand (second from right) meets with several dental leaders from the U.S.S.R. at the 1969 Annual Session, which was held in conjunction with the annual meeting of the Fédération Dentaire International in New York City. Dr. Hillenbrand retired at the end of 1969, making this the last Annual Session he attended as ADA's chief administrative officer.

The Hillenbrand Years
1946–1969

Dr. Harold Hillenbrand directed the affairs of the American Dental Association for nearly a quarter-century following World War II as its secretary/executive director from 1946 until his retirement in 1969, a period in which the ADA increased in membership, prestige, and influence. The first dentist to serve as an adviser to the U.S. delegation to the World Health Organization, he worked hard to make the ADA a leading voice in world dentistry.

A Chicago native and the son of a dentist, Hillenbrand graduated from the Loyola University School of Dentistry in 1930 and immediately joined the practice of his father, an 1898 alumnus of the Northwestern University School of Dentistry. Hillenbrand, the son, supplemented his income as an instructor at his *alma mater* and became actively involved with the Chicago Dental Society. He grew up speaking perfectly accented German and French, the result of his father's insistence that his nine children learn foreign languages and Latin. Two Hillenbrand children would enter the priesthood and become monsignors of the Roman Catholic Church.

▲ Dr. Harold Hillenbrand had a long and distinguished career as the ADA's chief administrator from 1946 to 1969. His title of secretary was changed to executive director in 1968. After his retirement, Hillenbrand stayed involved with the ADA as the Association's first and only executive director emeritus until his passing in 1986 at age seventy-nine. *(ADA file photo by Photo Ideas, Inc.)*

One of Hillenbrand's mentors at the Loyola University School of Dentistry, Dr. Harold Oppice, ADA president, 1950–1951, involved the young Chicago dentist in the affairs of the ADA. Hillenbrand helped prepare Oppice's 1939 testimony at congressional hearings in Washington, D.C. In 1942, Hillenbrand was named assistant editor of *The Journal of the American Dental Association* (*JADA*), a job he undertook while also editing *Illinois Dental Journal.* Three years later, in 1945, the twenty-nine-year-old Hillenbrand was named editor of *JADA*. When Dr. Harry B. Pinney announced his retirement in 1946 after nineteen years as the ADA's secretary, the Association's Board named Hillenbrand to replace him. For more than a year, Hillenbrand pulled double duty, filling the post of secretary as well as editor of *JADA* until 1947. In 1968, his title was changed from secretary to executive director.

Dr. Hillenbrand's tenure would exceed that of Dr. Pinney. Combined, the two secretaries served forty-three years at the helm of the ADA, from 1927 to 1969. When Hillenbrand replaced Pinney in 1946, the ADA had a membership of slightly more than sixty-two thousand and a staff of seventy-five people. The Association's budget was $600,000 a year, and the ADA

had total assets of about $2 million. The federal government allocated $50,000 for dental research funds, $6 million for public dental health funds, and nothing for dental education. In December 1969, when Hillenbrand retired as executive director, membership had nearly doubled to 112,000. There were 325 people on the staff, and the annual ADA budget had grown to $8 million. The ADA's total assets were $18 million, nine times what they had been in 1946. Federal support of dentistry had grown even more. The federal government appropriated $30 million a year for dental research funds, $200 million for dental public health funds, and $50 million a year for dental education.

Hillenbrand, whose gruff exterior could cow the most recalcitrant foe, was referred to fondly as "H. H." by younger ADA staff, who loved their crusty boss. He appreciated a well-stirred martini, and at a time when the effects of smoking were not fully understood and many physicians smoked, an ever-present cigarette was a Hillenbrand trademark.

In a lengthy editorial lauding his impact on the Association, *JADA* cited the eminence, effectiveness, total dedication, and bold imagination of Hillenbrand's leadership. Even after his

ADA Executive Director Emeritus Dr. Harold Hillenbrand (left) at the 1979 dedication of the Harold Hillenbrand Auditorium at ADA Headquarters, along with his wife Marie and Dr. Joseph P. Cappuccio, ADA president. *(ADA file photo by Photo Ideas, Inc.)*

retirement, Hillenbrand stayed involved with the ADA as the Association's first and only executive director emeritus. In a wide-ranging 1980 *JADA* interview, Hillenbrand expressed no regrets about his choice of dentistry as a career and the more than twenty-seven years he spent at the ADA. "I think I have had every opportunity to serve the dental profession over the years in every area in which I had, or claimed, a reasonable measure of competence," he said.

In 1970, the Hillenbrand Fellowship was established in commemoration of his lifetime of work for the Association. The fellowship is a training program and administrative internship for young dentists who exhibit leadership potential. In 1979, the auditorium at ADA Headquarters in Chicago was dedicated as the Harold Hillenbrand Auditorium.

Dr. Harold Hillenbrand died in Chicago at the age of seventy-nine on June 2, 1986. "Dr. Hillenbrand was an international statesman in dentistry," Dr. Abraham Kobren, ADA president, 1985–1986, eulogized. "His influence and dedication to the profession were felt throughout the world."

Thousands of army, air force, marine, and navy dentists accompanied them. U.S. Army dentists went into the field with high-speed handpieces powered by portable air compressors, a far cry from the foot-treadle drills used by an earlier generation of dentists on the battlefields of World War II.

Mobile dental units allowed marine and army dentists to bring their skills to every corner of Vietnam. As in previous wars, military dentists in Vietnam gained valuable experience in treating maxillofacial injuries they rarely would have seen in civilian life.

THE END OF AN ERA

Dr. Harold Hillenbrand, the ADA's longtime executive director, announced in 1969 that he would take early retirement at the end of the year at the age of sixty-three. Hillenbrand's twenty-three years at the helm of the ADA had resulted in a near doubling of the Association's membership and a more than thirteen-fold growth in the annual budget. Hillenbrand's stature in American dentistry was unparalleled in the long history of the ADA.

As an organization, the ADA came into its own during the final decade of the Hillenbrand Era. The Association broadened its mission and scope of activities to encompass a wide variety of socio-economic issues that were beginning to have a significant impact on the nation's health care community.

The ADA would continue its program of public outreach in the 1970s and would find itself embroiled during the decade in controversy with the federal government that would bring about major changes in the profession.

Chapter Five

An Advocate for the Profession, 1970–1979

The ADA's evolution from a professional association focused on the science and regulation of dentistry to a national advocate for the benefits of oral health accelerated during the 1970s. A decade in which society began to demand increasing accountability from its leading institutions, the 1970s saw further federal and state intrusion into the dental and medical communities. The ADA would emerge as a champion of public health with its initiatives targeting oral health for children. The Association's communications efforts would make its members among the best-informed professionals in the nation. Along the way, however, the ADA would settle a complaint filed by the Federal Trade Commission over dental advertising that would lead to a revision of the ADA's Principles of Ethics.

▶ Posters distributed for National Children's Dental Health Week during the 1970s.

NEW LEADERSHIP FOR CHANGING TIMES

Dr. Harold Hillenbrand cast a giant shadow over the ADA during the quarter-century following World War II. Hillenbrand, the Association's secretary/executive director from 1946 until his retirement in 1969, was the only executive director many postwar members ever knew.

Replacing him was another ADA veteran, Dr. C. Gordon Watson. A native of Idaho, Watson earned his dental degree at Northwestern University. During the late 1940s and 1950s, he maintained a private practice in San Diego, California, and served as secretary of the San Diego County Dental Society and editor of its journal.

Watson originally came to the ADA in 1960 to become Hillenbrand's right-hand man serving as assistant secretary for Administrative Affairs, a post he held until 1964 when he left to become the executive director of the California Dental Association. He would return six years later in 1970 to take over the executive director's position from Hillenbrand. Although Watson would labor in the shadow of his predecessor for the first few years of his tenure, he served capably through a contentious era in the Association's history.

The 1970 Annual Session in Las Vegas was the first since the retirement of Executive Director Hillenbrand, but he was on hand to greet delegates and introduce Watson as his successor. A sign of the high regard in which the nation's public health community held the ADA was the fact that the five surgeons general from the U.S. Public Health Service, Veterans Administration, and the U.S. Army, Navy,

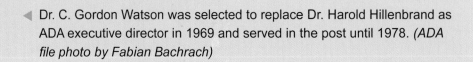

Dr. C. Gordon Watson was selected to replace Dr. Harold Hillenbrand as ADA executive director in 1969 and served in the post until 1978. *(ADA file photo by Fabian Bachrach)*

New Jersey Governor William Cahill (left) speaks with Dr. John S. Zapp at the 1971 Annual Session in Atlantic City. Cahill spoke at the opening session and Zapp, then deputy assistant secretary for health legislation at the U.S. Department of Health, Education, and Welfare, was the highest-ranking dentist in the federal government. Zapp would later serve as ADA executive director, 1993–2001. *(ADA file photo by Hess Commercial Studio)*

and Air Force were in attendance when the opening gavel came down.

Attendees discussed the burning issues of the day, including the need for an overall evaluation of prepaid dental programs, the necessity for members to participate in national legislative and political affairs, the inclusion of dentistry in national health programs, and the need for improved communication in dental education. Dr. F. Gene Dixon (founder of Delta Dental Plans and recipient of the 1989 ADA Distinguished Service Award) told a packed auditorium at the session that the era's unprecedented technological and societal changes like electronic data processing, space exploration, rapid population growth, and environmental concerns would be accompanied by similar upheavals in the dental and health care communities. Dixon predicted that larger government expenditures and expanded programs to provide health coverage for millions of Americans would have a huge impact on dentistry during the 1970s. What was left unsaid was that increasing government expenditures would inevitably mean increasing government intrusion into the practice of dentistry.

The ADA's Oral Health Education Program

The 1970s saw a concerted effort by the ADA to educate the public about the importance of good oral health. Since the publication of its first patient education pamphlet in 1909, the ADA had been distributing information and teaching the American public about the benefits of regular oral health care. In 1927, the ADA established its first department for developing and disseminating authoritative educational materials on oral health. These resources were originally distributed through printed materials and radio.

By the end of the 1950s, television had become the most effective way to transmit information to the general population, and the ADA embraced the technology. By the 1960s, the Association was using celebrities and television show sponsorship as a way to reach the public. In 1964 and 1965, in promotion of National Children's Dental Health

Some of the many dental health education brochures and pamphlets produced by the ADA in the 1970s.

Week, the ADA sponsored episodes of the award-winning and top-rated *Dick Van Dyke Show*. The regular sponsor of the show, Procter & Gamble, donated all of the commercial time for these shows to the ADA to air dental health messages. The shows were heavily promoted within the dental profession and they reached millions of people. The 1965 show was seen in over 14 million homes, almost 27 percent of the total TV audience. It was in the top fifteen of the most watched television shows during that week.

In the 1970s, the ADA sharply increased its production of educational audiovisual materials and public service announcements (PSAs). By 1982, the ADA was reaching a non-theatrical audience of 2.6 million people and a U.S. television audience of almost 48 million people.

By 1971, the ADA's dental health education program had grown to include the development of various printed materials (including brochures, pamphlets, and posters), PSAs for television and radio, educational slideshows and films,

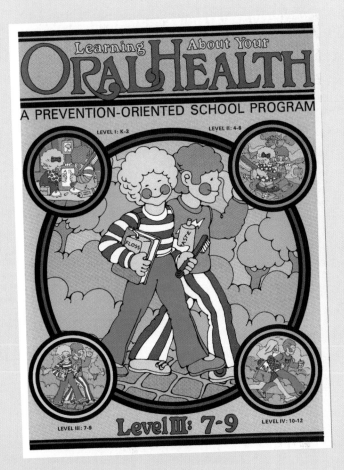

The ADA produced the curriculum packet for elementary and high school teachers, *Learning About Your Oral Health: A Prevention–Oriented School Program* in 1973. The program included separate volumes for grades K–3, 4–6, 7–9, and 10–12.

traveling exhibits for dental meetings and health fairs, and patient education seminars. The ADA continued to develop publicity and promotional materials for the Children's Dental Health Week/Month observance during the 1970s and 1980s.

In 1972, the House of Delegates authorized the development of materials for dental disease prevention programs aimed at the nation's teachers. As a result, the ADA produced comprehensive curriculum packets for elementary and high schools. Introduced in 1973 and re-released in 1982, the *Learning About Your Oral Health* program encompassed a variety of teaching aids, including guidelines for establishing a school program on preventing dental disease, curriculum guides, lesson plans, resource materials, plaque control kits, wall charts, and videocassettes. By 1982, the ADA was distributing eleven thousand teaching packets.

Today the ADA uses mainly the organization's Web site ADA.org to disseminate oral health education information in various formats. ADA. org features individual pages on many oral health topics such as anesthesia, dental implants, dentures, oral hygiene, and periodontal disease. The Association continues to produce and distribute patient education brochures, pamphlets, and other materials, which are made available through the ADA's online product catalog. Teaching aids, student resources, PSAs, Dental Minute news features, and video news releases are also accessible on ADA.org.

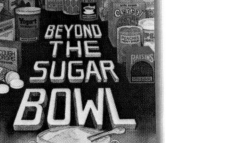

▶ Posters distributed by the ADA Order Department during the 1970s.

The 1970s were a decade in which dentistry and medicine were challenged by the emergence of government-subsidized health care. The introduction of Medicare and Medicaid in 1965 during President Lyndon Johnson's Great Society had opened the door to large-scale government intervention in the health care segment of the American economy.

The decade would see passage of a host of federal laws and regulatory pronouncements dealing with the practice of dentistry and medicine. In 1972, Congress passed the Comprehensive Health Management Training Act, and the federal government implemented an Economic Stabilization Program mandating wage and price controls for dentists and other small businesses. The next year, Congress added major amendments to the Social Security Act to expand eligibility and benefits under Medicare and Medicaid. In 1974, the National Health Planning and Resources Act became law.

The ADA believed then, as it had for more than a century, that private-practice fee-for-

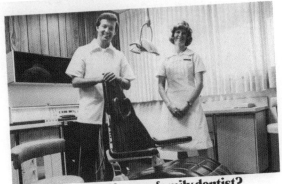

How good is your family dentist?

The best in the world. But you don't have to take his word for that. You can compare and easily see why American dentists are providing the finest care in the world. And improving all the time.

More dentists with better educations.

American dentists are generally better educated than their counterparts in other countries. Almost all students entering dental school have bachelor's degrees.

The number of students applying for dental school admission has also grown dramatically, while openings have risen at a slower rate. That means increased competition which results in a higher caliber individual entering the profession.

Dentists don't stop learning when they graduate from school.

Each year over half of all U.S. dentists enroll in continuing education programs. And the trend is increasing. In fact, formal programs exist in 44 states, and 14 of those states require it either for license renewal or continued dental society membership.

Who regulates the dental profession?

The state regulates them through licensing. In addition, the dentists themselves have a self-discipline system involving peer review.

Problems over dental care received by a patient are resolved by dental society peer review organizations. Should a patient, or his insurance company, challenge a dentist's work, the local or state peer review committee hears both sides of the grievance and almost always resolves it to the satisfaction of all parties.

American dentistry wants to prevent disease.

The emphasis is on prevention. American dentists believe that it's better for the patient's health, and more economical, to prevent disease rather than treat it.

The progress made in prevention was apparent in a major American Dental Association study made in 1970. It showed that in the preceding decade extraction of teeth dropped 7% despite a 14% increase in population. In the same decade, decay-fighting fluoride treatments rose 454%, orthodontic treatments increased 127% and tooth saving root canal treatments increased 124%.

Americans are keeping teeth that once were lost. The dental profession is making every effort to insure this kind of quality in the individual dental office, in group dental care insurance programs and in the country as a whole.

Ask your dentist.

The next time you see your family dentist, ask a few questions about what he or she is doing to assure quality dental care:
1. What educational programs do your local or state dental societies support?
2. Do you use trained assistants?
3. What new equipment and techniques do you use?
4. What preventive measures do you take for my dental health?
5. What can I do to prevent oral disease?

Your family dentist can give you professional dental treatment. And we can all work toward keeping America's dental health the best in the world. With regular preventive care.

American Dental Association
211 East Chicago Avenue
Chicago, Illinois 60611

service dentistry was the most cost-effective, most productive way to deliver dental services to the American consumer. In 1974, the ADA established a public relations and education campaign to promote the private-practice fee-for-service dentist, later dubbed the Public Education Program (PEP). Originally, the PEP initiative was designed to educate the public in strong labor communities that dental insurance could work without the destruction of the private-practice delivery system. PEP quickly broadened its scope to the importance of preserving the traditional patient/doctor relationship for maintaining the highest level of dental care and treatment in the world.

PEP staffers gave local dental societies the communications tools to boost the image of the private-practice dentist at a local level. The ADA developed a dentist spokesperson-training program. Speaker training seminars helped prepare thousands of U.S. dentists to "speak out for dentistry."

PEP was discontinued as a separate entity in 1979, and the program's activities and personnel were integrated into the normal structure of the ADA.

◄ Dr. Charles Smith (right), an ADA local society public relations chair, is interviewed about dental insurance on a local Buffalo, New York, talk show by host Stewart Dan in 1975. The interview was part of the ADA Public Education Program, a public relations and education campaign to promote the private-practice fee-for-service dentist.

▲ An attendee enters a mobile dental health unit on display at the 1971 Annual Session in Atlantic City. One of six ordered by the Baltimore City Health Department with federal urban renewal funding, the units provided dental screening and treatment services at public schools, day care centers, nursing homes, and public housing projects. *(ADA file photo by Hess Commercial Studio)*

DENTAL ACCREDITATION AND LICENSURE

During the 1970s, the ADA re-examined its handling of the oversight of dental education. From 1938 to 1974, the ADA Council on Dental Education (CDE) bore responsibility for accrediting U.S. dental education programs, including not only undergraduate dental programs leading to a DDS/DMD degree, but also postgraduate education programs in the dental specialties and allied dental education programs for dental assistants, hygienists, and laboratory technicians.

By 1973, the CDE's accreditation activity included more than twelve hundred educational programs. The unprecedented growth of the accreditation

▲ The exhibit booth of the National Institute of Dental Research at the 1971 Annual Session in Atlantic City publicizes NIDR's role in dental research and the development of new dental materials. The NIDR (now the National Institute of Dental and Craniofacial Research) was established in 1948 to improve and promote dental health through research. *(ADA file photo by Hess Commercial Studio)*

An Advocate for the Profession
1970–1979

1970

The ADA members are able to purchase professional liability insurance for the first time through the Association.

The *ADA News* is first published to keep members informed of Association activities and news and events affecting the dental profession.

1972

The American Association of Dental Schools split fifty-nine to fifty-nine on a vote to recommend either the DDS or the DMD as the preferred dental doctorate degree. Similarly, the ADA House of Delegates votes to allow continued awarding of both degrees.

1971

The ADA honors Dr. Gerald D. Timmons (ADA president, 1962–1963; speaker of the house, 1956–1961) with its first Distinguished Service Award in recognition of his tireless support of dental education.

1975

The ADA Commission on Dental Accreditation is established, taking over full authority and responsibility for the dental profession's accreditation program from the ADA Council on Dental Education.

Former ADA President Gerald D. Timmons is awarded the first ADA Distinguished Service Award in 1971.

program created new challenges for the CDE as it responded to the evolving demands of dental education. There was fear that the profession would lose its accreditation program if it was deemed unresponsive to the needs of the public. The ADA determined that the creation of a separate body responsible solely for dental accreditation was necessary. Therefore, in 1975, the ADA established the Commission on Accreditation of Dental and Dental Auxiliary Programs, renaming the body the Commission on Dental Accreditation four years later, to assume oversight of the accreditation of all dental education programs nationwide. The Commission continued the longstanding work of the CDE, making site visits to dental schools, establishing dental accreditation policies and

1976

The federal government for the first time sets standards for dental and medical devices when Congress passes landmark legislation directing the Food and Drug Administration to develop mandatory standards for Class II devices.

1979

The auditorium in the ADA Headquarters building is named the Harold Hillenbrand Auditorium to honor the longtime ADA executive officer.

1978

The ADA revises its Principles of Ethics to allow dentists to advertise following a complaint by the FTC in 1977.

The ADA establishes the Council on Dental Practice to study, evaluate, and disseminate information on dental business organization, economics, and practice management techniques so that dentists may continue to improve services to the public.

ADA staff members work on an early issue of the *ADA News* in October 1970. (ADA file photo by Allan Weber)

procedures, and establishing and approving dental educational standards. The Council on Dental Education retained responsibility for policymaking, specialty recognition, and licensure-related issues.

As early as 1929, the ADA had been involved in establishing licensing standards and the development of uniform national dental examinations in the basic and clinical sciences. Since 1979, the ADA has been a part of the Joint Commission on National Dental Examinations, the agency responsible for the development and administration of the National Board Dental Examinations, used to evaluate the competence of each dental school graduate for licensure. This fifteen-member Commission includes representatives of dental schools, dental practice,

DMD versus DDS

One of the oldest debates in the field of American dentistry involves the three letters dentists place behind their names to signify the degree that allows them to practice. Some schools award the Doctor of Dental Surgery degree, abbreviated DDS. Others grant the degree of Doctor of Dental Medicine, abbreviated DMD.

The argument over the dental degree designation has been going on almost since the ADA was founded in 1859. The Baltimore College of Dental Surgery, the world's first dental school (later merged with the University of Maryland), invented and awarded the first DDS degree in 1841. Harvard Dental School, the first dental school associated with a traditional university, started the controversy in 1869 when it awarded the first DMD degree. The DMD was a result of prefixing the Latin word for dentist, "Dentariae," to the university's already established "Mediciniae Doctoris" (Doctor of Medicine) degree because Harvard University transcribed its degrees in Latin. Since this was the first dental school associated with a university, its founders believed that all schools established thereafter would follow suit, but this was not to be the case.

As dental education grew quickly in the ensuing years, many other dental colleges across the nation opened and began awarding degrees. Most awarded the DDS while a couple of others opted for the DMD. By 1899, only two schools out of the fifty-seven existing at the time awarded the DMD. In 1926, in his landmark study on dental education for the Carnegie Foundation, William J. Gies noted the existence of two dental degree designations without further comment.

It was almost a century after Harvard University had awarded the first DMD that the ADA took the matter under advisement. In 1964, the ADA House of Delegates instructed the Council on Dental Education (CDE) to study the DDS/DMD degree confusion with the goal of unifying the degrees. In 1965, the CDE recommended that the ADA let the American Association of Dental Schools (AADS) decide the issue and the ADA let the matter drop without further action. However, the AADS could not come to a decision over which designation to adopt and in 1966 postponed further consideration of the issue indefinitely. By 1967, out of the fifty dental schools in the United States, ten were conferring the DMD and forty the DDS degree.

By 1970, the number of dental schools in the United States had grown to fifty-three, and the number conferring DMD degrees had grown to thirteen while the number conferring DDS degrees remained at forty. That year the ADA House of Delegates again took up the matter and again immediately referred it to the Council on Dental Education for action. In 1971, the CDE reported back to the House of Delegates that it supported the idea of awarding a single degree and again recommended that the matter be referred to the American Association of Dental Schools for final determination of the degree designation.

However, the AADS referred the matter to its House of Delegates in March 1972, which promptly deadlocked on the issue, fifty-nine to fifty-nine. The result was an AADS resolution that recommended support for the rights of individual dental schools to offer either degree, although expressing the wish that the two degrees be united as one.

For the second year in a row, the question of recommending one degree designation was deliberated by various ADA agencies: the Council on Dental Education, the Board, and the House. In the end the Association reached the same inconclusive answer as the AADS. The ADA House of Delegates voted in 1972 to support "the principle that degree determination is the prerogative of the individual educational institution" while urging dental schools to consider unifying the dental degree.

The ADA House of Delegates reconsidered the issue in 1984 and again in 1990, eventually postponing any resolution of the controversy indefinitely. As of 2009, the matter had not been reviewed again and there continue to be two dental degree designations awarded. By 2009, the number of dental schools in the United States had increased to fifty-eight, and the number conferring DMD degrees had grown to twenty-four while the number conferring DDS had dropped to thirty-four.

The ADA does not recognize a difference between the two degrees. Dentists who have a DMD or DDS have an equivalent education. Both degrees use the same curriculum requirements set by the ADA Commission on Dental Accreditation, generally three or more years of undergraduate education plus four years of dental school. State licensing boards accept either degree as equivalent, and both degrees allow licensed individuals to practice the same scope of general dentistry. Additional post-graduate training is required to become a dental specialist.

The exhibit booth of Health Science Products, Inc. at the 1971 Annual Session in Atlantic City shows equipment specifically designed for sit-down, four-handed dentistry, a technique developed in the 1960s by dental researchers at the University of Alabama School of Dentistry. The company was founded in 1969 to design and manufacture dental equipment to support this new mode of practice. *(ADA file photo by Hess Commercial Studio)*

state dental examining boards, dental hygiene, dental students, dental editors, and the public. The ADA established the first regional board to oversee licensing requirements in 1967, and by the early 1980s, more than thirty states were represented in membership on regional licensing boards. In the United States, state governments regulate dental licensing, and the laws regulating licensure vary from state to state. Currently, in order to be eligible for licensure, all states require the following: graduation from a dental school accredited by the ADA Commission on Dental Accreditation; successful completion of a written national board examination; and completion of a clinical examination or state-specific alternative, e.g., one year of accredited postgraduate education.

WAGE AND PRICE CONTROLS

The ADA got a first hint of the new reality of government intervention into aspects of the health care economy in 1971 when the administration of President Richard M. Nixon instituted wage and price controls in an attempt to avoid a recession. America had been living beyond its means since the mid-1960s, financing the war in Vietnam while trying to encourage the growth of the civilian economy. The result was an increasing problem with inflation and a sharp spike in unemployment as the 1970s began.

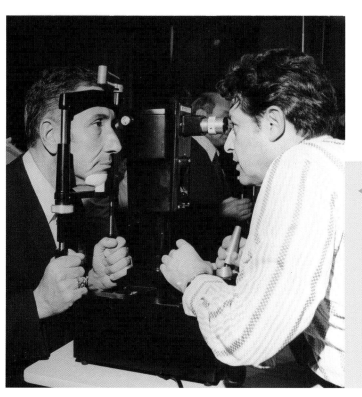

Dr. Milton E. Shaefer (left) is tested for glaucoma with a new device—the non-contact tonometer—as part of the 1972 Annual Session Health Screening Program in San Francisco. Optometrist Dr. Bernard Grolman, the inventor of the new instrument, administers the exam. Introduced in 1971, the instrument uses a puff of air to determine the presence of glaucoma and revolutionized the testing for the disease. *(ADA file photo by Cal Visuals Photography)*

A Nixon-appointed Cost of Living Council (CLC) was responsible for overseeing the wage and price controls. First instituted in late 1971, CLC wage and price controls had been gradually relaxed by early 1972, but were reinstated by 1973 as inflation rose again. Many American dentists and the ADA were unhappy with Nixon's economic policies. Subsequently, in October, the ADA filed suit against the Cost of Living Council, charging that the Council's administration of price controls discriminated against the nation's dentists. The ADA's suit accused the CLC of arbitrarily classifying dentists with other health care providers. The ADA argued that due to the unique nature of dental practice, the resulting "severe fee increase restrictions" hampered dentists from recovering increased costs. The ADA's suit also noted, "the regulations most acutely affect dentists whose incomes are lowest, principally young dentists." However, the ADA litigation was soon dropped as the wage and price controls proved to be ineffective in controlling inflation and the Nixon administration mostly abandoned them by April 1974.

THE ADA AND THE FTC

The ADA's legal action over wage and price controls was only a prelude to a broader confrontation between the Association and the Federal Trade Commission (FTC). In 1976 and 1977, the FTC would initiate a formal complaint against the ADA and two investigations of the dental profession. In 1976, the FTC launched an investigation into state restrictions on the manufacture and sale of dentures to consumers by anyone but a dentist. Then in 1977, the FTC filed a formal complaint against the ADA charging the

▲ Members of the House of Delegates wait in line to vote for ADA officers at the 1975 Annual Session in Chicago. *(ADA file photo by Photo Ideas, Inc.)*

illegal restraint of competition among dentists by preventing the solicitation of business by advertising. Finally, a 1979 FTC investigation targeted state regulations and professional restrictions affecting the delivery of dental care. This investigation focused on constraints on dental practice ownership, the restrictions on prepaid dental plans, and the expanded functions of allied dental professionals.

The FTC complaint against the ADA concerning advertising was part of a wider FTC investigation of similar rules by professional associations, including physicians, veterinarians, lawyers, architects, and others. The first professional health care association targeted by the FTC was the American Medical Association (AMA). In January 1976, the FTC announced an investigation of the AMA's code of ethics, which forbade advertising by physicians. At the same time, the FTC launched initiatives against states and professional societies that prohibited advertising by ophthalmologists, optometrists, and opticians.

In 1976 and 1977, the FTC would widen its investigations of the nation's health care community to include medical school accreditation, veterinary advertising, restrictions on the development of health maintenance organizations (HMOs), physician control of Blue Shield plans, marketing abuses in Medicare supplemental insurance, mouthwash advertising, and the sale and marketing

▲ Georgia Governor Jimmy Carter (second from left) lifts a glass of fluoridated water in a celebratory toast at the 1973 Thomas P. Hinman Dental Meeting in Atlanta along with (left to right) Dr. Charles Smith, Georgia Dental Association president, 1972–1973; Dr. Louis A. Saporito, ADA president, 1972–1973; and dentist and Tennessee Governor Winfield Dunn, 1971–1975. While governor, future U.S. President Carter signed the bill at the 1973 Hinman meeting making fluoridation mandatory in the state of Georgia.

▶ Outgoing president of the American Dental Hygienists' Association Konnetta Putman of Scarsdale, New York (left), meets with incoming president Austa White of Plainfield, Iowa, during the group's annual meeting held in conjunction with the 1974 ADA Annual Session in Washington, D.C. *(ADA file photo by Capitol and Glogau Photographers)*

In June 1977, the U.S. Supreme Court handed down a judgment against the Arizona Bar Association (*Bates & O'Steen v. State Bar Association of Arizona*, 1977) ruling that commercial speech is entitled to some First Amendment protection and that the state's prohibition of all advertising by professionals was a violation of the guarantee of free speech under the First Amendment to the Constitution. With the Supreme Court ruling, the struggle regarding dental and other professional advertising lost much of its steam. At the ADA's Annual Session in October 1977, the House of Delegates passed two resolutions on the subject, recommending that state and local dental societies not initiate disciplinary proceedings against dentists who truthfully advertise their services and fees, and not bar dentists from membership because of their advertising.

THE SHAPE OF A SETTLEMENT

The Bates decision of 1977 bolstered the ongoing FTC's complaint against the ADA concerning restrictions on dental advertising. However, defensive litigation by the ADA became unnecessary when in October 1978, the FTC approached the Association about negotiating a settlement. The Association moved toward such a

▲ ADA librarian Dorothy Carbonaro researches an inquiry in the ADA Library in 1974. Established in 1927 through member donations of books and journals, by the 1970s the Library had grown to be one of the world's largest dental libraries.

of hearing aids. The FTC actions were conducted against the backdrop of congressional investigations into dental and medical business practices that led to well-publicized hearings on charges that the medical appliance industry, including denture manufacturers, exploited the elderly.

◄ The ADA House of Delegates meets during the 1975 Annual Session in Chicago to consider the heaviest HOD agenda to that date. By the time the House had convened, 138 resolutions had been submitted by the Board of Trustees, constituent societies, and trustee districts.

Among the visitors to the American Dental Political Action Committee (ADPAC) exhibit booth at the 1976 Annual Session in Las Vegas were (left to right), ADPAC Vice-chair Dr. Jack T. Scott, ADPAC Chair Dr. William M. Creason, Mrs. Peggy Scott, and ADA President Frank F. Shuler. Creason reported to the 1976 House of Delegates that ADPAC had an overall success rate of 87 percent in supporting candidates for election to the U.S. Senate and House of Representatives in that year's elections. ADPAC was organized by a group of dentists in 1968 to help elect candidates to political office supportive of the legislative objectives of organized dentistry.

settlement by amending its Principles of Ethics to allow dentist members to advertise the availability of services and fees charged.

The settlement was relatively simple. The ADA agreed not to restrict, or to declare unethical, any truthful advertising or solicitation of patients by dentists. The ADA was allowed to maintain a proscription in its Principles of Ethics prohibiting advertising that is "false, misleading, deceptive, or fraudulent." The settlement was published in the *Federal Register* for public review and received final FTC approval in September 1979. The final order was issued with modifications in February 1983.

The other investigations never resulted in formal complaints or settlements between the ADA and the FTC. Prohibition against the provision of dentures by non-dentists and the business practices of dentists continue to be regulated on a state-by-state basis.

CHALLENGES MET

Dr. C. Gordon Watson served as ADA executive director during a difficult decade. ADA member dentists fought government wage and price controls

The duplicating center staff at the 1976 Annual Session in Las Vegas copy reference committee reports for distribution to delegates. The center handled a record one million pieces of paper during the session.

ADA News

One of the ADA's major benefits during the past century has been its member publications. During the 1940s–1960s, the ADA communicated news to its members through several publications. *The Journal of the American Dental Association* (*JADA*) included separate sections for Association reports and general news of the dental profession. The ADA published the bi-weekly *ADA Newsletter* to keep dental leaders informed of ADA policy decisions, programs, events, and other Association news. The ADA also published a daily newspaper throughout each Annual Session to keep attendees informed of daily events and important issues.

In 1970, *ADA Newsletter* was re-introduced as *ADA News*. Distributed to all ADA members, it quickly became one of the better-read publications in American dentistry. *JADA* continued to publish news and Association reports until the end of the 1970s when, through a series of redesigns, these sections became increasingly smaller and were phased out altogether by the 1990s. *ADA News* became the Association's

▲ A recent issue of *ADA News*.

main news source and *JADA* became focused on the publication of peer-reviewed clinical articles.

A small-format newspaper published every two weeks, the mission of *ADA News* has always been to report on current developments and news of interest to ADA member dentists. From the beginning, its pages have kept ADA members informed on a timely basis regarding the political, social, economic, and practice issues facing American dentists. Since 1970, *ADA News* has covered a broad spectrum of topics including current events, licensing issues, health legislation, practice management, conferences and meetings, scientific developments, ADA policy initiatives, membership benefits, dental education, and newsmakers in the dental profession.

Throughout its history, the ADA has also produced news publications as needed on specific topics such as state or federal legislation affecting the profession. Most current newsletters are published as electronic publications.

▲ ADA editorial staff (left to right), Editor-in-Chief Leland Hendershot, DDS, Managing Editor John Goetz, and News Editor Glenn Medcalf discuss one of the earlier issues of *ADA News* in October 1970. *(ADA file photo by Allan Weber Photography Unlimited)*

Dr. John M. Coady, ADA executive director, 1979–1985, works at his desk at the ADA Headquarters building in Chicago. *(ADA file photo by Photo Ideas, Inc.)*

A politically independent commission on the accreditation of dental educational programs was established in 1975. Another new body, the Council on Dental Practice, was established in 1978 to gather and disseminate information on the business of operating a dental practice, economic factors related to dental practice, and practice management techniques.

In December 1978, just as the ADA and the FTC began to come to a settlement, Dr. Watson resigned. Dr. John M. Coady, ADA's assistant executive director responsible for dental education and hospitals, was named acting executive director of the Association. The Board of Trustees then engaged in a nationwide search for a permanent replacement for Watson, but in August 1979, the Board abandoned the search and named Coady to the post permanently.

A native of Minooka, Illinois, Coady earned his dental degree from Loyola University School of Dentistry in 1953. He began a private practice in Morris, Illinois, but left in 1957 to pursue a master's degree in oral pathology at Loyola University. Coady returned to his practice in Morris and served as adjunct faculty at his *alma mater.* In 1963, he joined the ADA staff as assistant secretary.

Coady would preside over a rejuvenated ADA during his nearly six years at the helm of the organization. By the time of his 1985 retirement, the ADA would be considered one of the most influential health profession organizations in North America.

during the early years, and watched as inflation ate into earnings in the late 1970s. The FTC challenged longstanding ADA policy. Nevertheless, Watson's tenure as executive director during the 1970s resulted in many accomplishments. Because of his leadership, the ADA was able to show a strong defensive posture when the responsibilities and prerogatives of the ADA and the dental profession were legally and politically challenged.

The ADA increased its emphasis on public health during the decade, focusing on oral health for the nation's children. The Association began to realize the benefits of communicating with internal and external audiences. Watson first suggested that the Board of Trustees budget for national print and television marketing of the profession and its accomplishments.

Chapter Six
Benefits to Members, 1980–1989

The ADA celebrated its 125th anniversary in 1984 with renewed enthusiasm about the future. The Association had emerged from a lengthy challenge by the Federal Trade Commission over dental advertising and had revised its code of ethics allowing members to advertise their practices and fees.

Membership had climbed steadily, growing from 112,000 members at the dawn of the 1970s to more than 140,000 members at the beginning of the Association's 125th anniversary year. One factor fueling that membership growth was the corresponding rise in member benefits. The ADA promoted its benefit programs by stressing the "almost unlimited professional possibilities for its members."

The ADA entered the decade of the 1980s with better representation of the trustee districts. In addition, the Council on Dental Practice had been created in 1978 to focus on the business aspects of dental practice, a shift in Association emphasis that was welcomed by most members.

HELPING MEMBERS FINANCIALLY

A number of financial benefit programs were first offered to members during the 1970s and expanded in the 1980s. Group insurance coverage was among the most sought-after benefits that the ADA offered.

▶ Some of the many dental health education brochures and pamphlets produced by the ADA in the 1980s.

▲ Radiologist Dr. Robert Langlais explains effective X-ray procedures during a workshop on radiology at the 1980 Annual Session in New Orleans.

By 1984, the ADA group program offered life insurance coverage for members and their spouses. Members could also sign up for the ADA Disability Insurance Program, which provided long-term replacement income.

In 1970, the House of Delegates had approved a major expansion of the ADA's insurance coverage when it added various forms of liability, property, and casualty insurance lines, as well as professional liability insurance. In 1983, the Association introduced an office overhead expense program as part of its disability insurance package.

One increasingly important financial benefit for many members was the growth of financial planning instruments for retirement. By the mid-1980s, many baby-boomer dentists now approaching their forties were thinking seriously about how they would fund their retirements. As a result, in the mid-1980s, the ADA Members Retirement Program was expanded to include Keogh retirement plans as well as Individual Retirement Accounts.

In 1985, the ADA Council on Insurance expanded its investment offerings to include options in stocks, bonds, cash, and convertible instruments. When Congress passed the Tax Reform Act of 1986, *ADA News* kept dentist members fully briefed on the implications of the new law for practices and financial planning. In the 1980s, the Council on Dental Practice developed numerous seminars to help members run a successful practice on topics like marketing, financial planning, and tax strategies. One of the most popular offerings at Annual Sessions during the 1990s was a seminar on retirement planning.

In 1990, the Association endorsed a program to help dentists finance dental practice purchases. Young dentists faced ever-increasing costs in setting up a practice, and the program offered lower interest loans to ADA members at a time when the prime interest rate was 10 percent.

◄ Carrying colorful umbrellas festooned with doubloons, ADA officers and trustees march behind a brass band in typical New Orleans style to conclude the opening ceremony in the Louisiana Superdome at the 1980 Annual Session.

The Journal of the American Dental Association

A major benefit of being an ADA member is *The Journal of the American Dental Association* (*JADA*), which is widely recognized as the premier journal in American dentistry. Founded in November 1913 as *Official Bulletin of the National Dental Association*, *JADA* took its present name in 1922. By the time *The Journal* celebrated its fiftieth birthday in November 1963, it had become established as one of the most relevant and best-read dental journals in the world. Under the consecutive editorial direction of Dr. Harold Hillenbrand, 1944–1947; Dr. Lon W. Morrey, 1947–1963; and Dr. Leland C. Hendershot, 1963–1973, *JADA* steadily increased its number of editorial and advertising pages and upgraded the look of the publication.

JADA celebrated two major milestones in the 1980s. It published its one hundredth volume in 1980 and in 1988 celebrated its seventy-fifth anniversary. However, the 1980s proved to be some of the most difficult years in *JADA*'s history. Inflation early in the decade resulted in huge publishing cost increases for *The Journal*. Meanwhile, other dental publications entered the field and began to compete in terms of both content and advertising dollars. *JADA* succeeded by reinventing itself several times

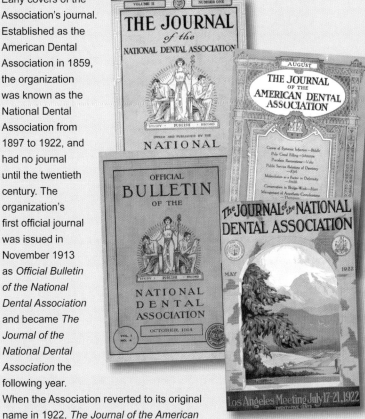

Early covers of the Association's journal. Established as the American Dental Association in 1859, the organization was known as the National Dental Association from 1897 to 1922, and had no journal until the twentieth century. The organization's first official journal was issued in November 1913 as *Official Bulletin of the National Dental Association* and became *The Journal of the National Dental Association* the following year. When the Association reverted to its original name in 1922, *The Journal of the American Dental Association* assumed its present title.

since 1980. Although it continued to cover basic dental research, *JADA* offered new features in response to changing membership needs, including a greater emphasis on clinical relevance, emerging trends, and practice management.

JADA added an online version in 1998, available on ADA.org. But the print version of *The Journal* continues to be the core publication read by most dentists each month. "*The Journal* is a direct reflection of the dental profession itself," then *JADA* Editor Roger H. Scholle wrote in 1980, "and this is its greatest strength. Since 1913, there is no better record of dentistry's progress and accomplishments."

Dr. Lon W. Morrey (right), *JADA* editor 1947–1963, consults with his successor Dr. Leland C. Hendershot, *JADA* editor 1963–1973, during the 1962 Annual Session in Miami.

TAKING CARE OF MEMBERS' HEALTH

Another growing concern of the ADA was the health of its members. As early as 1964, the ADA had offered a comprehensive health evaluation program for members that included free health screenings at ADA Annual Sessions. Members were generally able to get the results of their tests on site.

By the mid-1980s, the Annual Session Health Screening Program had come to include not only standard tests like electrocardiograms and X-rays but also a test for hepatitis. The introduction of hepatitis screening in 1979 resulted from a 1978 survey published in *JADA* that showed that nearly 14 percent of dentists engaged in dental practice had been exposed to hepatitis, an inflammation of the liver that could cause debilitating symptoms in victims. The introduction of a safe and effective hepatitis B vaccine in 1982 went a long way toward controlling the disease among members.

However, another more insidious viral infection would become the Association's and the world's focus through much of the 1980s.

DENTISTRY AND AIDS

In 1981, the U.S. Centers for Disease Control (CDC) first recognized AIDS (acquired immune deficiency syndrome) as a disease, and in 1982, researchers identified HIV (human immunodeficiency virus) as the likely cause of AIDS. At first, researchers thought that AIDS was a disease limited largely to the gay community and transmitted solely through sexual contact. It was soon discovered that AIDS could also be passed through the population by any exchange of bodily fluids including by contact with infected blood, by contaminated hypodermic needles, and even by infected breast milk from mother to child. The mysterious nature of AIDS and its transmission

ADA President Robert H. Griffiths demonstrates a method for marking dentures at the Operation IDENT exhibit at the 1981 Annual Session in Kansas City. Operation IDENT sent volunteer teams of dentists into long-term care institutions to mark oral prosthetic devices with wearers' identification information. *(ADA file photo by Anderson's Photography, Inc.)*

The ADA House of Delegates vote by a show of cards on one of the 125 resolutions presented for their consideration at the 1981 Annual Session in Kansas City. *(ADA file photo by Anderson's Photography, Inc.)*

The onset of the AIDS epidemic unleashed a flurry of CDC and ADA policy initiatives. In the mid-1980s, the CDC began to promulgate specific universal precautions designed to protect both health care workers exposed to blood-borne pathogens and the privacy of patients and workers.

In 1986, the ADA published and distributed a pamphlet to its members entitled *Facts about AIDS for the Dental Team*. The pamphlet, which was reprinted and reissued several times during the next decade, helped lay member concerns to rest at a time when fear of AIDS was widespread in American society.

The U.S. Centers for Disease Control (now called the Centers for Disease Control and Prevention) first issued recommendations for infection control practices for dentistry in August 1987. The recommendations included obtaining a complete medical history from patients, the use of protective attire and barrier techniques, hand-washing and care of hands, careful use and disposal of sharp

unleashed a wave of fear in the United States, resulting in a backlash by some against the gay community and those who had contracted HIV.

In the early 1980s, dentists became concerned about the possibility of the transmission of the AIDS virus among their patients and staff. The major worry involved oral bleeding. Infection control guidelines in place prior to the AIDS scare alleviated some of the concern about contracting the disease. Dentists had already been practicing precautions such as sterilization and barrier methods because of fears about hepatitis.

▶ A special issue of the Spider-Man® comic book promoting good dental habits published in cooperation with the Marvel Comics Group in 1982. Spider-Man later teamed up with the Fantastic Four® to fight oral disease in the *Heroes vs. Plaque* comic book and DVD produced by the ADA in 2004. *(Reprinted by permission of Marvel Entertainment, Inc.)*

instruments and needles, high-level disinfection and sterilization of reusable instruments, decontamination of environmental surfaces, decontamination of laboratory supplies and materials, routine sterilization of handpieces between patients, careful handling of biopsy specimens, and meticulous disposal of waste materials.

In October 1987, the ADA adopted a policy statement on AIDS, HIV infection, and the practice of dentistry. The statement said HIV-infected individuals should be treated with compassion and dignity and dentists should not turn away patients because of fear of contracting the disease. The following year, the ADA Council on Ethics, Bylaws and Judicial Affairs issued an advisory opinion to the ADA code of ethics indicating that it is unethical to deny dental care to individuals solely because they have AIDS or are HIV positive. By the end of the 1980s, attention had shifted from the fear of acquiring AIDS from a patient to the dentist's role in making early identification of AIDS infection. In a well-attended seminar at the 1986 Annual Session in Miami, Dr. Charles Barr, professor of dentistry at Mount Sinai School of Medicine, reported that dentists were often the first to recognize certain oral symptoms that indicated AIDS. Barr, who at the time had treated more than two hundred AIDS patients in his practice in New York, stressed that the danger of a patient transmitting AIDS to a dentist was almost non-existent if the dental team took proper barrier precautions.

Use of the CDC's universal precautions among dentists may have contributed to the low instance of HIV reported by the ADA Foundation's Health Screening Program in the late 1980s. The Program reported that of 1,195 dentists tested for HIV at the 1988 Annual Session, none tested positive for the AIDS virus, and in 1989, the Program reported that of the nearly 3,500 dentists tested for HIV, only two tested positive.

Attendees register during the opening day at the 1982 Annual Session in Las Vegas. The theme of the meeting, which drew about 28,000, was "Dentistry—A Caring Profession."

The Alliance of the American Dental Association

For much of its history, the Alliance of the American Dental Association was known as the Women's Auxiliary to the ADA. Founded in 1924 by a small group of dentists' spouses who attended the ADA's Annual Session, the Women's Auxiliary was initially a semi-organized social group with no political or official sanction. The House of Delegates remedied that in 1926 when it formally authorized the group to use the name. The onset of the Great Depression caused a sharp fall-off in Annual Session attendance, and in 1932, the Women's Auxiliary disbanded and gave the money in its treasury to the ADA Relief Fund.

The concept was revived during World War II, with the creation of the Women's Auxiliary Committee in 1944 to develop a more formal organization and to serve as a liaison to the growing number of state auxiliaries. In 1955, representatives from many state auxiliaries gathered at the ADA's Annual Session in San Francisco and formed a national Women's Auxiliary, which soon petitioned the ADA for official recognition. Full recognition was granted in 1958, and the Women's Auxiliary to the ADA was officially incorporated in 1962.

During the 1970s, the Women's Auxiliary took an increasingly active role in supporting the ADA and dental health. Auxiliary members worked closely with schools in their communities to encourage children's oral health. Members also raised funds for dental student loans and scholarships and sponsored high school programs on careers in dentistry.

Two major changes bracketed the 1980s. In 1979, the group changed its name to the Auxiliary to the American Dental Association, and in recognition that a growing number of dentists were women, their husbands became eligible for membership in the Auxiliary. In 1993, the organization's name was changed, once again, to the Alliance of the American Dental Association.

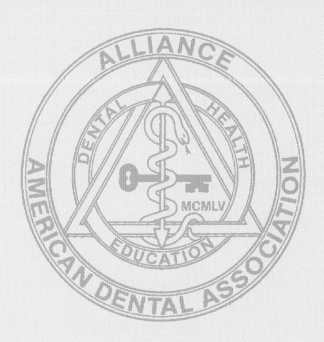

▲ The official seal of the Alliance.

Today the Alliance, made up of six thousand ADA member spouses, is committed to supporting the ADA through dental health education and legislative advocacy, and by promoting the well-being of the dental family. The Alliance hosts an annual Leadership Conference featuring topics such as oral health education, grassroots political activism, and fundraising. Alliance members have visited legislatures to discuss issues with lawmakers, distributed thousands of toothbrush kits to disadvantaged populations in their communities, visited local schools to promote good oral health, and participated in Give Kids A Smile Day® projects. The Alliance also helps foster social relationships among ADA members. The organization has an annual meeting held in conjunction with the ADA's Annual Session, as well as regional conferences at state and regional dental meetings.

Benefits to Members

1980–1989

1981

The ADA and cartoonist Charles Schulz collaborate on a *Peanuts* short film to demonstrate proper flossing techniques for children.

1984

The ADA celebrates its 125th anniversary with a special issue of *JADA*.

1983

The ADA publishes its first report on the future of dentistry.

1985

President Ronald Reagan commends the ADA for its support of fluoridation and the prevention of dental disease.

Dr. Irwin Mandel, director of clinical research at Columbia University School of Medicine, receives the first ADA Gold Medal Award for Excellence in Dental Research.

The ADA Research Unit at the U.S. National Bureau of Standards is named the Paffenbarger Research Center in honor of Dr. George C. Paffenbarger (the unit's director for its first fifty years) in recognition of his many contributions to the improvement of dental health care.

After the final payment, the mortgage on the ADA Headquarters is symbolically burned in a ceremony at Annual Session.

◀ Dr. Irwin Mandel (right) is presented the ADA's first Gold Medal Award for Excellence in Dental Research by ADA President John L. Bomba at the 1985 Annual Session in San Francisco.

1988

The ADA and the Fédération Dentaire Internationale co-host the World Dental Congress in Washington, D.C.

The Journal of the American Dental Association celebrates its seventy-fifth anniversary of publication.

1986

Dr. Harold Hillenbrand, ADA executive director 1947–1969, dies in Chicago at the age of seventy-nine.

1987

The U.S. Centers for Disease Control first issues recommendations for universal precautions.

NBC-TV's morning news program, *The Today Show,* airs a five-part series on American dentistry.

The ADA adopts its first policy statement on AIDS/HIV infection and dental practice.

1989

Dentists report a 90 percent success rate over twenty years in replacing missing teeth with dental implants.

◄ Dr. George C. Paffenbarger (right) receives the ADA Distinguished Service Award from ADA President Robert H. Griffiths at the 1982 Annual Session in Las Vegas. The ADA Research Unit was renamed in Paffenbarger's honor in 1985.

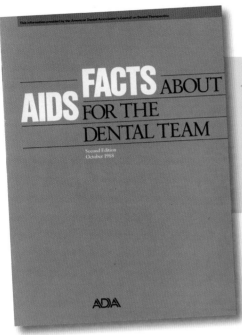

AIDS FACTS ABOUT FOR THE DENTAL TEAM

Second Edition
October 1988

ADA

In 1986, the ADA published and distributed to its members the pamphlet *Facts about AIDS for the Dental Team*. The pamphlet, reprinted and reissued several times as a *JADA* supplement during the next ten years, provided dentists and dental team members with accurate information on the disease and infection control at a time when fear of AIDS was prevalent.

The ADA's longstanding concern for the health of its members was brought into sharp relief by the AIDS crisis of the 1980s. The Association's calm, reasoned, science-based approach to the hysteria that sometimes surrounded the disease went a long way to reassuring members and the public that the dental office was a safe place to provide and receive dental care.

PLANNING FOR THE FUTURE

The 1980s were a decade in which the ADA began systematically planning for the strategic future of the organization. The landmark *Report of the American Dental Association's Special Committee on the Future of Dentistry,* published in 1983, was the ADA's first attempt to peer into the future and to assess how dentistry was doing and where it was headed.

Coordinated by Thomas J. Ginley, who would become the ADA's executive director in 1986, the *Report* outlined the external forces that had influenced the Association and its members in the nearly forty years since the end of World War II. It provided a comprehensive assessment of the dental profession's current state and future prospects. The *Report* would lead to major internal changes in the organization of the ADA during the latter 1980s.

A FOCUS ON PROGRAMS AND REVENUE

When Executive Director John Coady retired after six years on July 1, 1985, Thomas J. Ginley, a twenty-five-year veteran of the ADA staff, was appointed to take his place after an extensive search. Ginley was the first non-dentist to ever serve in the position.

A Chicago native, Ginley had earned his undergraduate, master's, and PhD degrees in

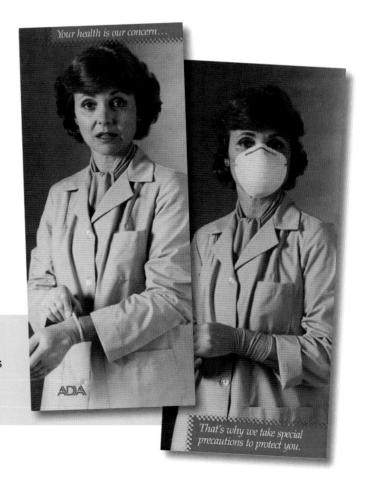

Your health is our concern...

ADA

That's why we take special precautions to protect you.

A 1986 brochure produced by the ADA for distribution to dental patients reassuring them that dentists wear gloves and masks to protect patients from contact with bacteria and viruses.

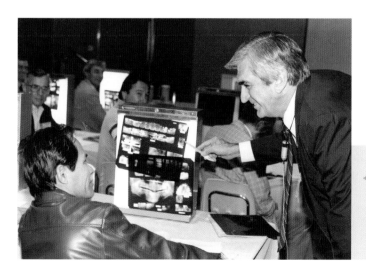

psychology at Loyola University. He joined the staff of the ADA in 1962 and served twenty-three years as a senior manager in the areas of dental education, accreditation, and policy administration.

As executive director, Ginley embarked on a program of streamlining operations at the Association, while increasing the budget for program activity. In a strategic report concerning the changes, published in *JADA* in 1986, Dr. Ginley remarked, "Dentistry has changed radically from what it was just twenty years

The Washington Office

In 1984, the ADA purchased a twelve-story office building to house the ADA's Washington, D.C., office. The 62,000-square-foot building is centrally located, just six blocks from the White House and a fifteen-minute walk from Capitol Hill.

The ADA has had a Washington presence since 1942, when the Association opened a part-time office in the nation's capital to deal with issues arising from dentistry's relationship with the military during World War II. The first head of the ADA Washington Office was Dr. C. Willard Camalier. A Washington, D.C., native, Camalier earned his dental degree from George Washington University in 1912. He served as ADA president, 1937–1938, and was the chair of the Association's War Service Committee during World War II.

A fixture in Association activities for more than fifty years, Camalier practiced in D.C. and was a natural to head the ADA's first Washington Office. He regularly provided dental care to senators, representatives, cabinet members, and regulatory officials in his Capitol Hill practice and he was said to have known half of Washington on a first-name basis. In 1959, the ADA elevated the status of the Washington Office when Camalier assumed full-time duties.

Since World War II, the Washington Office has fostered dialog and the exchange of ideas between the dental profession and the federal government. A typical day might see Washington Office employees hosting a breakfast meeting for congressional staffers; providing background briefings for news media; preparing testimony for an Association officer; working with regulatory agency staff to develop dental guidelines; or meeting with staff from other health care associations.

Through the ADPAC/Grassroots Network, the ADA Washington Office organizes and supports dentist volunteers who serve on dental action teams in each of the nation's 435 congressional districts. The Washington Office monitors continued federal support for the ADA's research efforts, including those of the Paffenbarger Research Center. It also lobbies Congress on behalf of the nation's dentists and dental students.

▲ The Washington Office building at the time of its purchase in 1984. Located just six blocks from the White House and a fifteen-minute walk from Capitol Hill, the Washington Office is the center of activity for ADA's advocacy efforts. The Association's offices occupy two floors of the building, while the rest is leased to tenants.

The ADA Division of Government and Public Affairs (DGPA) operates in both the Washington Office and the ADA Headquarters building in Chicago. DGPA works with constituent dental societies to provide them with information and expertise to enhance government advocacy efforts in each state, develops political and advocacy education for members and organizations, and assists other ADA staff in the creation of advocacy information and tools. Additionally, DGPA staff members represent the ADA at a number of national associations that focus on state government. This liaison activity raises the profile of the profession to state policymakers and assists constituent societies with their advocacy objectives.

ago. The way our members practice has changed, their patients and the disease patterns have changed, and what they expect from the ADA has changed. Our membership itself has changed; today we have more women dentists, more young dentists, more dentists involved in alternate practice settings. But the Association itself hasn't changed significantly since I started working here 23 years ago."

Ginley had worked with the previous executive director, Dr. John Coady, in the early 1980s to increase non-dues revenue. When he was named executive director, Ginley continued the initiative to curb the longtime reliance on dues income, including the establishment of for-profit ADA subsidiaries. His efforts resulted in a 30 percent increase in non-dues revenue between 1979 and 1990.

The reorganization under Ginley was designed to address contemporary issues while maintaining a long-range commitment to flexibility and adaptability. Broader member participation was achieved by increasing the number of

volunteers serving on the ADA's councils and commissions by a third, from 127 to 168. The majority of these agencies were expanded to eight, eleven, or sixteen members, in most cases allowing representation from each of the ADA's trustee districts. A number of councils and commissions with overlapping functions were consolidated, reducing the total number of these agencies from eighteen to fourteen.

Significant council changes were made to facilitate the ADA's involvement in community and professional relations. One of these changes was the establishment of a Council now known as the Council on Access, Prevention and Interprofessional Relations. The new Council's responsibilities covered broad community health issues such as fluoridation, oral health literacy, and access to care.

▲ Dr. Oliver McClintock of Anderson, Indiana, an attendee at more than fifty Annual Sessions, was the first member to register at the 1985 Annual Session in San Francisco.

◄ Outgoing ADA President Abraham Kobren (left) hands a wooden gavel, the traditional symbol of a presiding officer, to newly-installed ADA President Joseph A. Devine at the 1986 Annual Session in Miami. Devine was elected the year before. Successful candidates serve one-year as president-elect and begin their presidential term one year later at the Annual Session.

PROMOTION OF RESEARCH

Another outcome of the 1987 reorganization was the expansion of the responsibilities of the Council on Dental Research, resulting in a stronger ADA research position. The ADA continued to promote and support research across a wide range of scientific venues. The ADA Conference on Clinical Caries in 1983, held in conjunction with the National Institute of Dental Research (NIDR), highlighted the research activity in this area undertaken by the ADA Council on Dental Research. The Council also worked with the ADA Research Institute to host the annual Conference on Foods, Nutrition and Dental Health, 1981–1984, that brought together representatives from government, education, industry, and dentistry to discuss findings related to the caries potential of various food groups. The Council on Dental Research also worked with other ADA councils in organizing conferences on a number of contemporary topics, including hepatitis B outbreaks, mercury hygiene for dental office

► Celebrities are featured on a brochure for the ADA Public Service Radio Campaign that ran from 1979 to 1985. The ADA enlisted the support of a wide range of celebrities for the creation of radio public service announcements to promote dental health care. Topics included how to become a wise dental consumer, diet and dental health, caring for children's teeth, cleaning your teeth and gums, pregnancy and oral health, selecting a dentist, the dangers of chewing tobacco, and dental emergencies. The announcements were recorded and distributed on 45-rpm records that were mailed to 2,800 radio stations nationwide.

staff, pain research, behavioral science, reduction of dental anxiety, and temporomandibular joint dysfunction.

Research was a critical component of the ADA's non-dues income during the 1980s. Dr. Rafael L. Bowen, director of the Paffenbarger Research Center, assigned a number of his patents to the ADA. One Bowen patent, an improved composite resin material, produced substantial royalty payments for the ADA Health Foundation beginning in 1980. A measure of how important research was to dentistry could be gauged by the increase in NIDR congressional appropriations. In 1978, the NIDR secured grants and direct operations funding of just over $61 million. Six years later, in 1984, the NIDR was funded at $88 million, an increase of 43 percent.

INTO THE 1990S

The ADA came out of the 1987 reorganization with a far better focus on external influences on the Association and dentistry, as well as an awareness of and sensitivity to an increasingly diverse membership. The consolidation of two existing councils into a single council now called the Council on Government Affairs gave the ADA a more unified voice when dealing with regulators and congressional staff on Capitol Hill.

ADA President Arthur A. Dugoni and Chair of the Committee on Local Arrangements Dr. Frank Lock prepare to open the exhibit hall with the traditional ribbon-cutting ceremony at the 1989 Annual Session in Honolulu.

The establishment of a new commission later renamed the Committee on the New Dentist addressed the needs of recent dental school graduates entering the profession. The members of the new commission had to be younger than forty years of age at the time of their appointment. Aware of the increasing number of women and minority dentists, the ADA encouraged them to apply for vacancies on the commission.

With the completion of the 1987 reorganization, the ADA looked forward to confronting the challenges of the 1990s. The Association and the profession would experience remarkable changes during the decade, which began appropriately with the election of the ADA's first woman president.

A Healthy Smile Can Last a Lifetime

Brush and floss daily. Eat the right foods. See your dentist regularly

Poster distributed for Senior Smile Week in 1988. This ADA-sponsored nationwide dental health promotion took place from 1987 to 1995 and focused on oral health care for older adults.

Chapter Seven
The Changing Face of the Profession, 1990–1999

Dr. Geraldine T. Morrow's installation in 1991 as the first woman president in the ADA's 132-year history was an indicator of the remarkable changes the Association and American dentistry were experiencing in the early 1990s. Morrow, who practiced in Anchorage, was also the first Alaskan elected to head the ADA. A 1956 graduate of the Tufts University School of Dental Medicine and a longtime leader of the Alaska Dental Society, Morrow represented the changing face of the profession. As president-elect, she helped form a task force on women and minorities to reach out to both groups to help "keep organized dentistry strong."

Like all segments of the U.S. health care economy, the nation's dentists in the early 1990s were concerned with rapidly escalating costs. The rising cost of health care was a major political issue for many Americans who voted in the 1992 presidential election. The public's concern helped elect President William J. "Bill" Clinton, whose campaign had stressed providing affordable health insurance for the nation's citizens.

Another challenge that the ADA would face in this decade was working with government bodies, particularly the Occupational Safety and Health Administration, to establish reasonable occupational safety and health standards for the dental workplace.

Dr. Geraldine T. Morrow, the first woman president of the ADA, assumed office in 1991. Morrow, who practiced in Anchorage and was a longtime leader of the Alaska Dental Society, was also the first woman to be elected to the ADA Board of Trustees, 1984–1990. Her election as ADA trustee and president was indicative of the changing face of the dental profession at the end of the twentieth century.

Some of the many patient education brochures produced by the ADA during the 1990s.

THE STATE OF DENTISTRY

The ADA's 1991 Survey of Dental Practice offered a snapshot of the state of dentistry at the beginning of the 1990s. It revealed that the cost of dental care had increased rapidly for both patient and provider. Per capita expenditures for dental services more than doubled from 1980 to 1990. Although costs had increased, so too had the utilization of dental health benefit insurance plans. In 1980, just over one-third of payments to dentists had come from insurance and government sources. By 1990, that percentage had increased to just under a half of the $34 billion in dental payments in the United States.

Although 57 percent of the American population saw a dentist at least once a year, the percentage of total personal health care accounted for by dental spending actually decreased slightly during the 1980s. And even as patients were seeing general dentists and dental specialists on a more regular basis than in the past, many adults still suffered from untreated oral disease.

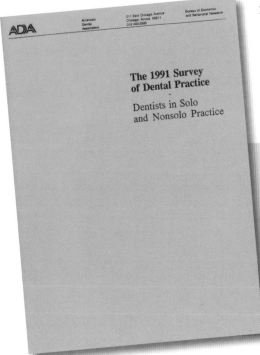

One volume of the ADA's 1991 Survey of Dental Practice. Other volumes include income, expenses, staffing, dental practice demographics, and patient populations. Since 1950, the ADA has conducted surveys, analyzed data, and published reports on a wide range of dental-related issues including dental practice, education, public opinion, consumer issues, and economics. As of 2009, most ADA Survey Center reports are available to members free of charge as downloads from the ADA's Web site, ADA.org.

Only among young patients had significant progress on oral health been made by 1990. Fully half of schoolchildren ages five through seventeen reported no decay in permanent teeth, a dramatic improvement from the 36.6 percent of children who reported no decay in 1980. Much of that improvement could be traced to the gradual success of fluoridation, which had been spreading across North America for more than forty years.

FACING ECONOMIC CHALLENGES

In the early 1990s, the dental profession was recovering from two difficult decades of financial stress. The 1970s had been marked by a twelve-year-long market decline on Wall Street that made it difficult for Americans to get any kind of return on their savings. In the 1980s, the American economy was wracked by the worst inflation since the early years of World War II. Wages, supplies, and commodities all increased at double-digit rates during a five-year period covering the late 1970s and early 1980s. It was not until the late 1980s that the balance of income versus expenses for most dentists finally evened out. The 101,000 private dental practices in the United States in 1988 were overwhelmingly solo practices, with eight of ten dentists choosing to practice by themselves. Another 13 percent of practices were made up of two dentists, while only 5.5 percent of practices had more than two practitioners.

Although private-practice dentists were in a stronger position in 1990 from an economic standpoint, most new dental school graduates carried increasing indebtedness as they went out into the workforce. For out-of-state residents at U.S. dental schools, the average tuition, fees, and other educational expenses, not including living expenses, was pushing $20,000 per year in 1990. The average dental school graduate of the class of 1990 was carrying $45,000 in debt when he or she graduated. This heavy indebtedness of new practitioners became a growing concern for the dental profession.

MEMBERSHIP DIVERSITY

By the early 1990s, the dental student population was becoming increasingly diverse. Dr. Geraldine T. Morrow's 1990 election as ADA president was testimony to women's increasing contributions to the dental profession. Just over 30 percent of graduates in 1991 were female, as were more than 35 percent of the first-year students that year.

The percentage of women in dentistry continued to rise over the decade. By the turn of the twenty-first century, nearly four out of ten dental students in the United States would be female, a number that Dr.

Patient education brochures produced and distributed by the ADA in the 1990s that addressed consumer concerns about the rising cost of dental care and insurance.

Lucy Hobbs Taylor, the first woman to receive a dental degree, would find of immense satisfaction.

In addition, the number of minority dentists was increasing dramatically during the 1990s. By 1995, there were nearly fifteen thousand minority dentists practicing in the United States, almost 13 percent of U.S. dentists. And those numbers were increasing rapidly with the entry of new graduates into the field.

The ADA strongly encouraged the growth of diversity in dentistry during the 1990s. Dr. William S. Ten Pas, ADA president 1995–1996, reported in his 1996 presidential address to the House of Delegates that the ADA had taken "great strides" in the 1990s in its efforts to create a broader base of participation in organized dentistry.

"We need greater diversity," Ten Pas told delegates, "because it is the right thing to do for this Association and this profession." The ADA, he said, needed to go beyond gender, age, and ethnicity and it needed membership that included educators, researchers, the uniformed services, and practitioners in various types of practice.

Dr. David A. Whiston, ADA president 1997–1998, confirmed Ten Pas's commitment when he told the

1998 House of Delegates that the Association had become more relevant, responsible, and representative of a changing profession.

NEW DEPARTMENTS ESTABLISHED

In 1992, ADA Executive Director Thomas Ginley retired at the age of fifty-four. Dr. William E. Allen delayed his retirement for several months to serve as interim executive director while a search was conducted for Ginley's permanent replacement. Allen practiced pediatric dentistry in California for thirty-eight years before serving as director of the ADA Washington Office, 1981–1988, and as ADA associate executive director, 1988–1992.

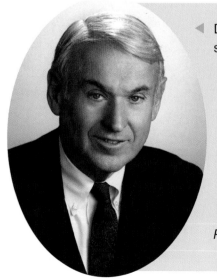

Dr. William E. Allen served as interim executive director, 1992–1993. Allen had previously served as director of the ADA Washington Office and as ADA associate executive director. (ADA file photo by Stuart–Rodgers–Reilly Photography)

▲ Members examine ADA publications on display in the exhibit hall at the 1991 Annual Session in Seattle. The ADA Department of Product Development and Sales offers a variety of professional materials, patient education brochures, posters, gifts, e-Books, and DVDs for order at every Annual Session and in the ADA's annual product catalog. In 2001 the catalog was made available on the Internet as well as in print.

In 1993, Dr. John S. Zapp, an Idaho native who had nearly a quarter-century of experience dealing with government policy issues, was selected the ADA's next executive director. He came to the ADA from the American Medical Association, where he had spent nearly twenty years in its Washington, D.C., office, most recently as the AMA's vice president for government affairs.

◀ Dr. John S. Zapp served as ADA executive director, 1993–2001. During his administration, the ADA established a Division of Information Technology, a Department of Dental Informatics, and created a Web site now called ADA.org.

One of his first tasks as the new executive director was to work with a Board of Trustees committee to evaluate a recent study on the effectiveness of the Association's structure and processes. In 1992, shortly before Zapp joined the ADA, the Board had hired an outside consultant to study a number of governance issues involving the structure and function of the Board, the duties of Association officers, the responsibilities and size of councils and commissions, the constitution and bylaws, and policies of the House of Delegates.

The subsequent restructure plan, implemented at the end of 1993, included the establishment of the Survey Center of the Division of Information Technology, the Department of Dental Informatics, and the Health Policy Resources Center. At the same time, the Salable Materials Program was made a stand alone department (now called the Department of Product Development and Sales). The study would also lead to a 1999 amendment to the ADA's constitution and bylaws that made the treasurer's position an elective office.

The ADA and the
FDI World Dental Federation

The ADA's 1996 Annual Session was held in conjunction with the World Dental Congress. This meeting of the world's dentists sponsored by the FDI World Dental Federation is part of a tradition that dates back a half-century. The 1996 gathering of the world's dentists, in Orlando, Florida, was billed as the "ADA/FDI World Dental Congress," in recognition of the longstanding relationship between the two organizations.

The FDI is an international federation of national dental societies from every continent. Founded in 1901 in Paris under the name Fédération Dentaire Internationale, the Federation, with the exception of the Red Cross, is the world's oldest international health association. Its principal goals as established by its founders were to sponsor International Dental Congresses every five years, maintain and strengthen the bonds of fellowship between national dental societies, encourage the advancement of dental science, collect and collate scientific data in the dental field, publish an international dental journal, and bestow the Willoughby Dayton Miller Prize, a distinguished service award.

The FDI's long-range objective, since its beginning, has been the attainment of the highest possible level of dental health for people worldwide. To that end, the Federation has been particularly active in the field of oral health for children.

For much of its first half-century of existence, the FDI enjoyed periods of growth followed by retrenchment during the two world wars of the twentieth century. It was not until the late 1940s that the Federation emerged as a true international organization. The person perhaps

FDI President Harvey J. Burkhart (right) talks with Dr. Daniel F. Lynch, chair of the ADA International Relations Committee, shortly before Burkhart's death in 1946. Dr. Burkhart was instrumental in establishing an International Dental Congress in conjunction with the ADA's 1947 Annual Session that led to the rebirth of the FDI. Lynch would later serve as president of the ADA, 1954–1955.

most responsible for this was Dr. Harvey J. Burkhart. A prominent dentist at the turn of the twentieth century, Burkhart was much involved in ADA affairs during his lifetime, serving as ADA president, 1898–1899. In 1915, he became the first director of the Rochester Dental Dispensary, founded by philanthropist George Eastman. The clinic became so successful under his directorship that Eastman, with Burkhart's guidance and assistance, soon founded other dental clinics all over Europe in the years leading up to WWII. Now internationally respected, Burkhart was asked by some FDI members to assist them in resuscitating the organization made inactive because of the war. Though Burkhart was quite elderly at the time, his connections helped bring the world's dentists together to convene an International Dental Congress in conjunction with the ADA's 1947 Annual Session. The Congress went a long way toward giving the FDI the support and affirmation it needed to go forward after the war. However, Burkhart was not able to see the results of his efforts, as he died suddenly in 1946 before the Congress took place.

Until the post-World War II period, the FDI had a reputation of being oriented to the needs of its European member associations. Similarly, the ADA during the first half of the twentieth century was primarily focused on serving its members in the United States. Dr. Harold Hillenbrand served as the bridge to bring the two organizations closer together. Hillenbrand, ADA executive director 1946–1969, spoke fluent French and German and steered the ADA to an internationalist outlook during his tenure. In 1971, shortly after retiring from the Association, Hillenbrand was named the first American to serve as president of the FDI.

ADA President William S. Ten Pas (left) and FDI/World Dental Federation President Heinz Erni open the 1996 ADA/FDI World Dental Congress in Orlando. *(ADA file photo by Christie Photographic Studios)*

▶ The exhibit floor at the 1993 Annual Session in San Francisco shows the typical large attendance at the commercial and scientific exhibits during the ADA's annual meeting. *(ADA file photo by Dave Bush Photographers)*

DRIVING CHANGES IN DENTAL CARE

When Dr. John S. Zapp was hired as ADA's executive director, America was in the midst of a contentious national debate on health care. In 1993 President Bill Clinton, a Democrat, had appointed a White House Task Force to recommend reform on the structure and finance of health care in the United States.

Among the resulting Clinton health care initiatives was a proposal to require health plans to cover preventive dental services for children, as well as emergency care for adults. Long a champion of children's oral health issues, the ADA was

sympathetic to President Clinton's goal of ensuring that the nation's children were provided with adequate dental insurance.

But the ADA took exception to some of the overhauls contained in health care legislation sent to Congress as a result of the Clinton initiatives. The Association argued that policymakers in Washington did not have a good handle on how dentistry was delivered in the United States. Many ADA members felt that dentistry already provided cost-effective and efficient care and did not need the proposed health system reforms.

As it happened, the Clinton health care plan ran into tremendous resistance from the medical and hospital community. When the Republican Party engineered a

◀ Outgoing ADA President Jack H. Harris (right) congratulates newly installed President James H. Gaines at the 1993 Annual Session in San Francisco. During his first interview with *ADA News*, Dr. Gaines cited health system reform and rising dental student indebtedness among the most prominent issues facing the profession at the onset of his term.

The Changing Face of the Profession
1990–1999

1991

Dr. Geraldine T. Morrow assumes office as the first woman president of the ADA.

1993

The ADA adopts a slogan calling attention to the profession's cost effectiveness: "Dentistry: Health Care That Works."

Drs. William E. Allen and Michael L. Perich are named co-recipients of the 1993 ADA Distinguished Service Award, the first time in the twenty-three-year history of the award that multiple winners are selected.

1992

Hurricane Andrew damages sixty south Florida dental offices in its rampage across populated areas south of Miami.

1995

The ADA launches ADAOnline, its first Web site, to communicate to members and the public.

The newly renamed ADA Health Foundation channels nearly $600,000 into dental research, education, and other charitable projects.

1998

The National Institute of Dental Research celebrates its fiftieth anniversary and is renamed the National Institute of Dental and Craniofacial Research.

1996

According to an ADA survey report, there are 7,425 Asian dentists actively practicing in the United States, about 5 percent of all active practitioners.

1997

According to an ADA survey report, there are 3,680 Hispanic dentists and 2,505 African American dentists actively practicing in the United States out of a total of 138,435.

An ADA survey reveals that 84 percent of U.S. dentists offer tooth-whitening services to patients.

1999

The U.S. House of Representatives approves ADA-sponsored patients' rights legislation by a vote of 275–151.

Community water fluoridation is named one of the ten greatest public health achievements of the twentieth century by the U.S. Centers for Disease Control and Prevention.

Ask your dentist about *tooth whitening.*

ADA

▲ A 1996 ADA patient education brochure describing how tooth whitening could improve your smile and well-being.

major resurgence in the 1994 off-year congressional elections, the Clinton health care proposal failed. The ADA emerged from the debate with confidence in its ability to muster grassroots support and to lobby for Association positions on complex issues.

Health care costs, and how Americans would pay for them, remained a priority issue for Washington policymakers throughout the 1990s and into the twenty-first century. The ADA and its members would learn to deal with new methods of financing dentistry's delivery, including preferred provider organizations, health maintenance organizations, and direct payment mechanisms.

Dr. Richard W. D'Eustachio, ADA president 1994–1995, summed up the realities that America's dentists faced in the final years of the twentieth century. In an *ADA News* interview at the beginning of his term, D'Eustachio talked about where the profession was headed.

"The marketplace is going to change, and dentistry is going to change with it," D'Eustachio said. "It's the marketplace that's driving this, and it's a machine that's been gearing up for some time. The ADA has to be in a position to help our members address these changes."

DENTISTRY'S COMMITMENT TO SAFETY

At the beginning of the 1990s, the ADA and dentistry ended up in the spotlight over allegations of a dentist having transmitted AIDS to several patients. It was the only case in which the disease was allegedly transmitted by a U.S. health care worker to patients. Though the Centers for Disease

◀ Participants in the 1993 Health Screening Program are tested for tuberculosis and are given a head, neck, and oral examination. The program drew record crowds at the 1993 Annual Session in San Francisco. *(ADA file photo by Dave Bush Photographers)*

Dudley the Dinosaur

Since the 1920s, the ADA has taken a continued interest in the dental health of the nation's children. The Association has routinely used cartoon characters and children's celebrities to reach children and teach them good oral health care. Through the years, ADA's dental health education program for children has featured many popular characters, including Mickey Mouse®; Dennis the Menace®; Kukla, Fran and Ollie®; Casper the Friendly Ghost®; Charlie Brown; Kermit the Frog®; Spider-Man®; and the Fantastic Four®. The ADA has also created many characters for use in educational and promotional materials. One of the most successful of these has been Dudley the Dinosaur.

In 1990, Dudley the Dinosaur was introduced, capitalizing on the contemporaneous craze among children for all things dinosaurian. Dudley the Dinosaur first appeared in the animated film *Dudley Visits the Dentist*, released in December 1990 and still being distributed, that shows children what to expect during a dental visit.

Other films featuring Dudley, his sister Dee Dee, Grandpa Rex, and friends include *Dudley Goes to Camp Brush and Floss, Dudley's Classroom Adventure, Dudley Visits the Dentist, Dudley and Dee Dee in Nutrition Land,* and *Brushing Magic.* Dudley and his friends have been featured in a variety of ADA public service announcements and marketing materials including

▶ A storyboard for an ADA public service announcement features Dudley the Dinosaur, his sister Dee Dee, and his brother Baby Digby warning the public about baby bottle tooth decay.

AMERICAN DENTAL ASSOCIATION
"BABY DIGBY"
30 SECOND PUBLIC SERVICE ANNOUNCEMENT

Dudley: Shhh... | **Dee Dee:** Can Baby Digby have some of this to go nitey nite? | **Mom:** When it's time for baby to sleep, we don't give him a bottle of milk, formula or any juices.

Mom: Sweet liquids can stay in baby's mouth and cause Baby Bottle Tooth Decay. | **Mom:** Between feedings, at naps and bedtime, if needed, we only give baby a bottle of plain water. | **Dee Dee:** Only water.

Mom: No Baby Bottle Tooth Decay for you... | Healthy Teeth and a beautiful smile. | **Dee Dee:** He's so Cute!

 ADA American Dental Association | 211 East Chicago Ave. Chicago, IL 60611 (312) 440-2589

videos, practice promotional materials, posters, patient education brochures, classroom materials, and plush dolls. Dudley the Dinosaur was the first bilingual public service cartoon series produced in the United States.

Before there was Dudley the Dinosaur, ADA Salable Materials program had used a different cartoon creature with a similar name. The earlier character, Dudley the Dragon, was featured in a 1971 comic book written in verse for preschoolers and primary grade children that taught them how to take care of their teeth. It was an immediate hit, and an animated short film version of the comic book came out a year later. Both versions were sold through the ADA Catalog continuously until 1985.

It was five years later, in 1990, that Dudley the Dinosaur first appeared as ADA's new ambassador to children. By 2009 Dudley the Dinosaur had aired over one million times on U.S. television, surpassing Smokey the Bear® as the most televised animated public service character. Today's Dudley the Dinosaur is an ADA icon well-known to ADA members, their staffs, and younger patients. Countless dentists, dental team members, and their children have met Dudley at ADA Annual Sessions and other events in his role as ambassador for good dental health.

10

SO WITH THAT, DUDLEY THE DRAGON BEGAN RIGHT AWAY, | TO LEARN TO FLOSS AND BRUSH AND FIGHT OFF TOOTH DECAY

HOWIE SHOWED DUDLEY THE PROPER POSITION, | FOR HOLDING THE BRUSH LIKE A ROD WHEN YOU'RE FISHIN'.

▲ This 1971 ADA-produced comic book originated the cartoon character Dudley the Dragon who taught children the importance of proper oral health care.

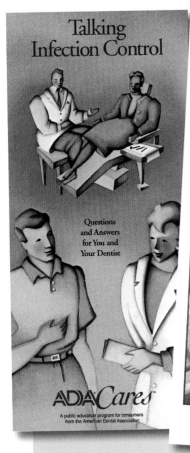

Amid growing fear due to the spread of AIDS in the early 1990s, the Association sought to alleviate public concerns about the health risks of visiting a dentist. These ADA brochures educated patients about standard infection control procedures in the dental office.

Control and Prevention (CDC) became involved and studied the case, the method of transmission between the dentist and his patients was never fully explained. The case was widely covered in the media. There were calls for compulsory HIV/HBV testing for health care workers and mandatory disclosure of their status. The case focused attention on the importance of infection control in the dental office and on the right to know versus the right to privacy.

The AIDS crisis resulted in a strong response by federal and state regulatory agencies responsible for overseeing public and workforce safety. In 1991, the Occupational Safety and Health Administration (OSHA) issued its Bloodborne Pathogens Standard, which greatly affected how dentists and their teams performed their duties. The standard was created to protect health care workers from workplace exposure to bloodborne diseases. The ADA worked with OSHA to develop a standard acceptable to dentistry.

The ADA advocated for the revision of other OSHA regulations affecting the dental profession, such as the Ergonomics Standard in the late 1990s. In 1997, ADA President Gary Rainwater told a U.S. House of Representatives Committee that OSHA seemed to be moving in the right direction. However, he said, the profession would continue to be proactive in legislation that could affect individual dental practices.

Bugs Bunny visits children at Kid Camp during the 1997 Annual Session in Washington, D.C. Kid Camp provides day care for children of visitors attending ADA Annual Session. *(ADA file photo by Richard Greenhouse) (Bugs Bunny used courtesy of Warner Bros. Entertainment Inc.)*

Community Water Fluoridation

A Great Public Health Achievement

When the U.S. Centers for Disease Control and Prevention (CDC) listed the "Ten Great Public Health Achievements" in the United States of the twentieth century, nobody in dentistry was particularly surprised that fluoridation of the nation's water supply was on the list.

The CDC unveiled its list in April 1999 to give attention to the dramatic increases in lifespan in the U.S. during the past one hundred years. According to the CDC report, since 1900, "the average lifespan of persons in the United States has lengthened by greater than 30 years; 25 years of this gain are attributable to advances in public health."

Community water fluoridation was commended along with other significant public health achievements including vaccination, motor vehicle safety, safer workplaces, control of infectious diseases, decline in death from coronary heart disease and stroke, safer and healthier foods, healthier mothers and babies, family planning, and recognition of tobacco use as a health hazard.

▶ A patient education brochure on the benefits of fluoride produced and distributed by the ADA in commemoration of the sixtieth anniversary of community water fluoridation in 2006.

The inclusion of fluoridation paid tribute to an oral health initiative that began in 1945 when Grand Rapids, Michigan, became the first U.S. community to fluoridate its water supply. In 1950, the ADA went on record in support of fluoridation when it passed a resolution recommending the fluoridation of community water supplies when approved by the local dental society. "Fluoridation safely and inexpensively benefits both children and adults by effectively preventing tooth decay, regardless of socioeconomic status or access to care," the CDC reported. "Fluoridation has played an important role in the reductions in tooth decay and of tooth loss in adults."

Fluoridation continued to make inroads, even into the twenty-first century. In 1999, the same year that the CDC saluted fluoridation, an estimated 144 million Americans had access to a fluoridated water supply, almost 65 percent of America's population. By 2006 that increased to nearly 70 percent, close to the U.S. Department of Health and Human Services' 75 percent goal identified in its 2000 landmark statement of national health objectives, *Healthy People 2010*.

Fluoridation Facts

◀ *Fluoridation Facts* is an informational pamphlet on community water fluoridation, which the ADA has produced and published in many editions since 1952.

Dr. Gerrit Hagman (center) presents the 1997 Annual Session best table clinic award to Dr. Arthur Van Stewart (right) and Robert H. Staat, PhD (left). Their table clinic was on the timely safety control topic "Clearance of Water Line Biofilms Using Hydroperozide Ions." *(ADA file photo by David Buehrens)*

▶ ADA President A. Gary Rainwater is interviewed in 1997 about the ADA Seal of Acceptance for the PBS show *Healthweek*. Much favorable coverage for the Seal program was generated in light of a short-lived controversy involving the AMA. The medical organization was criticized when a home health appliance manufacturer received exclusive use of the AMA's endorsement in exchange for royalties generated. In contrast, the media praised the ADA Seal of Acceptance evaluation methods, which involved vigorous product testing and scrutiny of advertising claims. *(ADA file photo by Richard Greenhouse)*

THE ELECTRONIC REVOLUTION

In the late 1990s, nothing would have a more profound effect on dentistry than the electronic revolution that was taking place across all segments of society. The transition to desktop computers that had begun in the late 1980s accelerated dramatically throughout the 1990s, and the ADA and the dental profession adapted to electronic communications.

The growth of the Internet was little short of astounding. Increasingly, member dentists were using the Internet for a host of tasks. In 1996, the ADA signed contracts with two vendors to develop electronic dental claims processing. At the time, seven of ten U.S. dentists had a personal computer in their office. About half of the dental computer users had a telephone modem connected with the growing World Wide Web.

In 1998, the ADA previewed a virtual dental practice for more than six hundred members in attendance at the Association's Annual Session in San Francisco. The Session's Technology Day event attracted standing-room-only crowds eager to see demonstrations of practice management software, electronic insurance claims processing, Internet marketing tools, e-mail chat groups, and Internet conferencing. "Investing in technology is not a luxury....It's a necessity," one exhibitor told attendees.

◀ At the 1995 Annual Session in Las Vegas, ADA librarian Mary Kreinbring gives attendees a demonstration of ADAOnline, the Association's recently launched Web site later renamed ADA.org. *(ADA file photo by Wendell Donahoo)*

ADA Business Enterprises, Inc.

One of the ADA's more successful initiatives involved the creation of for-profit subsidiaries to address the changing business world and to increase non-dues revenue. In 1989, the Board of Trustees established the ADA Holding Company, Inc. (HCI), to endorse companies that would provide a variety of goods and services to ADA members and other dental professionals. In 1995, HCI established ADA Financial Services Company (FINCO) to provide financial products and services. A year later, in 1996, ADA Electronic Commerce Company (ECCo) was set up to promote electronic commerce within the dental profession. The subsidiary quickly endorsed an electronic clearinghouse for processing dental claims and worked closely with a software vendor to help members more easily process electronic claims.

All for-profit subsidiaries were eventually merged into HCI in 1999 and the company's name was changed to ADA Business Enterprises, Inc. (ADABEI). The company worked closely with suppliers and vendors through the ADA Member Advantage Program, founded in 2001, to address various business and leisure needs for members. By 2008, the program's offerings had grown to encompass a wide range of services and products, including credit cards, practice financing, real estate loans, credit card

▷ ADA Business Resources brochures market credit card processing, office management, and customized staff apparel, some of the many products and services available to ADA members through the program.

processing, payroll management, telephone services, staff apparel, patient financing, postage meters, health savings accounts, and patient record-keeping systems. In 2009, the program was revamped and renamed ADA Business Resources to reflect its new commitment in providing the best products and services available for practice management.

ADABEI contributed some of its profits to the ADA Foundation's activities. The subsidiary was a contributor to ADA 9/11 emergency funds, and by 2002, had donated more than $1 million to the ADA Foundation. In 2005, ADABEI contributed $50,000 in seed money to the Foundation's Disaster Response Fund to assist dentists affected by Hurricane Katrina.

◁ Dr. Barry Freydberg presents his "Nothing but the 'NET!" seminar at the 1997 Annual Session in Washington, D.C., on how to access and use the Internet. He warned that dental offices not linked to the Internet would soon become outdated.
(ADA file photo by Richard Greenhouse)

By the time ADA President S. Timothy Rose left office in 1999, the Association had entered into what he called e-life. The ADA's Web site, ADAOnline, launched in 1995 and later renamed ADA.org, was clearly the Association's communication vehicle of the future. "Electronic commerce in all its manifestations will clearly provide a major opportunity for the American Dental Association," Rose told delegates at the 1999 Annual Session. With the promise of new technology, the ADA and dentistry looked ahead to the new millennium with confidence and optimism.

Chapter Eight
The ADA in a New Millennium, 2000–2009

Like the rest of America, the ADA and the dental community found themselves deeply affected by the worst attack on America's shores since Pearl Harbor when terrorists piloted two hijacked jet airplanes into the World Trade Center (WTC) in New York City on September 11, 2001. Before the Twin Towers in New York had fallen, a third hijacked jet plowed into the Pentagon in suburban Washington, D.C., and a fourth plane had crashed in a field in Pennsylvania after altering its flight plan and changing course for the nation's Capitol. The public feared that other American landmarks, including the White House and the Sears Tower in Chicago, would soon become targets. To be on the safe side, the ADA closed its offices in Chicago and Washington in late morning, reopening the next day.

The four attacks on the morning of September 11 killed nearly three thousand Americans. Several ADA members with offices in New York City lost their practices in the WTC attack. Others had patients who lost their lives. Air travel was disrupted across North America for almost a month. The lifting of travel restrictions in early October and the government's encouragement of a return to normalcy allowed the ADA to host its scheduled Annual Session in Kansas City from October 13–17.

A number of members from the New York and Washington areas would be otherwise occupied and unable to attend the 2001 Annual Session. Dr. Jeffrey Burkes, chief dental consultant for New York City, spent several months leading

ADA President D. Gregory Chadwick (second from right) and ADA Fourth District Trustee Dr. Bernard McDermott (right) tour military dental facilities at Fort Sam Houston in San Antonio, Texas, in 2002 with hosts (left to right) U.S. Army Dental Command Chief of Staff Ronald Lambert and Commander Robert Leeds. The tours were a show of support for dental officers in the military.

147

The ADA Library

ADA members, whether they live in Chicago, Seattle, or rural Tennessee, have long had a dental library to call their own. Housed in the Association's Chicago headquarters building, the ADA Library provides information services to local dentists, visiting members, and ADA members nationwide. In 2007 the Department of Library Services celebrated eighty years of service to ADA members and staff.

The Association established the ADA Library in 1927 as a national repository of dentistry, which would collect and make generally available all the published information of interest to the dental profession. There were only a handful of dental libraries at the time, located at dental schools, and they were inaccessible to most of the ADA membership.

The idea for an ADA Library was proposed as early as 1923. In his address to the House of Delegates at the 1923 Annual Session, ADA President John P. Buckley urged the establishment of a dental library by the Association: "The standing or character of a profession can best be judged by its literature… [and] organized dentistry should have a library of its own… The library should contain everything in the way of reference, be complete in every particular, all dental literature, national and international, properly indexed…This would not only augment and encourage our research workers; but would reflect greatly to the credit of our profession."

The ADA had begun to collect book and journal resources as early as 1922. *JADA* published notices requesting donations of dental books and journals. The book collection of the Library was given

The ADA Library in 1957, when the ADA's offices were located in a building at 222 East Superior Street in Chicago.

a good beginning by ADA member Dr. William H. DeFord, who donated his large private library of dental and medical books before his death in 1932.

In 1939, the ADA Library assumed responsibility for publication of the *Index to Dental Literature* (*IDL*), which had been founded and edited by Dr. Arthur D. Black, son of G. V. Black, and a former dean of Northwestern University Dental School. Before the *IDL* was available, it was almost impossible to find articles on a specific topic or by a particular author within the large number of published dental journals. The *IDL* covered the dental literature back to 1839 but ceased publication in 2001, when the National Library of Medicine (NLM) assumed sole responsibility for indexing the dental literature in the MEDLINE database, now available on NLM's PubMed Web site.

In 1948, Dr. Arthur H. Merritt, a prominent dentist who served as president of the ADA, 1939–1940, began to donate funds for the purchase of rare, historical dental books for the Library and bequeathed money to the collection upon his death in 1961. As a result, the ADA Library today has one of the best institutional collections of rare and historical dental books dating back to the eighteenth century. The Library has a strong dental history collection and also houses the archives of the Association.

The main services in the early years were much the same as those offered by the Library today: journal articles, book loans, bibliographies, and reference assistance. In the days before photocopiers, library staff assembled topical binders of articles clipped from journals. ADA members could then borrow these

The ADA Library in 1929, when the ADA's offices were located in a rented space at 58 East Washington Street in Chicago. This is one of two existing photographs of the Library, the only surviving interior images of that era's ADA central office.

▲ The ADA Library in 1977 in its original location on the nineteenth floor of the current ADA building at 211 East Chicago Avenue in Chicago.

subject files. The Library still maintains a large collection of current journal articles arranged by subject to answer reference questions on any dental topic, but now journal articles are usually scanned and sent to members in electronic format.

In 2009, the Library has a comprehensive book collection, receives over six hundred journal titles each year, has a Web catalog listing books and journals in the collection, and lends books to members all over the country. ADA Library staff members respond to a daily array of reference questions on standard topics, new technologies, practice management issues, and emerging trends in dentistry. Today, the average dental practitioner still lacks easy access to a local dental library, and the ADA Library continues to support the information needs of ADA members.

▲ The ADA Library in 2009. The library moved to its present space on the sixth floor of ADA Headquarters as part of a major building renovation in 2002.

a forensic dentistry team identifying dentures and dental records of WTC victims. "It's 24/7 here," Burkes told the *ADA News* in October. "We never shut down. It could be 2 a.m. or 2 p.m. – the work is the same."

Military dentists assisted in the identification of victims from the Pentagon attack. Forensic dental experts from all of the service branches began gathering at Dover Air Force Base in Delaware on September 13 for the arduous task of reconstructing fragments of victims' dental work.

Other Association members were donning uniforms in October 2001 as U.S. forces began hitting terrorist enclaves in Afghanistan. Dental members of Reserve and National Guard units called up during the emergency were extended a dues waiver by the ADA for the duration of their military service.

The ADA responded quickly to the events of September 11. Before the rubble had even stopped smoking, the Association established the ADA American Tragedy Fund, a special temporary fund for the dental community designed to help dentists, their families, and other victims impacted by the attack. Among the first to contribute to the fund were the ADA Endowment and Assistance Fund, which donated $100,000, and ADA Business Enterprises Inc., which contributed $10,000.

HEADQUARTERS RENOVATION

The ADA began the twenty-first century with a new chief executive. Dr. John S. Zapp retired after eight years as the Association's executive director in March 2001. Dr. James B. Bramson was selected to be his replacement, and he

assumed the position in July 2001. A graduate of the University of Iowa College of Dentistry, Bramson began his dental career as a private practitioner in Iowa. He first came to the ADA as a Hillenbrand Fellow in 1986 and stayed on as director of both the Council on Dental Practice and the Commission on Relief Fund Activities, 1990–1997. He left the Association to serve four years as executive director of the Massachusetts Dental Society before returning to Chicago as ADA executive director.

Bramson's administration, which ended in 2008, was marked by initiatives to marshal the Association's resources to add value to membership and to increase non-dues revenue. One initiative

was to develop a customer service culture within the organization. A central Member Service Center was established to facilitate the response to member calls. Another important achievement was overseeing a multi-year renovation project in which the ADA Headquarters building received a much-needed modernization. Though the project began under his predecessor, most of the remodeling of the forty-year-old building was completed during Dr. Bramson's tenure. The outcome was an open floor plan and space-saving design that freed up more space for lease to tenants to increase non-dues revenue.

DENTISTRY IN THE NEW MILLENNIUM

In the new millennium, the ADA continued to pursue the objective set forth in its constitution "to encourage the improvement of the health of the public and to promote the art and science of dentistry." Though there remained many goals to achieve, there was good news in both these areas at the beginning of the twenty-first century.

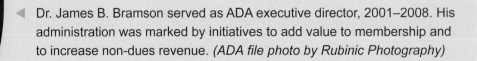

◀ Dr. James B. Bramson served as ADA executive director, 2001–2008. His administration was marked by initiatives to add value to membership and to increase non-dues revenue. *(ADA file photo by Rubinic Photography)*

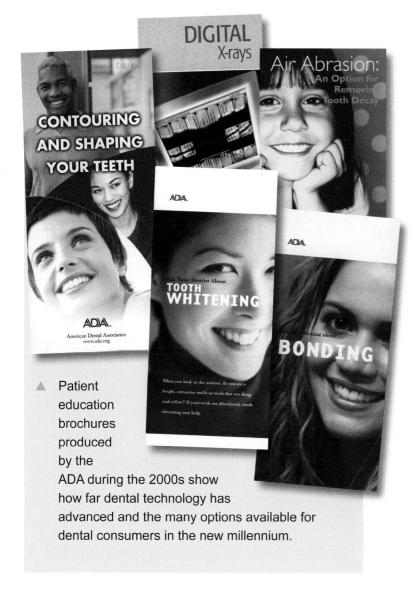

▲ Patient education brochures produced by the ADA during the 2000s show how far dental technology has advanced and the many options available for dental consumers in the new millennium.

In 2002, the ADA reported that there were just under 170,000 professionally active dentists in the United States. The vast majority of them, about 157,000, were private practitioners. The remaining 13,000

dentists worked for government, were in the military, or taught in one of the nation's fifty-six dental schools.

The future held promise of a more diverse profession. Although in 2000, nearly 83 percent of U.S. dentists were males, many more women had begun entering the profession. During the 1990s, 34 percent, or 12,130, of the nation's new dentists were female, and 66 percent, or 23,500, were male.

The percentages were even higher for new dentists who would enter the profession during the first decade of the twenty-first century. Almost 39 percent of the dental school class of 2002 were female, as were 44 percent of first-year dental students that year. Dental students were also more racially diverse. Minority students made up 35 percent of the graduating class and 32 percent of first-year dental students in 2002.

While the per capita cost of personal health care continued to increase at a rapid rate, from $3,983 in 2000 to almost $4,700 in 2002, the average per person expense for dental services was still a small portion of

▶ In 2003, dental leaders share a lighter moment at the first-ever congressional briefing on women's oral health: (from left) Rear Admiral Dushanka V. Kleinman, U.S. Public Health Service chief dental officer; Dr. Linda C. Niessen, Baylor College of Dentistry; Dr. Kathleen S. Roth, ADA Ninth District trustee (ADA president, 2006–2007); Dr. Marjorie K. Jeffcoat, *JADA* editor; and Dr. Barbara J. Steinberg, Drexel University College of Medicine. The "Women's Oral Health: Implications Across the Lifespan" briefing was presented by the ADA and the Society for Women's Health Research in cooperation with the Congressional Caucus for Women's Issues and drew over fifty Capitol Hill staffers and oral health advocates. *(ADA file photo by Anna Ng Delort)*

ADA Governance

The inclusive nature of the ADA encourages member involvement in policy and decision-making. Because of the volunteer focus of the Association, dentists from every walk of life serve on the ADA Board of Trustees, in the House of Delegates, and on the councils, commissions, and committees that make up the governing structure of the ADA. More than seven hundred members serve on these bodies annually.

BOARD OF TRUSTEES

The ADA Board of Trustees provides organizational leadership while acting as the steward of the Association's mission and resources. The Board partners with staff, plans strategies, identifies priorities, builds consensus, and implements the directives of the House of Delegates.

As the managing body of the ADA, the Board conducts the business of the Association and proposes an annual budget to the House. The Board also appoints the executive director, manages ADA property, reviews reports of councils and special committees, and makes recommendations to the House of Delegates.

The Board traditionally meets seven times a year and is composed of twenty-three members: one representative from each of the seventeen trustee districts that encompass the United States and its jurisdictions; the president-elect, first vice president, and second vice president; and the president, treasurer, and executive director, who serve as *ex officio* members, without the right to vote. The speaker of the House of Delegates also attends all Board meetings but is not a member of the Board of Trustees.

ADA immediate Past President Richard W. D'Eustachio presents Dr. William S. Ten Pas with the insignia of office of ADA president at installation ceremonies during the annual meeting of the House of Delegates at the 1995 Annual Session. The traditional transfer of office occurs at every ADA Annual Session. *(ADA file photo by Wendell Donahoo)*

The Association's constituent dental societies are organized into seventeen districts, each of which has a trustee elected to serve on the Board of Trustees. The following is the territorial organization of the trustee districts:

First District:	Connecticut, Maine, Massachusetts, New Hampshire, Rhode Island, Vermont
Second District:	New York
Third District:	Pennsylvania
Fourth District:	Delaware, District of Columbia, Federal Dental Services, Maryland, New Jersey, Puerto Rico, Virgin Islands
Fifth District:	Alabama, Georgia, Mississippi
Sixth District:	Kentucky, Missouri, Tennessee, West Virginia
Seventh District:	Indiana, Ohio
Eighth District:	Illinois
Ninth District:	Michigan, Wisconsin
Tenth District:	Iowa, Minnesota, Nebraska, North Dakota, South Dakota
Eleventh District:	Alaska, Idaho, Montana, Oregon, Washington
Twelfth District:	Arkansas, Kansas, Louisiana, Oklahoma
Thirteenth District:	California
Fourteenth District:	Arizona, Colorado, Hawaii, Nevada, New Mexico, Utah, Wyoming
Fifteenth District:	Texas
Sixteenth District:	North Carolina, South Carolina, Virginia
Seventeenth District:	Florida

The ADA Board of Trustees meets in 1973. The twenty-three-member Board is currently composed of one representative from each of seventeen trustee districts plus the elected officers and the executive director. *(ADA file photo by Photo Ideas, Inc.)*

ADA President-elect John S. Findley, President Mark Feldman, and Speaker of the House of Delegates J. Thomas Soliday (left to right) preside at a Board of Trustees meeting in August 2008.

HOUSE OF DELEGATES

The House of Delegates, as the legislative and governing body, is the supreme authority in the ADA. As such, it speaks for the membership of the Association and for the dental profession in the United States. The House establishes official policy, sets the annual member dues, and approves the annual operating budget.

The House is composed of 473 delegates representing 53 constituent societies, 5 federal dental services, and the American Student Dental Association. The body meets once a year during the Association's Annual Session, usually held in October. The officers of the House are the speaker and the secretary. The executive director of the Association serves as secretary of the House.

Dr. T. Howard Jones takes a phone call at his desk at ADA Headquarters in Chicago during his term as president, 2002–2003. One of five elected officers, the president serves as the primary official representative of the Association in its contacts with government, civic, business, and professional organizations for the purpose of advancing the ADA's objectives and policies. Presidents serve one-year terms, during which they spend about a quarter of their time at ADA Headquarters, the Washington Office, or traveling on ADA business. The other elective offices are president-elect, first vice president, second vice president, speaker of the House of Delegates (all one-year terms), and treasurer (a three-year term).

TRIPARTITE STRUCTURE

As of 2009, the ADA had more than 157,000 dentist members from 53 constituent (state-territorial) and 545 component (local) dental societies. The ADA is the largest and oldest national dental association in the world. For more than ninety years, the ADA, together with the state and local dental societies, has functioned as a three-tiered system called the tripartite. While retaining their autonomy as associations, the national, constituent, and component organizations work together for members. With a few exceptions, ADA members hold membership at all three levels.

Under the tripartite structure, a dentist practicing in Chicago would be a member of the Chicago Dental Society, the Illinois State Dental Society, and the national ADA. In most locations, dentists join and pay their dues through the state dental society. The tripartite structure provides a consistent voice in advocacy issues, supports uniform educational standards, promotes ethical dental practice, and coordinates activities. The result is a more comprehensive set of resources for members and a unified voice for the profession.

The ADA House of Delegates takes a vote during the 2003 Annual Session. The legislative and governing body of the Association, the House is the supreme authority in the ADA. *(ADA file photo by Lagniappe Studio)*

A 2002 ADA "Healthy Smiles" billboard over Provo, Utah, promotes the dental profession. Over one thousand billboards like this one were distributed for use by dental societies across the country.

U.S. Secretary of Health and Human Services Tommy Thompson (second from right) meets with ADA leaders during the 2001 Washington Leadership Conference: (left to right) Drs. Robert M. Anderton, D. Gregory Chadwick, Thomas J. Hughes, and S. Timothy Rose. The annual conference draws state and local dental society representatives from across the country, many of them leaders of ADA grassroots political action teams, to Capitol Hill for meetings with administration officials to discuss state and national policy issues important to dentists. *(ADA file photo by Anna Ng Delort)*

the total, only $246 in 2002. Nearly two-thirds of patients who saw general dental practitioners in 2003 were covered by some sort of private dental insurance.

At a time when the federal government was encouraging the spread of health maintenance organizations (HMOs) and preferred provider organizations (PPOs), managed care was making inroads into the nation's dental practices. By 2002, 5.4 percent of gross billings for general dental practitioners and more than 9 percent of gross billings for oral and maxillofacial surgeons were from managed care entities such as HMOs or PPOs.

Americans were becoming more aware that regular visits to the dentist were key to overall physical health. Nearly three out of four U.S. children visited the dentist in 2001. About two-thirds of adults made at least one visit to the dentist during the year, although those aged sixty-five and older continued to lag younger members of the population, with 56 percent making annual visits to the dentist in 2001.

Perhaps the best news for America's dental community was the continuing progress made in treating children's caries. By the late 1990s, well

Steve Gruninger (right), assistant director of safety and biocompatibility in the ADA Division of Science, discusses latex hypersensitivity with toxicologist Dr. Milton Marshall at the 2003 annual meeting of the American Association for Dental Research. Staff from the ADA Division of Science, the Paffenbarger Research Center, and the Health Policy Resources Center presented thirty-nine scientific presentations, informational sessions, and posters at the meeting covering a wide variety of topics on dental materials, dental education, and dental practice trends.

over half the nation's children had no decay in their permanent teeth. That was more than double the number of children who had no decay in their permanent teeth during the early 1970s.

THE ADA FOUNDATION THRIVES

A dental assistant visits the Health Screening Program at the ADA Annual Session and learns of a potentially life-threatening condition—early detection allows her to get an operation to reverse the problem. An Arkansas dentist opens a $2,500 check—it's the earliest help he receives after his office is damaged in a deadly tornado. An unemployed mother of five receives oral health care to restore her broken teeth and, newly confident, re-enters the job market. These stories—stories of research, education, charitable assistance, and access to care—have one thing in common: the ADA Foundation.

▶ Dr. Samuel D. Harris (second from left) celebrates his ninety-eighth birthday in 2001 with the help of (left to right) Dr. Jack Gottschalk, a Harris Advisory Committee member and chair of The Dr. Samuel D. Harris National Museum of Dentistry Board of Visitors; Dwight S. Edwards, director of development for the ADA Foundation; and Dr. Anthony R. Volpe, ADA Foundation president. Harris, who died in 2003 just shy of his one hundredth birthday, was a leader in pediatric dentistry and a generous dental philanthropist who contributed millions of dollars to establish and support the National Museum of Dentistry in Baltimore and to endow the ADA Foundation's Samuel D. Harris Fund for Children's Dental Health. In appreciation of his previous generosity, the three guests flew to Florida to deliver best wishes, a Foundation baseball cap, and a birthday cheesecake to Dr. Harris. The following day, he pledged a million dollars each to the Foundation and the museum.

The ADA in a New Millennium
2000–2009

2000

The *ADA Legal Adviser* becomes the first ADA print publication to be offered to members online only.

Of the total 166,383 professionally active dentists in the United States, 26,011 are female, about 16 percent of the total.

The ADA hosts a headquarters building open house for members attending the Annual Session in Chicago.

2002

Former U.S. President George H. W. Bush addresses the ADA Annual Session in New Orleans.

2005

The ADA and the Kellogg School of Management at Northwestern University team up to offer an Executive Management Program for dental professionals.

2001

The ADA formally recognizes the specialty of oral and maxillofacial radiology.

A full-text version of *The Journal of American Dental Association* becomes available in electronic format.

The ADA Catalog goes online.

2003

Dr. Eugene Sekiguchi assumes office as the first Asian American president of the ADA.

The ADA Health Foundation merges with the ADA Relief Fund, ADA Endowment and Assistance Fund, Inc., and ADA Emergency Fund, Inc. and is renamed the ADA Foundation.

The ADA Institute for Diversity in Leadership is established to prepare a diverse group of dentists to become leaders within the profession and in their communities.

The first "Give Kids A Smile®" day is held as part of National Children's Dental Health Month.

2009
ADA Annual Catalog
Helping You Deliver the Best in Patient Care.

Better Together!
CDT 2009-2010 plus the CDT Companion.
See page 21 for details!

It's easy to place your order!
Online: www.adacatalog.org
Phone: 800.947.4746
Fax: 312.440.3542

211 East Chicago Avenue
Chicago, Illinois 60611-2616

CDT 2009-2010 with CDT Companion Kit
K010
Member: $84.95 / Nonmember: $127.45

ADA American Dental Association®
America's leading advocate for oral health

◄ The 2009 print edition of the ADA Annual Catalog, which offers to member dentists a wide selection of effective and affordable products for patient education and practice management.

2006

Dr. Kathleen S. Roth is installed as the second woman president of the ADA.

The ADA Foundation launches *Our Legacy—Our Future*, the nationwide initiative spearheaded by the Foundation to raise awareness of the needs of dental education.

The *ADA Professional Product Review*, created to assist dentists with product selection for their practices, begins publication.

The ADA Foundation leads a major relief effort to aid dentist victims of Hurricane Katrina.

2008

Dr. Thomas S. Underwood is presented the first ADA Humanitarian Award.

The ADA Center for Evidence-Based Dentistry is established and launches a Web site the following year.

2007

The ADA, the ADA Foundation, and GlaxoSmithKline launch OralLongevity™, a three-year collaborative initiative to address the oral health needs of older adults.

The ADA Library celebrates its eightieth year of service to ADA members.

2009

Dr. Kathleen T. O'Loughlin becomes the first female executive director of the ADA.

The ADA celebrates the 150th anniversary of its founding.

The ADA elects Dr. Raymond F. Gist, its first African American president, who will serve his term in 2010–2011.

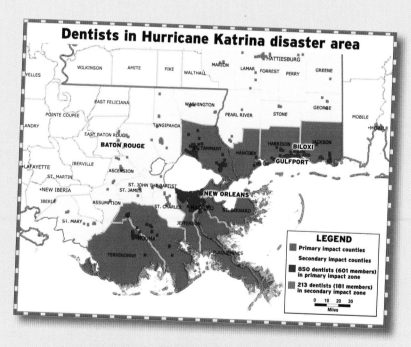

Dentists in Hurricane Katrina disaster area

LEGEND
- Primary impact counties
- Secondary impact counties
- 850 dentists (601 members) in primary impact zone
- 213 dentists (181 members) in secondary impact zone

0 10 20 30 Miles

▲ Dr. Eugene Sekiguchi, the first Asian American president of the ADA, speaks to the House of Delegates at his installation during the 2003 Annual Session. *(ADA file photo by Lagniappe Studio)*

▲ A map created by the ADA Health Policy Resources Center using data from the ADA's Distribution of Dentistry database shows the number of ADA members in Louisiana and Mississippi affected by Hurricane Katrina. The devastating storm hit the area in August 2005 leveling homes and businesses, leaving thousands homeless, and claiming hundreds of lives. The dental profession responded by providing aid and assistance to dentists and dental organizations impacted by the storm.

ADA Councils, Commissions, Committees

ADA COUNCILS

One key to the Association's ability to respond quickly to issues and challenges is contained in the design and makeup of the ADA's council structure. The Association's councils serve as policy-recommending agencies. Each council is assigned to study issues relating to its special area of interest and to make recommendations on those matters to the Board of Trustees and the House of Delegates.

Most councils are composed of one member from each of the seventeen trustee districts of the Association and meet two to three times a year, either at the ADA Headquarters office in Chicago or the Washington, D.C., office. Council members, who serve four-year terms, must be ADA dentist members in good standing. In 2009, there were eleven councils organized by subject area to cover the multiple challenges the profession faced in the twenty-first century.

The **Council on Access, Prevention and Interprofessional Relations** provides leadership, vision, and coordination of the ADA's activities to advance oral health care within the health delivery system, to promote prevention as the cornerstone of oral health, and to improve access to oral health services for underserved populations.

The **Council on ADA Sessions** is responsible for the development and continuous improvement of every aspect of the ADA Annual Session, in order to maintain its stature of being the premier meeting in the worldwide dental community.

▽ The Council on Dental Benefit Programs meets in the ADA boardroom in 2006 including members (from left) Drs. Mark Kampfe, Steve Hogg (back), Pat Boyle, and Steve Simpson. The Association's councils make recommendations on their special areas of interest to the Board of Trustees and the House of Delegates.

▶ Members of the 2005 Component B Test Construction Committee, (left to right) Dr. Jacqueline Plemons from the Baylor College of Dentistry and Lynn Tolle from Old Dominion University, study possible cases for the national boards. The Test Construction Committee is part of the Joint Commission on National Dental Examinations, which provides written examinations to assist state boards in determining qualifications of dentists and dental hygienists seeking licensure.

The **Council on Communications** advises the Association on the external image and brand implications of Association plans, programs, services, and activities, in order to preserve and enhance the trusted image of the Association and the profession.

The **Council on Dental Benefit Programs** promotes quality dental care through the development, promotion, and monitoring of dental benefit programs for the public, and by the development and maintenance of dental coding systems and quality assessment and improvement tools and methodologies.

The **Council on Dental Education and Licensure** is responsible for policies and issues related to dental education, dental licensure, continuing dental education, specialty definitions and recognition, and dental career guidance, and acts as liaison to other education and licensing agencies.

The **Council on Dental Practice** develops resources and policies and disseminates information intended to help the dentist and dental team manage the day-to-day activities of a dental practice, grow professionally, and continuously improve the delivery of dental services to the public. The Council provides resources and assistance in practice management and marketing, dental team liaison activities, emergency preparedness and forensics, disaster planning and recovery, telemedicine, and dentist well-being and disability support.

The **Council on Ethics, Bylaws and Judicial Affairs** oversees the enforcement of the *ADA Principles of Ethics and Code of Professional Conduct* and reviews proposed changes to the ADA's constitution and bylaws. The Council seeks to enhance

Dr. Nick Bouzis (left) looks on as Dr. Randall Ogata (center), ADA Committee on the New Dentist chair, speaks with U.S. Congressman and dentist Dr. Charlie Norwood (second from left) after his keynote address drew two standing ovations at the ADA's 15th National Conference on the New Dentist in 2001. Dr. Norwood spoke about the recent passage of patients' bill of rights legislation in the U.S. House of Representatives and encouraged the young audience to be politically active members of the Association.

the ethical conscience of dentists by promoting the highest moral, ethical, and professional standards in the provision of dental care to the public.

The **Council on Government Affairs** recommends policies related to legislative and regulatory issues, including the formulation of proposed federal legislation. The Council disseminates information to assist constituent and component societies on state legislative and regulatory matters, and serves as the Association's liaison with agencies of the federal government.

The **Council on Members Insurance and Retirement Programs** oversees the administration of sponsored and endorsed insurance and retirement programs and aids member dentists in the management of personal and professional risk through educational activities and informational programs. The Council offers resources on dental liability and other practice-related insurance coverage.

The **Council on Membership** seeks to increase and enhance membership to preserve the ADA's place as the unified voice of dentistry. The Council monitors membership trends, encourages the development and promotion of member benefits, and collects and disseminates information on members' needs.

The **Council on Scientific Affairs** is the primary ADA source of timely, relevant, and emerging information on dental science and oral health. The Council conducts and evaluates studies on scientific matters; makes recommendations to the ADA's policymaking bodies on scientific issues; directs *ADA Professional Product Review*, the Seal of Acceptance, and evidence-based dentistry programs; and interacts with government agencies and other organizations regarding the scientific aspects of dentistry.

At the 1996 Annual Session, Dr. John Warford, the chair of the American Dental Political Action Committee (ADPAC), shows off a print advertisement of a snarling cartoon dog above the headline, "This should be muzzled. Not your practice." which was designed to draw attention to ADPAC's role in bringing dentistry's message to Washington, D.C. *(ADA file photo by Christie Photographic Studios)*

ADA COMMISSIONS

Equally important to the smooth operation of the ADA are the activities of the Association's two commissions. The commissions are independent agencies that report directly to the House of Delegates. Commission members typically serve four-year terms.

The **Commission on Dental Accreditation** is the only national accrediting body for dentistry and allied dental fields that is recognized by the United States Department of Education. The Commission formulates and adopts accreditation standards for programs in pre-doctoral dental education, advanced and specialty dental education, and allied dental education; conducts periodic site visits with regular review of written and quantitative data; and accredits more than thirteen hundred programs nationwide.

The **Joint Commission on National Dental Examinations** provides written examinations to assist state boards in determining qualifications of dentists and dental hygienists seeking licensure. The Commission maintains the regulations for conducting the dental and dental hygiene national board exams and serves as a resource for the dental profession in the development of written examinations.

ADA COMMITTEES

In addition to the councils and commissions there are two permanent ADA committees, representing specific objectives or segments of the Association.

The **American Dental Political Action Committee** (ADPAC) provides bipartisan financial assistance to congressional candidates who support issues of importance to dentists and their patients, oversees a grassroots network of politically active dentists, and works closely with state dental political action committees. Every year about one-third of ADA members join ADPAC by making a contribution.

The **Committee on the New Dentist**, composed of one member from each of the seventeen ADA trustee districts, is a standing committee of the Board of Trustees. The Committee represents the perspective of new dentists on ADA councils and commissions, makes recommendations for programs to assist new graduates' transition to the practice of dentistry, and promotes the participation of new dentists in organized dentistry.

As the ADA entered the new millennium, the ADA Foundation (ADAF) was a major strength. The charitable arm of the Association, the Foundation is America's leading charitable organization dedicated to enhancing clinical dentistry and the nation's oral health. Led by volunteers and supported through contributions from dentists, patients, and corporations, the Foundation provides grants for sustainable programs in dental research, education, access to care, and assistance for dentists and their families in need.

▲ Officials from the Infant Welfare Society of Chicago and the Children's Memorial Foundation accept oversized checks for proceeds from the ADA's annual staff raffle in 2001. Pictured are (left to right) Executive Director John S. Zapp (in festive costume); Dr. Gus Souri of the Infant Welfare Society; Dr. Cynthia Mears, MD, of the Children's Memorial Foundation; ADA Foundation Executive Director Barkley Payne; and Dudley the Dinosaur. The staff conducts a dental charity raffle each year in December and the proceeds are matched by the ADA Foundation.

Between 1995 and 2000, the Foundation provided more than $3 million in funding for a host of programs focused on dental research, education, scholarship, and access projects. The Foundation continues to support the activities of its two research agencies: the Research Institute at the ADA's Chicago headquarters and the Paffenbarger Research Center (PRC) on the campus of the National Institute of Standards and Technology in Gaithersburg, Maryland. Both the PRC and the Research Institute have given the ADA and its Foundation a strong presence in the communities of government, industry, and dental education. The collaborative efforts forged by the ADAF and its research arms have played a vital role in improving the quality of dental care provided to the American public, and in developing innovative clinical materials and new technologies.

In 2003, the ADA leadership decided to bring together all of the charitable organizations under one umbrella to increase the charitable impact of the ADA and its members. Accordingly, the former ADA Health Foundation was renamed the ADA Foundation. At the same time, the ADA Relief Fund, the ADA Endowment and Assistance Fund, and the ADA Emergency Fund were merged into the Foundation.

In 2009, the ADAF supported and funded a broad range of programs including scholarships and fellowships, research and recognition awards, access to care projects, community water fluoridation initiatives, local oral health promotion programs,

The ADA Seal of Acceptance

The ADA Seal of Acceptance program, administered by the ADA Council on Scientific Affairs (CSA), has long been recognized for the benefits it has brought to dentistry and the public.

In the 1860s, shortly after its founding, the ADA showed concern for the public's safety by issuing a statement on safe dentifrices. In 1930, the ADA created guidelines to evaluate dental products for safety and effectiveness, and the first Seal of Acceptance was awarded in 1931 to a brand of cod liver oil. The first toothpastes with fluoride received the Seal in the 1960s. In 1984, President Ronald Reagan gave the Association a certificate of commendation for the outstanding self-regulatory efforts of its Seal program.

Though participation in the program is strictly voluntary, dental manufacturers apply for the ADA Seal of Acceptance in order to assure both dentists and consumers of the safety and effectiveness of their products. Not all products submitted for the Seal meet the ADA's stringent requirements. ADA Seal designation represents a major commitment for manufacturers, requiring significant resources to test products before submitting them to the ADA.

Products must meet the ADA Seal program's acceptance criteria with respect to safety, effectiveness, composition, labeling, package inserts, advertising and other promotional material. When evaluating Seal product submissions, the CSA utilizes recognized and published technical standards, including official ADA guidelines, specifications developed by the ADA and approved by the American National Standards Institute (known as ANSI/ADA standards), and specifications of the International Organization for Standardization (known as ISO standards).

A company must provide objective data on each product from clinical and laboratory studies. All proprietary studies for the product as well as a list of all other studies conducted using the final product must be submitted. The ADA may choose to conduct additional evaluations, in the ADA Laboratories or external facilities. Participating manufacturers pay submission fees and annual maintenance fees, which cover a portion of the Seal program's cost.

Today, both over-the-counter therapeutic and cosmetic consumer products have been accepted, including toothpastes, toothbrushes, floss, denture adhesives and cleaners, and tooth-whitening products. In 2009, more than three hundred products from more than one hundred different companies carried the ADA Seal. When using the Seal, accepted products must display an approved Seal statement. This statement gives the indications for which the product was accepted, further providing guidance to the consumer.

For many years, the ADA Seal was granted to both consumer goods and professional products used or prescribed by dentists in their practices. However, the professional side of the program was phased out from 2005 to 2007. It was replaced by *ADA Professional Product Review* (the *Review*), a publication that was launched in July 2006. Issued quarterly with *JADA* in print and also available online, the *Review* was designed to meet dental practitioner product information needs, as identified by ADA member research. The *Review* has gained members' attention as a source of unbiased, scientifically sound comparisons of professional dental products. Each issue typically features three product categories and includes extensive laboratory performance data and clinician feedback. The *Review*'s technology updates, expert panel discussions, product test results, and buyers' checklists help dentists make responsible product choices.

▶ *ADA Professional Product Review* was launched in July 2006 to meet the need of today's dentists for objective, comprehensive, and clinically relevant product information. Product testing for both the *Review* and the Seal of Acceptance are conducted at the ADA Laboratories in Chicago.

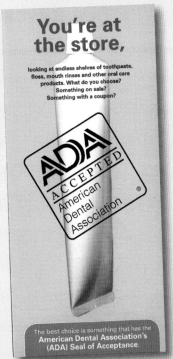

◀ A 2005 brochure for the ADA Seal of Acceptance program describing the Seal as a symbol of safety and effectiveness.

▲ ADA staff member Lerone Fong assists Dr.
Steve Able and dental hygienist Lisa Weber at
the debut ADA Pavilion during the 2004 Annual
Session in Orlando. The Pavilion was designed
to provide ADA members with a single area at
Annual Sessions for information on member
resources and services. *(ADA file photo by
Lagniappe Studio)*

the retraining of dentists with medical disabilities,
and charitable assistance grants for dentists and their
families in need.

Recognizing the importance of dental education
for the future of dentistry and the well-being of the
public's oral health, in 2004 the Foundation launched
Dental Education: Our Legacy—Our Future, a major
initiative "to raise awareness of the challenges facing
dental education in the U.S. and to promote a culture
of philanthropy within dentistry to address these
issues." The purpose of *Our Legacy—Our Future*
was not to create another fundraising program; it
will not collect a single dollar of its own. Instead, it
is designed to serve as a flexible support tool to raise
awareness for the needs in dental education and to
enhance visibility for the fundraising campaigns of its

collaborative organizations—dental schools, specialty
groups, and other dental organizations. As of May
2009, there were 138 collaborative organizations. It
is estimated that by the end of 2014, the collaborative
organizations will collectively raise $1.3 billion to
address the critical issues facing the future of dental
education.

THE ELECTRONIC ADA

The digitization of society that the ADA had
participated in during the 1990s picked up its pace
in the twenty-first century. The ADA accelerated
its adaptation of electronic media as an efficient
way to communicate with its more than 150,000
members. A number of e-mail publications were
launched during the 2000s that provided not only

The mobile dental unit, Tomorrow's Dental Office Today (TDOT), showcasing the latest dental office technology, premieres at the ADA's 2004 Annual Session. TDOT was a fully functioning technology-driven dental operatory and office involving all aspects of a modern dental practice. Its purpose was to promote the advancement of modern technology in dental practice. The traveling operatory spent several years on display at dental meetings and provided access to dental care to underserved areas nationwide. It was then donated for use in Mississippi in an area that was devastated in 2005 by Hurricane Katrina. *(ADA file photo by Lagniappe Studio)*

general news and information but also addressed specific issues of interest to members such as new product information and government affairs.

Members in attendance at the 2000 Annual Session in Chicago got an introduction to the inroads the World Wide Web was making in dentistry when Dr. Paul Landman, a general dentist, performed a cosmetic dental procedure live on the Internet. The ADA's first Webcast, "Get Connected to a New Smile," was performed from Landman's office in Chicago. The Webcast, which was viewed by several hundred attendees at the 2000 Annual Session, was archived on the ADA Web site.

Also at that 2000 Annual Session, ADA Business Enterprises, Inc. offered discounted Internet

Dr. Angela Scarfarotti was one of the more than one hundred dentists who evaluated handpieces during the Hands-on Evaluation program during the 2008 Annual Session. The program was initiated in 2005 to allow dentists to test and evaluate products for *ADA Professional Product Review*, a quarterly publication that provides clinically relevant information on dental equipment and materials for practicing dentists. *(ADA file photo by Lagniappe Studio)*

▲ The inaugural class of the ADA Institute for Diversity in Leadership meets in September 2003 at ADA Headquarters. The class of eight dentists representing private practice, dental education, and the federal dental service are (seated left to right) Drs. Flauryse Baguidy, Jose-Luiz Ruiz, Gayle Kawahara; (standing left to right) Drs. Donald Dexter, Jr., Marija LaSalle, Ronald Evans, Jeannette Peña Hall, and John Jow.

service to members. The dial-up service was substantially cheaper than several of the more popular commercial services. In 2001, the ADA Catalog went online, allowing members to browse the inventory and place online orders for practice management books, continuing education videotapes and CD-ROMs, reference materials, and patient education brochures.

In January 2001, *The Journal of the American Dental Association* made a major announcement: each new *JADA* issue would be available for accessing and downloading through ADA.org, with full text and graphics. Coverage expanded until, by

2009, members were able to access all issues on the Web back to 1995.

By the early 2000s, the Internet had become such a part of everyday life that most members had a computer in their office or home with access to the World Wide Web. At Tech Day at the 2002 Annual Session, members flocked to demonstrations of Personal Data Assistants (PDAs). One consultant, Dr. Barry Freydberg, told attendees, "You can't practice without water and electricity today. You won't be able to practice without the Internet. The Internet will be the Evernet."

▶ Dr. Kathleen T. O'Loughlin became the first woman to serve as executive director of the ADA when she was appointed to the position in June 2009.

PROMOTING INCLUSION

In the twenty-first century, the ADA continued to actively promote organizational inclusion. These efforts traced back to a 1958 initiative by the ADA to end membership discrimination by any of its constituent and component dental societies. With ADA's outright ban on discrimination in 1965, African American dentists were able to join the ADA regardless of where they lived.

In the latter part of the twentieth century the ADA undertook further initiatives aimed at creating a more diverse and inclusive organization. These efforts included regularly consulting with leaders of the National Dental Association (a national organization representing African American dentists) and fostering liaison activities with two newer organizations, the Hispanic Dental Association and the Society for American Indian Dentists, both established in 1990. The ADA also actively sought to advance dental school enrollments among ethnic and racially diverse groups.

In the twenty-first century, the ADA again stepped up its efforts to foster diversity. In 2000, the Board of Trustees created a Standing Committee on Diversity to monitor diversity issues throughout the ADA on a continuing basis. The committee also makes recommendations to the Board on diversity initiatives and offers perspective and advice to the Board regarding its diversity deliberations.

Between 2003 and 2008, the ADA Institute for Diversity in Leadership enrolled nearly seventy dentists, representing a cross section of ethnicity, race, and gender. The year-long program is designed to develop the leadership skills of ADA members from groups who are traditionally underrepresented in leadership roles in various sectors of society, including organized dentistry.

Diversity and inclusion have become characteristic of ADA membership in the twenty-first century. In 2009, the ADA elected Dr. Raymond F. Gist, its first African American president, who will serve his term in 2010–2011. With more than 157,000 members, the ADA has become a force for progress and change in American health care.

GOING FORWARD

The ADA reached another milestone in 2009 when the ADA Board of Trustees announced the appointment of Dr. Kathleen T. O'Loughlin as the first woman to serve as executive director. Prior to her appointment, O'Loughlin had been consulting on dental curriculum development and dental hygiene accreditation and served on the boards of several non-profit dental organizations. A resident of Massachusetts and a graduate of Tufts University School of Dental Medicine, she brings to the Association a varied experience of twenty years in private dental practice and public health dentistry, ten years in dental education and research, and a decade of key leadership roles in management and business operations. With the appointment of Dr. O'Loughlin, the Association looks forward to new initiatives and new challenges in the twenty-first century.

Chapter Nine

The ADA Today...and Tomorrow

The twenty-six dentists who gathered in Niagara Falls in 1859 with a mission to establish dentistry as a profession based on educational and scientific standards would be amazed by the strides their organization has made in the past century-and-a-half.

In its 150th year, the ADA is America's leading advocate for oral health, with more than 157,000 members. Seventy percent of dentists are ADA members, a level of participation unmatched among health care associations, which gives the ADA a powerful voice in legislative and regulatory arenas.

The ADA is a member-driven organization committed to the public's oral health, ethics, science, and professional advancement, leading a unified profession through initiatives in advocacy, education, research, and the development of standards.

To fulfill its modern mission, the ADA of today works on many fronts to care for the public and support the profession.

CARING FOR THE PUBLIC

The many opportunities and challenges faced by the ADA and its members in the twenty-first century will undoubtedly revolve around the increasing complexity of oral health care. In recent years, the

▶ The ADA building plays host to many Association meetings and conferences throughout the year. Members visiting Chicago are always welcome to visit for a guided tour of the building, including the Division of Science laboratories, the ADA Library, and the administrative offices.

The Family Sculpture

The sculpture in front of the ADA Headquarters building has become a Chicago neighborhood landmark and an icon for the Association. The piece is composed of three figures—man, woman, and child—in modified abstract form. The sculpture, which epitomizes the family of man and reflects dentistry's concern for humankind, has appeared on ADA brochures in the past. Today passersby stop to have their pictures taken with the piece, and art classes pause to appreciate what ADA staff have affectionately named *The Family*.

In 1964, Joseph O'Connell (1927–1995), a Minnesota artist known for his public and religious sculpture, was commissioned to create a work for the front of the newly constructed ADA Headquarters building. He was given a free hand to develop an appropriately themed piece. Funding for the sculpture came from the ADA Fine Arts Fund, which was set up specifically for supplying artwork for the new building and composed of donations from ADA members, dental organizations, and commercial sponsors.

In his studio, the artist made plaster models of the figures, which were cut into pieces and shipped to a foundry in Detroit. There the sections were cast in bronze and welded together. Each figure in the group is more than twice life-size, with the tallest almost fifteen feet high. The entire sculpture weighs approximately sixteen thousand pounds. The finished work was shipped to the ADA on a flatbed truck and installed in May 1969 in a courtyard on the west end of the building façade.

In November 2006, the sculpture was removed and stored in a warehouse during a major renovation of the lobby. The renovation enclosed parts of the building's east and west courtyards behind a glass wall. During the sculpture's eighteen-month absence, local residents phoned the ADA and asked about the work, concerned that *The Family* might have left home, never to return. They were relieved to learn that the sculpture was merely on an extended vacation.

When the renovation was completed in April 2008, the sculpture was reinstalled near its original location, just slightly closer to the street, where it continues to be a vital part of the neighborhood and a symbol of the dental profession's long tradition of service.

▲ Construction of *The Family* sculpture nears completion in the foundry in 1969.

▲ *The Family* sculpture as it originally appeared in the west court of the new ADA Headquarters building in Chicago in 1969. The figures of man, woman, and child are more than twice life-size and the tallest figure stands fifteen feet high. The sculpture was commissioned especially for the ADA building and symbolizes dentistry's concern for humankind.

▲ *The Family* is carted away for eighteen months of storage while the lobby of the ADA building undergoes a major renovation in 2006–2008. The artwork was missed by residents in the Streeterville neighborhood of Chicago, who contacted the ADA to inquire about the missing figures. Fortunately, all "Family" members returned home safe and sound.

▲ Discussing issues at the first American Indian/ Alaska Native Oral Health Access Summit in November 2007 are (left to right) Jean Othole of the Indian Health Service, and Drs. Alyssa York, David Keim, Ronald L. Tankersley (ADA president 2009–2010), Roger Newman, Howard Pollack, and Marty Leiberman. The summit, hosted by the ADA in Santa Ana, New Mexico, brought together leaders in organized dentistry and public health dentistry to address oral health disparities for native populations. *(ADA file photo by Gary Podschun)*

steepest recessions since World War II, access to care for underserved and economically disadvantaged families has become even more important.

The ADA took the lead in providing information for member dentists and their staffs when it published *State and Community Models for Improving Access to Dental Care for the Underserved*, a landmark 2004 white paper. The paper was of interest to a variety of stakeholders, including the dental community, health care professionals, policymakers, and public health and human service advocates, who understood how lack of access to good oral health care affects the overall health, self-esteem, ability to learn, and employability of underserved Americans. The ADA followed up the 2004 white paper with a comprehensive report about access to oral health care for American Indians and Alaska Natives.

ADA has addressed such issues as access to care for the underserved, including children and the elderly; the changing dental workforce; fluoridation; and oral health research. Each of these issues will affect how dentistry is practiced in the years to come. By bringing together its members, the public, government agencies, and private oral health industry leaders, the ADA helps ensure that all Americans are informed about their oral health and have the opportunity to receive high-quality dental care.

FOCUS ON ACCESS

Increasing access to dental care for those who need it most has been a strategic initiative of the Association for many years. As the nation experiences one of the

GIVE KIDS A SMILE®

Give Kids A Smile® (GKAS) day is an annual volunteer event that provides free preventive, restorative, and educational services to children from low-income families. Established nationally by the ADA in 2003, GKAS was organized on the St. Louis Dental Society model, demonstrating the importance of grass-roots programs within communities.

By 2005, Give Kids A Smile was firmly established all over the United States. GKAS has become a cornerstone of one of the ADA's most challenging issues: providing access to care for all Americans. On February 6, 2009, more than 46,000 volunteers, including 12,558 dentists, cared for 463,000 kids in need.

GKAS day takes place on the first Friday in February nationwide, but recent expansion efforts have given GKAS a year-round presence as well. The GKAS National Advisory Board, composed of ADA, business, and public health representatives, was created in 2007. The Board addresses access to care issues throughout the year with evolving initiatives including fundraising, the awarding of grants, and building a network of GKAS program champions.

ORALLONGEVITY™

As the average American life span has increased, raising awareness of the oral health needs of older Americans has become a critical goal of U.S. dentistry. Demonstrating that oral health is not just for the young, the ADA Foundation (ADAF) established grants in 2004 for pilot programs addressing access-to-care issues for older adults. The ADAF received an unprecedented 178 grant applications and provided grants for six pilot

programs in 2005. The next year, the ADAF House of Delegates passed a resolution concerning strategies to address oral health issues of vulnerable elders. The ADA, the ADAF, and GlaxoSmithKline launched the OralLongevity™ program in the fall of 2007. The program encourages seniors to visit their dentist's office where they can receive information and guidance from trusted professionals.

In 2008, the OralLongevity intiative passed a number of milestones, including an advertising campaign in *AARP The Magazine* (AARP, formerly known as the American Association of Retired Persons) that reached eight million older adults, a one-day program at the National Museum of Dentistry in cooperation with Elderhostel programs, and the distribution of educational DVDs and brochures to dental professionals and consumers.

> Give Kids a Smile started as an annual one-day event in February 2003 to provide free dental care to underserved children. It has expanded into a broader initiative to increase access to care year-round.

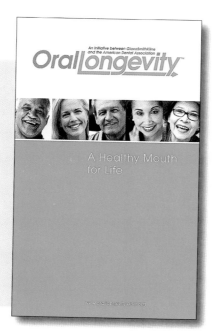

► Brochure describing the ADA collaborative OralLongevity™ intiative, launched in 2007 to raise awareness of the oral health needs of older Americans.

CDHCs will work in medically underserved communities as an integrated member of the dental team with the approval, consultation, and review of a dentist. The CDHC will be in a position to link patients who could not otherwise access care with health providers by coordinating the logistics of appointments and helping eligible patients apply for charitable and public dental programs. CDHCs will be trained to promote oral health, provide preventive services, and assist patients in navigating the oral health care delivery system so that they may receive comprehensive services from a dentist.

CHANGING DENTAL WORKFORCE

Unfortunately, some Americans still do not have access to a dentist in 2009, most commonly those in rural and disadvantaged urban areas. Most states have seen the introduction of legislation to modify workforce roles and scopes. Those efforts range from establishing Expanded Function Dental Assistants to creating a new "mid-level" position. The primary motivation behind most of these efforts is the access-to-care issue.

The ADA believes that all Americans should have access to oral health care and that the dental team should be supervised by a dentist to ensure the highest level of care. In 2008 the ADA House of Delegates made a $5 million commitment to improving oral health care access by strongly supporting development of the Community Dental Health Coordinator (CDHC) workforce model.

ADVOCATING FLUORIDATION

The Centers for Disease Control and Prevention named fluoridation as one of ten great public health achievements of the twentieth century in 1999. Grand Rapids, Michigan, was the first community in the world to fluoridate its water supply (1945). Sixty years later, almost a third of Americans using community water systems still have no fluoridation. In 2008, water fluoridation was on the ballot in at least eighty-nine communities in several states.

The ADA continues to advocate the fluoridation of community water supplies and the use of fluoride-containing products as safe and effective measures for preventing tooth decay, particularly among children. This has been the Association's position since an official policy on fluoride was first adopted in 1950. Providing sound scientific information about fluoridation is a key element of the ADA's oral health literacy initiatives.

► In recognition of the sixty-year anniversary of public water fluoridation, a public health milestone, the ADA and the Centers for Disease Control and Prevention hosted a National Fluoridation Symposium at ADA Headquarters in Chicago in July 2005.

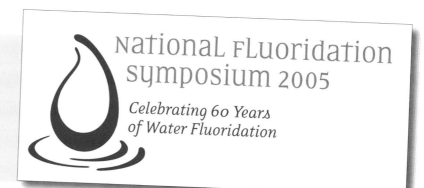

National Fluoridation Symposium 2005

Celebrating 60 Years of Water Fluoridation

The ADA Paffenbarger Research Center is located in Gaithersburg, Maryland, on the campus of the National Institute of Standards and Technology, an agency of the U.S. Department of Commerce. One of the world's premier dental research centers, the PRC has played a major role in the development of modern dental materials and equipment. The PRC celebrated its eightieth anniversary in 2008.

ORAL HEALTH SCIENCE AND RESEARCH

ADA-funded scientific research has revolutionized the practice of dentistry and improved the oral health of Americans. Groundbreaking dental innovations such as panoramic X-rays and composite materials were developed at the ADA Paffenbarger Research Center (PRC) in the twentieth century. Today, ADA scientists are working on bone grafting materials for jaw augmentation that will enable a one-step process for dental implants.

Announcement promoting the first of several ADA-sponsored EBD Champion Conferences, providing training in evidence-based dentistry. The goal of these workshops is to develop a network of clinical and academic dentists to serve as a resource to their local dental communities in the evidence-based approach to preventive care and treatment. The ADA Center for Evidence-Based Dentistry, established in 2008, launched an EBD Web site in 2009, offering systematic reviews and other EBD resources.

Another priority in recent years has been the ADA's evidence-based dentistry (EBD) initiative. EBD is an approach to oral health care that integrates clinically relevant scientific evidence with the dentist's clinical expertise and the patient's treatment needs and preferences. With hundreds of clinical trials published yearly in the dental and medical literature, the amount of EBD information available is overwhelming for a solo practitioner.

An annual EBD Champions Conference and a one-week intensive continuing education course, offered in collaboration by the ADA and The Forsyth Institute, were created to teach dentists how to obtain, appraise, and implement the array of new treatment options available.

Launched in March 2009, the ADA's EBD Web site (ebd.ada.org), which was supported by a grant from the National Library of Medicine and the National Institute for Dental and Craniofacial Research, provides systematic reviews and summaries of scientific evidence to assist dentists in clinical decision making.

In addition, one of the summaries posted on the EBD Web site is published each month in *The Journal of the American Dental Association*. This *JADA*

The Evidence-Based Dentistry
CHAMPION CONFERENCE*

May 2 and 3, 2008 Chicago, IL
Co-Sponsored by the American Dental Association and the *Journal of Evidence-Based Dental Practice*

Apply and become a Champion for Evidence-Based Dentistry.

By attending this Conference, the Evidence-Based Dentistry Champions will serve as a resource to their local dental communities by promoting the application of an evidence-based approach to patient treatment and prevention of disease. Applications to become an EBD Champion or to attend as an observer can be found at **www.ada.org/goto/ebdconf.**

*Supported by an Educational Grant from Procter and Gamble

ADA.
American Dental Association
www.ada.org

Evidence-Based
Dental Practice

▶ ADA Test Equipment Designer Nick Njegovan measures the comparative performance of major brands of polishing systems in the laboratories at ADA Headquarters in Chicago. Studies conducted here by the ADA Department of Research and Laboratories of the Division of Science include tests on various dental materials and equipment for the quarterly *ADA Professional Product Review* (published by the Council on Scientific Affairs), evaluations of consumer products for the ADA Seal of Acceptance, and other critical research issues. Much of the testing equipment is designed by ADA staff engineers and scientists and fabricated in the research department's machine shop.

feature, titled "Critical Summaries," offers a critique of one systematic review and an assessment of its underlying evidence.

ORAL SYSTEMIC HEALTH

Advances in scientific technologies and improved clinical research methods have heightened awareness of the relationships of oral health to general health. This is leading to a change in the way dentists, other health care providers, and their patients are looking at oral health issues and their relationship to systemic health.

Like other areas of scientific inquiry, the oral health profession is continuing to promote improved methods of risk assessment, prevention, disease management, chemotherapeutics, and disease interventions leading to better-quality health outcomes. Clinical researchers are helping to unravel the mysteries of oral cancer causation, detection, and treatment, along with the complex relationships of oral conditions such as chronic periodontitis to inflammatory diseases, osteonecrosis, diabetes, pneumonia, cardiovascular diseases, and pregnancy. Preliminary studies have suggested that pregnant women who have periodontal disease may be at an elevated risk of delivering pre-term and/or low birth weight babies, although further studies need to be completed to determine if or how definitive care may improve pregnancy outcomes.

▲ In 2009, Dr. Rafael L. Bowen marked his fifty-third year on the staff of the ADA Paffenbarger Research Center, where he is emeritus director and a full-time research scientist. The inventor of the original composite resin material, he also led the evolution of contemporary adhesive bonding agents, formulated the glass-ceramic inserts for composites, and is responsible for over forty patents. He was named the ADA's first distinguished scientist in 1994 and received the 1999 Distinguished Service Award, the ADA's highest honor. *(ADA file photo by Anna Ng Delort)*

ADA President-elect Robert M. Brandjord (left) and ADA President W. Richard Haught participate in a Board of Trustees strategic discussion in 2005, following presentations by a panel of dental and medical experts on the emerging link between oral health and overall health. The forum covered salivary diagnosis as well as the association between periodontitis and certain systemic diseases. The meeting resulted in the development of an ADA position statement on oral-systemic relationships.

The ADA promotes and supports well-designed clinical studies to further advance knowledge and understanding of how preventing and treating oral conditions may improve the overall health and wellness of patients.

SUPPORTING THE PROFESSION

More than 75 percent of ADA members own or are employed by a private dental practice. In addition to educating the public and improving access to oral health care, the ADA works to ensure that dentists have a positive environment in which to practice.

The ADA has played a significant role in shaping twenty-first-century policies affecting private dental practices, including health care reform, occupational regulations, tax laws, small-business issues, and tax deductions on student loan interest. ADA activities in Washington, D.C., assure that government decisions affecting dental care are made with input and counsel from organized dentistry.

DENTAL EDUCATION AND THE PROFESSION'S FUTURE

Active ADA membership, the future of dental education, and the health of our communities are inextricably linked. The aging of the American population is reflected in the membership of the American Dental Association. Between 2010 and 2020, as much as 30 percent of the membership of the ADA will retire from active clinical practice.

From left, Drs. Zeb F. Poindexter III, Orrin D. Mitchell, Wisdom F. Coleman, Jr., and Joseph S. Gay enjoy a break during the 2004 Washington Leadership Conference. The annual ADA-sponsored conference brings hundreds of dentist volunteers in political advocacy to the nation's capital to discuss important policy issues and to meet with their elected officials. Many of the participating dentists are active with their local ADA grassroots action teams. *(ADA file photo by Anna Ng Delort)*

U.S. Representative George Miller (D-California) (left) listens to the concerns of his constituents (from left) Drs. William van Dyck, Brian Scott, and Donald Schinnerer at the 2005 Washington Leadership Conference (WLC). During this annual conference many dental leaders schedule meetings with their members of Congress. In addition, congressional leaders from both parties are usually among the scheduled WLC speakers. In 2009, there were two dentists serving in Congress, Representative Mike Simpson (R-Idaho), one of the 2009 WLC speakers, and Representative John Linder (R-Georgia). *(ADA file photo by Anna Ng Delort)*

The needs in dental education are pressing and include faculty shortages, outdated facilities, escalating costs, declining public support, and lack of diversity. To avert a crisis in the dental profession and the oral health of the public, the ADA is actively addressing these challenges. With the collective support of more than one hundred other organizations, the ADA Foundation spearheaded *Dental Education: Our Legacy— Our Future,* a national initiative designed to raise awareness about these critical challenges and further promote philanthropy to address the issues.

In the late twentieth century the number of dental schools declined, but that trend has reversed. From 1986 to 2001, seven dental schools, all private institutions, closed their doors. From 1997 through 2009, five new schools, four of them private, opened. Despite the challenges facing dental education, a number of groups, public and private, are discussing potential new dental schools, prompted by concern about access to care and changing demographics. The need for support of dental education has never been greater.

THE CHANGING FACE OF DENTISTRY

The 2000 Census indicated that 12.3 percent of the U.S. population is African American and 12.5 percent is Hispanic. Yet, African Americans make up only 6 percent of dental school enrollment and Hispanics represent only 6 percent as well. Only 2 percent of ADA members are African American and 2 percent

▶ The goal of the ADA Foundation's *Dental Education: Our Legacy—Our Future (OLOF)* initiative is to raise awareness of the challenges facing dental education in the U.S. and to promote a culture of philanthropy within dentistry. *OLOF* seeks to help its more than 135 partners—dental schools and universities, dental foundations and associations—to build long-term financial support for dental education.

DENTAL EDUCATION
OUR LEGACY-OUR FUTURE

Dental Emblem and Color

DENTAL EMBLEM

The traditional symbol or emblem for the dental profession is widely used and recognized by dentists and dental organizations.

As its central figure, the design uses a serpent entwined about an ancient cautery (a wound-cauterizing instrument), which is known as the rod of Asclepius, the Greek god of healing. A traditional symbol of medicine, the rod of Asclepius is also used by the American Medical Association (AMA) and other health related entities. The dental emblem is sometimes referred to as a caduceus, a symbol that is often confused with the rod of Asclepius and used to imply medical affiliations. However, a true caduceus is a staff entwined by two serpents, not one, and is sometimes surmounted by wings.

In the dental emblem, the rod of Asclepius is encompassed by the Greek letter "delta," for dentistry, and the Greek letter "omicron," for odont, the Greek word for tooth. In the background of the design are thirty-two leaves and twenty berries, representing the permanent and primary teeth.

The suggested colors for the insignia are background in lilac (the official academic color of dentistry); omicron in gold; delta in black; cautery in gold outlined in black; and leaves, berries, and serpent in white outlined in black on the lilac background.

The dental emblem has been in use since 1940. It was created and adopted at the urging of Josephine Hunt, director of the ADA Library, 1927–1948.

In 1938, Hunt suggested to Dr. Lon Morrey, head of the ADA Bureau of Public Relations, that the dental profession adopt an official insignia similar to the medical profession's traditional symbol. The rod of Asclepius had been adopted by the AMA in 1912. Morrey made a quick sketch of the design incorporating the rod, with input from Hunt and others on staff, and gave it to Melville Stenfels, a freelance artist employed by the ADA, to create the final design and camera-ready artwork.

The Bureau of Public Relations first presented the design to the Board of Trustees for approval in 1938. In 1940, after some study of the matter, the Board presented the design to the House of Delegates, which adopted it as the official emblem of dentistry.

The House of Delegates reaffirmed the use of the emblem in 1965, once again at the prompting of the director of the ADA Library, Dr. Donald Washburn. The ADA Library was routinely receiving requests for images of the emblem, and Washburn wanted assurance that the organization had an official policy on it. In 1964 he submitted a proposal for an emblem of a different design to the House of Delegates. After studying the matter for a year, the House re-adopted the use of the original 1940 design as the official emblem of dentistry since its use had become widespread. Use of the emblem is now a standing policy of the ADA.

COLOR OF DENTISTRY

In 1897, the National Association of Dental Faculties chose the color lilac for trimming dental schools' graduation gowns and caps. Since then, the color has become associated generally with the dental profession and is used traditionally to embellish dental banners, emblems, insignia, signs, symbols, and publications.

The official emblem of dentistry dates back to 1940 and was formally adopted by the ADA in 1965. It incorporates the color lilac, traditionally used to denote dentistry since the nineteenth century.

California dentist Dr. Newton Gordon tells his audience how he became a leader in his profession and community during the program "Community: Celebrating Diverse Leadership in Dentistry" at the 2003 Annual Session in San Francisco. He has served not only as a dental school professor and a hospital chief of dentistry, but also as president of his local dental society, member of his state dental board, and executive director of an oral surgery society. *(ADA file photo by Lagniappe Studio)*

▲ The ADA Member Service Center handles about 15,000 inbound calls per month. MSC staff answer many callers' inquiries, refer more specialized questions to the appropriate department, and take orders for books and products in the ADA Catalog.

are Hispanic. Today 18 percent of ADA members are women, and in 2009 the ADA appointed its first female executive director.

An inclusive environment that values and embraces membership diversity is essential to the profession and the Association. To that end, the ADA is working with dental schools to provide scholarships and mentors for dental students of diverse racial and ethnic backgrounds. The ADA also sponsors the Institute for Diversity in Leadership, an all-expenses-paid leadership program for members of racial, ethnic, and/or gender groups that have been traditionally underrepresented in dentistry. Northwestern University faculty facilitate the Institute curriculum, continuing the longstanding tradition of collaboration

▷ Dr. Grace Yi-Ying Su, a member of the 2006 class of the ADA Institute for Diversity in Leadership, appears on the brochure for the 2009 program. The Institute is a personal training program designed to enhance the leadership skills of a dozen selected applicants belonging to racial, ethnic, and/or gender backgrounds traditionally underrepresented in leadership roles. Through three seminars held over the course of a year, the program helps participating dentists enhance skills needed to successfully make a difference in their communities, organizations, or the dental profession.

▶ The March 2005 issue of *JADA* salutes the efforts of military dentists by presenting stories of dentists serving in Iraq and Afghanistan. A longtime supporter of Federal Dental Service dentists, the Association has advocated for FDS pay increases, backed appropriate military rank recognition for military dentists, and obtained significant additional funding for military dental research.

between the Association and the University, whose Chicago campus sits a block away from the ADA Headquarters building. This relationship can be traced back to more than one hundred years ago when Dr. G. V. Black served as ADA president, 1900–1901, during his tenure as second dean of Northwestern University Dental School.

Traditionally, the majority of ADA member dentists have been in private practice, but the

settings in which dentists serve their country and their communities are continually changing. For example, ADA membership also includes those employed in academia, research, corporations, and in the U.S. legislature. Additionally, there are approximately three thousand member dentists in the Federal Dental Services (FDS) who serve the country in the army, navy, air force, Department of Veterans Affairs, and the U.S. Public Health Service. Of note are the many ADA FDS members who currently provide care to the armed forces in Iraq and Afghanistan. The ADA has and will continue to meet the unique needs of these dentists and to support their diverse professional interests.

MEMBERSHIP VALUE

From 362 members in 1899 to 157,000 members in 2009, the ADA's growth over the last century has been driven by the Association's focus on value for its members.

ADA membership helps dentists stay well informed through *ADA News, The Journal of the American Dental Association* (*JADA*), ADA.org, and various electronic newsletters. In 2008, 3.7 million scientific articles were downloaded from the online version of *JADA,* dentistry's best-read journal.

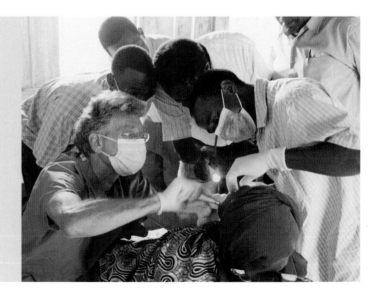

▶ Dr. Jack Levine (left) performs dental surgery on a refugee patient during an ADA/Health Volunteers Overseas visit to a refugee camp in Tanzania in 2008. In a two-week period, a four-person ADA/HVO volunteer team was able to train a dozen refugee dental workers in addition to treating many patients. Health Volunteers Overseas is a private nonprofit organization committed to improving health care in developing countries through training and education. The Oral Health Initiative of HVO is sponsored by the ADA through its Division of Global Affairs, and all volunteers must be ADA members. *(Photo courtesy of Dr. Christine Lathuras)*

◁ Members of the 2008 ADA/Kellogg Executive Management Program for Dentists celebrate completion of the program along with faculty and ADA staff. This joint program of the ADA and the Kellogg School of Management of Northwestern University is based on core courses taken by Kellogg MBA students. Not a practice management course, the curriculum features advanced business subjects such as business strategy, organizational leadership, and finance. Shown are (front row from left) ADA Senior Vice President for Membership Wendy-Jo Toyama, with class members Dr. Vishruti Patel, Dr. Wenli Loo, Dr. Irene Gula, Dr. Shab Krish, Dr. Karin Irani, Ms. Gelsys Resto, Dr. Lynn Wan, Dr. Wandy Tsai, Dr. William Leon, ADA staff member Connie Paslaski, and Northwestern Professor Thomas Prince; (back row from left) Northwestern Associate Dean Vennie Lyons, with class members Dr. Rawley Fuller IV, Dr. Donald Deems III, Dr. Samuel Smiley, Dr. Primitivo Roig Jornet, Dr. Allan Jacobs, Dr. Alejandro Aguirre, and ADA staff member Joe Martin.

With a comprehensive Web site to provide timely information, one of the world's largest libraries devoted to dentistry, and a survey center dedicated to researching dental economic and demographic trends, ADA members have at their fingertips a wealth of information they cannot get anywhere else in the world. The ADA also supports the lifelong learning needs of its members by certifying continuing education providers and offering CE opportunities via online courses and society seminar courses.

Most ADA members are solo practitioners who have the added challenge of managing a business in addition to treating patients. But they need to focus on patient care while keeping their practices financially healthy.

▷ The sesquicentennial of the ADA was a focal point of the 2009 Annual Session in Hawaii. Attendees could view an exhibit on ADA history and pick up a 150th anniversary commemorative lapel pin.

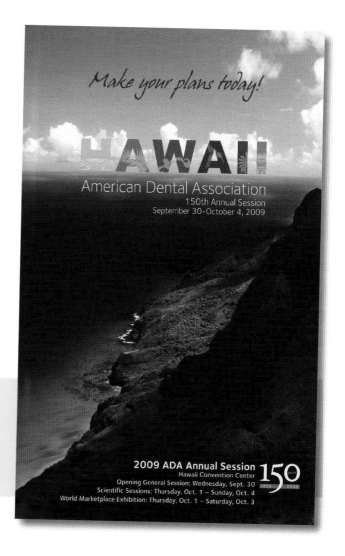

Make your plans today!

HAWAII
American Dental Association
150th Annual Session
September 30–October 4, 2009

2009 ADA Annual Session 150
Hawaii Convention Center
Opening General Session: Wednesday, Sept. 30
Scientific Sessions: Thursday, Oct. 1 – Sunday, Oct. 4
World Marketplace Exhibition: Thursday, Oct. 1 – Saturday, Oct. 3

ADA Annual Session

When ADA members attend an ADA Annual Session, they are taking part in the largest dental meeting and one of the best-attended trade shows in North America. They may not know the Annual Session started as a small meeting of dentists eager to exchange knowledge and set high ethical standards for the profession. Early ADA meetings consisted mainly of committee reports and scientific discussions.

For the first fifty years, the attendance at ADA's annual meeting was rarely more than a few hundred because the total membership was small. In 1911, of the more than thirty-five thousand U.S. dentists, fewer than a thousand were ADA members. Membership grew dramatically after the reorganization of 1912 and the establishment of the tripartite in 1922. Attendance at Annual Session grew accordingly, reaching a new record of thirty-five thousand in 1972.

Though the attendance varies greatly based on the year and the location, total attendance (dentists, dental staff, exhibitors, and guests) averaged close to thirty-eight thousand for the twenty-year period 1989–2008. The popular destinations of Orlando, Las Vegas, and San Francisco drew between forty and fifty-six thousand attendees during that period.

The ADA has met every year since its founding in 1859 except for two years when major wars caused disruptions in supplies and transportation. The ADA did not meet in 1861 due to the American Civil War nor did it meet in 1945 because of World War II. In 1943, 1944, and 1946, the House of Delegates met, but there were no accompanying scientific or trade events.

For the ADA's first 150 years, Niagara Falls, New York, the site of the first meeting and a popular nineteenth-century vacation spot, holds the record for the most Annual Sessions at thirteen. The meeting was last held there in 1902. Many nineteenth-century sessions were held in smaller resorts or cities.

▲ Attendees at the 1890 Annual Session gather on the steps of the Elms Hotel in Excelsior Springs, Missouri. The town was a popular spa resort of the day, known for the alleged medicinal properties of its natural spring waters. Membership and meeting attendance was small through the first fifty years of the ADA's existence and many of the early Annual Sessions were held in resort towns, including Niagara Falls, New York; Saratoga Springs, New York; Old Point Comfort, Virginia; Asbury Park, New Jersey; Put-in-Bay, Ohio; and White Sulphur Springs, West Virginia.

◄ Dr. Todd Ehrlich demonstrates a CAD/CAM system at the ADA's Live Operatory Center at the 2008 Annual Session in San Antonio. New in 2008, the LOC features free CE programs on high-tech dental products and procedures. Besides CAD/CAM, the program in San Antonio presented demonstrations of 3-D imaging and lasers. *(ADA file photo by Lagniappe Studio)*

▲ Attendees eager to provide testimony at an open hearing of the Reference Committee on Dental Education and Related Matters line up for their turn at the microphone during the 2006 Annual Session in Las Vegas. Reference committee hearings allow ADA members and invited representatives from the communities of interest to present their views on relevant issues. The reference committees make recommendations to the HOD on pending resolutions and may amend or propose new resolutions. *(ADA file photo by Lagniappe Studio)*

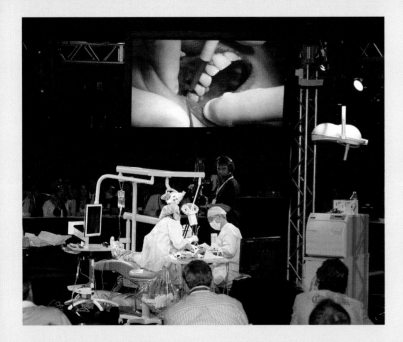

Participants get a close-up view as Dr. Edward Allen demonstrates root coverage and grafting in an Education in the Round (EIR) course at the 2008 Annual Session in San Antonio. Presenting live-patient procedures in a fully functional dental operatory, EIR was introduced at the 2007 Annual Session as an innovative CE option. Each EIR course features high-definition images captured on intraoral cameras and displayed on 60-inch flat-screen monitors, as well as an interactive format between speaker and attendees. *(ADA file photo by Lagniappe Studio)*

Since the mid-twentieth century, Annual Sessions have been limited to larger cities or resorts with many hotels and larger convention facilities. The second most frequent site for Annual Session is San Francisco, which has hosted the meeting eleven times, and the third is Chicago with nine sessions. In ADA's sesquicentennial year of 2009, Honolulu, Hawaii, hosted the Annual Session and the culmination of the ADA's 150th anniversary celebration.

The core of the conference lasts four days and includes scientific sessions and technical exhibits, but many meetings of committees and related dental organizations are held before and after Session. The House of Delegates, which sets official ADA policy, meets at the beginning and the end of the conference. At the last House session, the ADA's new officers and trustees are installed for the coming year.

With access to almost two hundred continuing education courses, Annual Session attendees can avail themselves of valuable educational opportunities. The meeting brings together leaders in dental practice, research, the academic community, and industry to share practical advice and information that members can use in their practices and careers. Recent educational innovations include a Live Operatory Center featuring CAD/CAM technology and live-patient demonstrations; Education in the Round with live-patient procedures in a fully functional dental operatory; and ADA365, a pre-course self-study package and online community.

A major draw at Annual Session is the World Marketplace Exhibition where attendees can view hundreds of exhibits on the latest dental products, technology, and services. Also popular is the ADA Foundation's free Health Screening Program, which not only gives individuals a snapshot of their health, but has also guided the profession on topics and policies related to the risks that dental professionals may face. In addition, the ADA Annual Session allows members the opportunity to network with peers, catch up with old friends, and take part in activities sponsored by the more than two hundred alumni and professional associations in attendance.

Since 2001 the ADA Distinguished Speakers Series at Annual Session has featured some of America's most famous personalities. These include such varied individuals as former President George H. W. Bush, ABC-TV newscaster Barbara Walters, seven–time Tour de France winner Lance Armstrong, former astronaut Jim Lovell, and former Secretary of State Colin Powell.

Today's Annual Session offers something for everyone: educational events, commercial exhibits, policymaking, noted speakers, networking, health screenings, social events, children's programs, local tours, and meetings of related dental organizations. And it all began with those twenty-six dentists meeting in Niagara Falls to create a dental society with high professional standards.

Staff members at the ADA Pavilion respond to questions about member benefits and services at the 2007 Annual Session in San Francisco, one of the ADA's most popular conference cities. The 2007 session drew over 47,000 attendees. Close to 14,000 of those were dentists, almost 30 percent of the total. Other participants included students, dental assistants, dental hygienists, lab technicians, dental dealers, exhibitors, and guests. The technical exhibits of the average Annual Session feature six hundred exhibiting companies. *(ADA file photo by Lagniappe Studio)*

To save members' time and money, the ADA offers various business resources through its for-profit subsidiary, ADA Business Enterprises, Inc. In addition, ADA Insurance and Retirement Plans help member dentist protect their famlies, incomes, and practices.

ADA patient education materials have come a long way since the Association's first brochure, *The Mouth and The Teeth*, was published in 1909. The ADA Catalog now offers hundreds of patient education materials on contemporary oral health issues including tooth whitening, meth mouth, and oral piercings. Many materials are also available in Spanish and on DVD.

Finally, membership in the ADA means the opportunity to build friendships, camaraderie, and community. When members gathered in Hawaii on September 30 thru October 4, 2009, for the ADA's 150th Annual Session, they were participating in one of the largest, best-attended trade shows in North America.

THE NEXT 150 YEARS

The ADA's first constitution was adopted in 1860 at its second Annual Session. An essay titled *The Claims of Dentistry Upon Dentists* was presented at that meeting by prominent dentist and early ADA member

▲ Banners along Chicago's North Michigan Avenue proclaim the ADA's 150th anniversary in June 2009.

◀ Contents of an ADA time capsule are displayed at the ADA Sesquicentennial Celebration in Chicago. The capsule was sealed into a column when the ADA Headquarters building was dedicated in February 1966 and opened forty-three years later in April 2009. Contents included photos of the building's groundbreaking and construction, contemporary ADA publications, congratulatory telegrams, and four Chicago newspapers from the dedication day. In 2009, plans were under way for a new time capsule to be opened in fifty years, at the ADA's two hundredth anniversary.

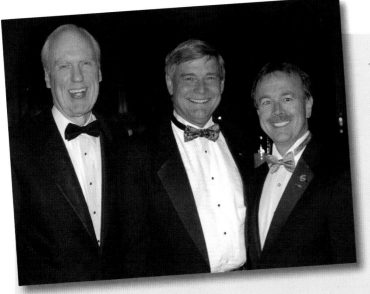

Dr. David A. Whiston, ADA president 1997–1998, President-elect Ronald L. Tankersley (president 2009–2010), and Dr. Ralph L. Howell, Jr., president of the Virginia Dental Association (left to right) were among the attendees at the ADA Sesquicentennial Celebration in June 2009. Guests at the event included state society presidents, state executive directors, current and past ADA officers, and sponsors.

ADA President John S. Findley, ADA Executive Director Kathleen T. O'Loughlin, and FDI World Dental Federation Executive Director David C. Alexander (left to right) enjoy the ADA Sesquicentennial Celebration held in Chicago in June 2009.

J. Foster Flagg. In his essay, Dr. Flagg stated, "This act [of forming the Association] may well be regarded with pride as the consummation of the exertions of our predecessors. It now rests with us to fitly prosecute a work so nobly begun . . ."

While time, technology, background, and education differentiate the current 157,000 members from the 26 founders, all ADA members of the last 150 years have something fundamental in common—a commitment to public health and a pride in their profession.

This "work so nobly begun" now rests with the exertions of a future generation of member dentists. By holding steady to the core values of its founders, the ADA will continue to thrive for another 150 years. Quality oral health care for all Americans will surely depend upon it.

The June 2009 sesquicentennial event brought together eleven former presidents of the ADA: (seated from left) Drs. Eugene Sekiguchi, Kathleen S. Roth, S. Timothy Rose, and T. Howard Jones; (standing from left) Drs. D. Gregory Chadwick, W. Richard Haught, A. Gary Rainwater, James H. Gaines, Jack H. Harris, Mark Feldman, and David A. Whiston.

Chapter Ten
Dentistry Tomorrow: The Next Fifty Years

As the ADA commemorates the last 150 years, it also anticipates the next fifty years. A broad cross-section of ADA members from various backgrounds were invited to share their vision of what changes would occur in dentistry by 2059.

RAFAEL L. BOWEN, DDS, DSc

Distinguished Scientist, Emeritus Director, ADA Paffenbarger Research Center
Dr. Bowen joined the ADA staff in 1956;
in 2009 he marked his fifty-third anniversary at PRC.
ADA Member, fifty-five years

In 2059, it should be possible to determine whether an oral cavity contains any *Streptococcus mutans* by use of a convenient indicator solution. If present, these specific bacteria will then be selectively eliminated with an oral rinse containing a germicide with sufficiently high molecular mass to disable its penetration through oral or gastrointestinal membranes, thereby preventing untoward systemic effects.

Esthetic composite reparative materials will have superior bonding, dimensional stability, strength, durability, and biocompatibility in comparison to the best materials available today.

By 2059 dentists could become primary sources for diagnosing treatable systemic diseases with the use of advanced salivary analytic technologies.

L. JACKSON BROWN, DDS

Editor, *Journal of Dental Education*
Managing Vice-President, ADA Health Policy Resources Center, 1996–2007
ADA Member, thirty-nine years

Many believe we may be on the doorstep of a new era. New scientific breakthroughs have the potential to be a countervailing force to the shift in the epidemiology of traditional dental diseases. Advances in oral biology and craniofacial research are poised to produce new diagnostic and therapeutic options that will change the future character of dental and oral health practice. This progress in oral biology is part of the general advance of human biology. The surge of knowledge is cumulative, irreversible, and accelerating. As research expands the knowledge base of dental practice, new and effective options for prevention, diagnosis, and therapy will develop.

GORDON J. CHRISTENSEN, DDS, MSD, PhD

Director, Practical Clinical Courses
Senior Consultant, *Clinicians Report*
JADA Contributor
ADA Member, forty-nine years

In 2059, potentially pathologic occlusal diseases, including bruxism, clenching, occlusal trauma, malocclusion, abfractions, and TMD will still plague many in the population. Digital devices will assist in determining occlusal prematurities and constructing occlusal splints.

Orthodontic diagnosis and treatment will be determined and simplified by digital devices coordinated by practitioners.

Dental caries will still be present, but significantly reduced. Caries of mature persons will dominate operative dentistry. Greatly improved polymer and ceramic restorations will simulate tooth structure nearly exactly, and in-office and laboratory milling of restorations made from digital images will dominate indirect restorations.

Cone beam radiography will be the norm.

The proven relationship of periodontal disease to systemic disease will further integrate dentistry and the other specialties of medicine.

MAJOR GENERAL RUSSELL J. CZERW, DDS, MSS

Chief, U.S. Army Dental Corps
Commanding General, Fort Sam Houston and Army Medical Department Center and School
Delegate, U.S. Army, 2009 ADA House of Delegates
ADA Member, nine years

Leveraging of dental technology and incorporation of the latest research will yield environmentally friendly offices, focused on holistic preventive and regenerative oral procedures. I envision a profession in which caries is essentially eliminated; missing teeth are replaced with stem cell-generated buds that are engineered to anatomical form; dental offices communicate via a common National Electronic Dental Record; and the use of digital radiography/photography is a standard. Also, I see resurgence in charitable attitudes within the profession, with providers routinely scheduling time in prisons, serving the homeless, and in government-assisted dental clinics. Our profession will continue to become the template that the world will strive to emulate in the provision of oral health care.

SHERI B. DONIGER, DDS

Director of Enrichment Activities, Board of Directors, American Association of Women Dentists
Editor, *Woman Dentist Journal*, 2006–2009
ADA Member, twenty-six years

As we are the most respected and ethical of all professions, our standards may not be raised much higher, but dentistry will commit to greener practices to reduce the amount of waste for the future generations to come to our planet. I believe dentistry will become a greener place to be with LEEDS buildings, comprehensive electronic data, a decrease in the total amount of environmental toxins, and a concerted effort to save electricity and our natural resources. Being well-respected community members, dentists will lead the way to the future health of the sustainable planet, both in body and in environment.

ARTHUR A. DUGONI, DDS

President, ADA Foundation
Dean Emeritus, Arthur A. Dugoni School of Dentistry, University of the Pacific
ADA President, 1988–1989
ADA Member, fifty-nine years

Dentists in the decade ahead will participate in successful dental practices using expanded knowledge based on the biomedical sciences. The future holds more non-invasive options, less mechanical/surgical repair, and more care dependent upon an in-depth knowledge of chemistry, biology, microbiology, physiology, internal medicine, and pharmacology.

Closely allied with medicine, these practices will be conducted by knowledgeable practitioners skilled in preventive and self-assessment techniques, dietary counseling, information management and risk assessment, clinical pharmacology, general medicine, physical diagnosis, and the diagnostic sciences. Armed with the latest advances, from twenty-first-century science and technology, they will provide state-of-the-art integrated health care to an appreciative population, enhancing their general health, and the length and quality of their lives.

CLIFTON O. DUMMETT, DDS

Distinguished Emeritus Professor of Dentistry, USC School of Dentistry
Author, *The Hillenbrand Era: Organized Dentistry's Glanzperiode* (1986)
Author, *NDA II: The Story of America's Second National Dental Association* (2000)
ADA Member, sixty years

Advancements in dentistry from 1859 to 2009 are primary indicators of dentistry in 2059. Academia will be comfortable with problem-based learning (PBL) as a boon to educating administrators, researchers, specialists, teachers, and advocates of the public's health. Nevertheless, producing competent practitioners to protect and preserve oral health will remain the basic function of dental education. Researchers in dentistry will expand activities and procedures in management of oral/systemic diseases. ADA support of professional diversity will achieve total success in all phases of American dentistry, thereby maintaining our nation's world leadership in dental care.

ERNEST L. GARCIA, JR., DDS

Member-at-Large, ADA Foundation Board of Directors
Delegate, Thirteenth District, 2009 ADA House of Delegates
President, Hispanic Dental Association, 2006–2007
ADA Member, twenty-seven years

My vision for dentistry in fifty years sees dentists being rewarded for what we prevent rather than what we produce. I see state and regional board exams replaced by one national exam that allows freedom of movement for all who pass. I see equal and accessible care for all who seek it. I see dental school education emphasizing cultural competency, being community based, and available to anyone regardless of socio-economic status. Finally, I see the profession of dentistry in its finest hour.

JANE GILLETTE, DDS

Alternate Delegate, Eleventh District, 2009 ADA House of Delegates
ADA EBD Champion
Section Editor, *Journal of Evidence-Based Dental Practice*
ADA Member, eleven years

The next fifty years of dentistry will be a ray of light in health care. Personalized dental medicine will be delivered to patients based on their individual risk for a disease. Risk assessment, treatment, and management of dental disease will be facilitated by electronic clinical decision support delivered at the point of care based upon high-quality systematic reviews. This evidence-based approach will not only improve patient health outcomes, but the face of dental research and the profession of dentistry.

ALBERT H. GUAY, DMD

ADA Chief Policy Advisor
ADA Trustee, First District, 1991–1992
ADA Member, forty-eight years

In the future, we will experience a replay of the medieval "Surgeons of the Long Coat"— "Surgeons of the Short Coat" scenario. The profession will evolve in two directions, differentiated by their reliance on science and their affiliation with a research university. Non-dentist technicians—taking the "Short Coat" developmental route—will provide about 90 percent of the care dentists provide today. Those taking the "Long Coat" route of evolution will become more closely allied with medicine. The prevalence of infectious oral diseases will greatly diminish. Oral and maxillofacial surgery and orthodontics will expand, while the future of the other specialties is uncertain.

ROGER P. LEVIN, DDS

Chairman and CEO, Levin Group
JADA Contributor
ADA Member, twenty-seven years

Practice management in 2059 will be based on the science and development of ideal practice models. These models will be systemized to allow for the highest quality of clinical care and patient satisfaction. The dental experience for patients will be greatly improved as dental staff will have a clear understanding of practice management systems and how to apply them to maintain patient comfort and support. The overall experience of dentistry will encompass a person's dental needs as well as some medical needs. Certain medical screenings will become a routine part of the preventive process in dental practices, elevating the importance of dental practitioners to patients' overall health.

RUCHI NIJJAR, DDS

Vice-Chair, ADA Committee on the New Dentist, 2008–2009
Instructor, Arthur A. Dugoni School of Dentistry, University of the Pacific
ADA Member, eight years

Service. Advancement. Fellowship. No matter how far we look into the future, dentistry will always be about serving the public, progressing technological advancements, and continually growing with lifelong learning and fellowship. Our profession will change dynamically. New knowledge, new practices, and probably a whole bunch of "news" we don't even see coming will all be normal in another fifty years. What will stick around are the relationships. The doctor-patient relationship that is renewed every time a patient steps into our office will stay around, will stay strong, and will maintain our very privileged profession.

MALVIN E. RING, DDS, MLS

Author, *Dentistry: An Illustrated History* (1985)
Editor, *Journal of the History of Dentistry,* 1969–1988
ADA Member, sixty-one years

Scientists have long wondered how sharks were able to grow new teeth when one or more of their teeth broke off as they were consuming their prey. Now researchers have discovered that a single gene, named Osr2, appears to be the controlling factor. Species that are not destined to have a second—or third—set of teeth are lacking this gene. But when this necessary gene was transplanted into mice, they developed new teeth behind their last permanent ones, a backup similar to those in sharks. It is conceivable, and highly likely, that fifty years from now, this gene therapy will be another tool in the dentist's armamentarium.

KATHLEEN S. ROTH, DDS

ADA President, 2006–2007
ADA Trustee, Ninth District, 2001–2005
ADA Member, thirty-six years

In the year 2009, it is a wonderful honor and privilege to be a practicing dentist within the United States. The profession is a strong, well-respected community of the health care system, and as I look forward, trying to envision what my profession will look like for my grandchildren, I am encouraged as well as envious! Using quality science as our backbone, improving oral health for America will be a dynamic, fulfilling career for both men and women, with strong personal satisfaction and technology challenging the practitioner to continuously strive for improved delivery systems, disease prevention and management.

EUGENE SEKIGUCHI, DDS

Associate Dean, International, Professional and Legislative Affairs, USC School of Dentistry
ADA President, 2003–2004
ADA Trustee, Thirteenth District, 1998–2002
ADA Member, thirty-five years

The future of dentistry is great. Dentistry will evolve to become the health profession that specializes in treating the orofacial structures, restoring stomatognathic function, and diagnosing diseases of the entire body.

Exponential growth in our knowledge and skills will make us a gatekeeper of our patients' health. New health care delivery systems will place value on treatment to maintain and preserve health, as most diseases are preventable. The role of all health professionals will be preventing disease, preserving and maintaining quality of life, not just curing and treating the ravages of disease and trauma to restore form and function. Dentists and other health professionals will be rewarded more for keeping people healthy than for treating them after disease has taken its toll.

REPRESENTATIVE MICHAEL K. SIMPSON (R-IDAHO)

Six-term Congressman, U.S. House of Representatives, Idaho
First ADA member, Nonpracticing Dentist category
Representative Simpson is one of only two dentists serving in Congress (2009).
ADA Member, eighteen years

If I wanted to return to my practice tomorrow, having not practiced for ten years, I'd have to go back to school because of how quickly things are changing. Technology is improving at such a tremendous rate. It is not unreasonable to suspect that in the future, prevention and cosmetic dentistry will be more important than restorative dentistry. There will always be a need for restorative work; however, dental disease and decay could become a part of the past.

As an elected official, I think about the future of our nation's health care system. I am certain that Congress will expand the availability of both medical care and dental care. One way or another, we will improve access.

WAYNE STEPHENS

DDS-MBA Candidate 2010, College of Dental Medicine and Graduate School of Business,
Columbia University
President, American Student Dental Association, 2007–2008
ADA Member, four years

The information technology revolution, evidence revealing the interrelatedness of various medical conditions, and changing social mores will be the main drivers of the dentistry of tomorrow. The next generation of dentists will be part of diverse, interdisciplinary health care teams. In the integrated world of the future, the 1990s slogan of the ADA "Dentistry, health care that works" will need to be expanded to "Dentistry, an essential part of a health care system that works." Our profession can display visionary leadership today by increased promotion of interdisciplinary collaboration.

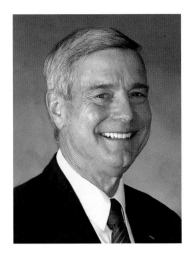

RONALD L. TANKERSLEY, DDS

ADA President, 2009–2010
ADA President-elect, 2008–2009
ADA Trustee, Sixteenth District, 2004–2008
ADA Member, thirty-eight years

Advances in biotechnology will result in the dental profession morphing from one largely compensated for mechanical skills to one largely compensated for medical screening, diagnosis, problem solving, and the use of advanced technologies.

Increased oral health literacy, an enhanced understanding of periodontal disease, and improved caries-prevention modalities will dramatically reduce oral disease among the young. However, the aging population will present increasingly complex diagnostic, management, and restorative challenges. Meeting these challenges will require closer collaboration between a diverse health care community and social support services.

An interconnected health care system will encourage large, multi-disciplinary groups with increased efficiency and coordination of care.

ROBERT V. WALKER, DDS

Professor and Past Chairman of the Division of Oral and Maxillofacial Surgery,
UT Southwestern Medical Center
Chair, Board of Directors, Baylor Oral Health Foundation
Chair Emeritus, American Trauma Society
ADA Member, sixty-two years

Technology is advancing so rapidly in dentistry, it reminds one of the third of Arthur C. Clarke's three "laws" of prediction: "Any sufficiently advanced technology is indistinguishable from magic." Sadly, much technical and bioscience-based dental care done today is, indeed, considered almost a product of magic. But it is not. Technology and bioscience related to oral and total health care have grown enormously. Where dentistry became a highly successful part of the health care professions during the last two decades, the prediction is that it will transition into a SIGNIFICANT player in health care during the next fifty years.

JANE A. WEINTRAUB, DDS, MPH

Lee Hysan Professor and Chair, Division of Oral Epidemiology and Dental Public Health,
UCSF School of Dentistry
Director, Center to Address Disparities in Children's Oral Health, UCSF School of Dentistry
ADA Member, twenty-five years

U.S. dentists will provide increasingly sophisticated and technological care based on advanced knowledge of biology, genomics, tissue engineering, and biomaterials, including growing new teeth from patients' stem cells—for those who can afford it. Earlier disease stages will be treated as infections rather than by removing diseased tissue. There will be more merging of medical and dental care, and a broader range of providers, especially for the increasingly diverse populations traditionally underserved by the dental profession. Changing people's behaviors to prevent oral diseases will remain a challenge, and public health interventions will continue to be needed.

Appendix A

Annual Session Sites

1859	Niagara Falls, NY	1909	Birmingham, AL	1960	Los Angeles, CA
1860	Washington, D.C.	1910	Denver, CO	1961	Philadelphia, PA
1861	No meeting due to the Civil War	1911	Cleveland, OH	1962	Miami, FL
1862	Cleveland, OH	1912	Washington, D.C.	1963	Atlantic City, NJ
1863	Philadelphia, PA	1913	Kansas City, MO	1964	San Francisco, CA
1864	Niagara Falls, NY	1914	Rochester, NY	1965	Las Vegas, NV
1865	Chicago, IL	1915	San Francisco, CA	1966	Dallas, TX
1866	Boston, MA	1916	Louisville, KY	1967	Washington, D.C.
1867	Cincinnati, OH	1917	New York, NY	1968	Miami, FL
1868	Niagara Falls, NY	1918	Chicago, IL	1969	New York, NY
1869	Saratoga Springs, NY	1919	New Orleans, LA	1970	Las Vegas, NV
1870	Nashville, TN	1920	Boston, MA	1971	Atlantic City, NJ
1871	White Sulphur Springs, WV	1921	Milwaukee, WI	1972	San Francisco, CA
1872	Niagara Falls, NY	1922	Los Angeles, CA	1973	Houston, TX
1873	Put-in-Bay, OH	1923	Cleveland, OH	1974	Washington, D.C.
1874	Detroit, MI	1924	Dallas, TX	1975	Chicago, IL
1875	Niagara Falls, NY	1925	Louisville, KY	1976	Las Vegas, NV
1876	Philadelphia, PA	1926	Philadelphia, PA	1977	Miami, FL
1877	Chicago, IL	1927	Detroit, MI	1978	Anaheim, CA
1878	Niagara Falls, NY	1928	Minneapolis, MN	1979	Dallas, TX
1879	Niagara Falls, NY	1929	Washington, D.C.	1980	New Orleans, LA
1880	Boston, MA	1930	Denver, CO	1981	Kansas City, MO
1881	New York, NY	1931	Memphis, TN	1982	Las Vegas, NV
1882	Cincinnati, OH	1932	Buffalo, NY	1983	Anaheim, CA
1883	Niagara Falls, NY	1933	Chicago, IL	1984	Atlanta, GA
1884	Saratoga Springs, NY	1934	St. Paul, MN	1985	San Francisco, CA
1885	Minneapolis, MN	1935	New Orleans, LA	1986	Miami, FL
1886	Niagara Falls, NY	1936	San Francisco, CA	1987	Las Vegas, NV
1887	Niagara Falls, NY	1937	Atlantic City, NJ	1988	Washington, D.C.
1888	Louisville, KY	1938	St. Louis, MO	1989	Honolulu, HI
1889	Saratoga Springs, NY	1939	Milwaukee, WI	1990	Boston, MA
1890	Excelsior Springs, MO	1940	Cleveland, OH	1991	Seattle, WA
1891	Saratoga Springs, NY	1941	Houston, TX	1992	Orlando, FL
1892	Niagara Falls, NY	1942	St. Louis, MO	1993	San Francisco, CA
1893	Chicago, IL	1943	Cincinnati, OH	1994	New Orleans, LA
1894	Old Point Comfort, VA	1944	Chicago, IL	1995	Las Vegas, NV
1895	Asbury Park, NJ	1945	No meeting due to WWII	1996	Orlando, FL
1896	Saratoga Springs, NY	1946	Miami, FL	1997	Washington, D.C.
1897	Old Point Comfort, VA	1947	Boston, MA	1998	San Francisco, CA
1898	Omaha, NE	1948	Chicago, IL	1999	Honolulu, HI
1899	Niagara Falls, NY	1949	San Francisco, CA	2000	Chicago, IL
1900	Old Point Comfort, VA	1950	Atlantic City, NJ	2001	Kansas City, MO
1901	Milwaukee, WI	1951	Washington, D.C.	2002	New Orleans, LA
1902	Niagara Falls, NY	1952	St. Louis, MO	2003	San Francisco, CA
1903	Asheville, NC	1953	Cleveland, OH	2004	Orlando, FL
1904	St. Louis, MO	1954	Miami, FL	2005	Philadelphia, PA
1905	Buffalo, NY	1955	San Francisco, CA	2006	Las Vegas, NV
1906	Atlanta, GA	1956	Atlantic City, NJ	2007	San Francisco, CA
1907	Minneapolis, MN	1957	Miami, FL	2008	San Antonio, TX
1908	Boston, MA	1958	Dallas, TX	2009	Honolulu, HI
		1959	New York, NY		

Presidents of the American Dental Association

ADA presidents begin and end their one-year term at the ADA's Annual Session. They are elected at the previous year's meeting and serve as president-elect for one year prior to their term as president.

There was no president to preside at the ADA's organizing meeting in 1859. Dr. William W. Allport served as chairman. The first election of officers was held at the ADA's second meeting in 1860.

1860-61	William H. Atkinson	1898-99	Harvey J. Burkhart	1936-37	Leroy M. S. Miner	1974-75	Lynden M. Kennedy
1861-62[1]	William H. Atkinson	1899-00	B. Holly Smith	1937-38	C. Willard Camalier	1975-76	Robert B. Shira
1862-63	George Watt	1900-01	Greene V. Black	1938-39	Marcus L. Ward	1976-77	Frank F. Shuler
1863-64	William H. Allen	1901-02	James A. Libbey	1939-40	Arthur H. Merritt	1977-78	Frank P. Bowyer
1864-65	John H. McQuillen	1902-03	Llewellyn G. Noel	1940-41	Wilfred H. Robinson	1978-79	Joseph P. Cappuccio
1865-66	Christopher W. Spalding	1903-04	Charles C. Chittenden	1941-42	Oren A. Oliver	1979-80	I. Lawrence Kerr
1866-67	Chauncy P. Fitch	1904-05	Waldo E. Boardman	1942-43	J. Ben Robinson	1980-81	John J. Houlihan
1867-68	Ambrose Lawrence	1905-06	Mark F. Finley	1943-44	Charles R. Wells	1981-82	Robert H. Griffiths
1868-69	Jonathan Taft	1906-07	Adelbert H. Peck	1944-45[5]	Walter H. Scherer	1982-83	Burton H. Press
1869-70	Homer Judd	1907-08	William Carr	1945-46	Walter H. Scherer	1983-84	Donald E. Bentley
1870-71	William H. Morgan	1908-09	Vines E. Turner	1946-47	Sterling V. Mead	1984-85	John L. Bomba
1871-72	George H. Cushing	1909-10	Burton L. Thorpe	1947-48	Harvey B. Washburn	1985-86	Abraham Kobern
1872-73	Phineas G. C. Hunt	1910-11	Edward S. Gaylord	1948-49	Clyde E. Minges	1986-87	Joseph A. Devine
1873-74	Thomas L. Buckingham	1911-12	Arthur R. Melendy	1949-50	Philip E. Adams	1987-88	James A. Saddoris
1874-75	Mason S. Dean	1912-13	Frank O. Hetrick	1950-51	Harold W. Oppice	1988-89	Arthur A. Dugoni
1875-76	Aaron L. Northrop	1913-14	Homer C. Brown	1951-52	LeRoy M. Ennis	1989-90	R. Malcolm Overbey
1876-77	George W. Keely	1914-15	Donald M. Gallie	1952-53	Otto W. Brandhorst	1990-91	Eugene J. Truono
1877-78	Frederick H. Rehwinkel	1915-16	Thomas P. Hinman	1953-54	Leslie M. Fitzgerald	1991-92	Geraldine T. Morrow
1878-79	Henry J. B. McKellops	1916-17	Lafayette L. Barber	1954-55	Daniel F. Lynch	1992-93	Jack H. Harris
1879-80	Luther D. Shepard	1917-18	William H. G. Logan	1955-56	Bernard C. Kingsbury	1993-94	James H. Gaines
1880-81	Cyrus N. Peirce	1918-19	Clement V. Vignes	1956-57	Harry Lyons	1994-95	Richard W. D'Eustachio
1881-82	Henry A. Smith	1919-20	John V. B. Conzett	1957-58	William R. Alstadt	1995-96	William S. Ten Pas
1882-83	William H. Goddard	1920-21	H. Edmund Friesell	1958-59	Percy T. Phillips	1996-97	A. Gary Rainwater
1883-84	Edwin T. Darby	1921-22	Thomas B. Hartzell	1959-60	Paul H. Jeserich	1997-98	David A. Whiston
1884-85	John N. Crouse	1922-23	John P. Buckley	1960-61	Charles H. Patton	1998-99	S. Timothy Rose
1885-86	William C. Barrett	1923-24	William A. Giffen	1961-62	John R. Abel	1999-00	Richard F. Mascola
1886-87	Walter W. Allport	1924-25	Charles N. Johnson	1962-63	Gerald D. Timmons	2000-01	Robert M. Anderton
1887-88	Frank Abbot	1925-26	Sheppard W. Foster	1963-64	James P. Hollers	2001-02	D. Gregory Chadwick
1888-89	Charles R. Butler	1926-27[4]	Henry L. Banzhaf	1964-65	Fritz A. Pierson	2002-03	T. Howard Jones
1889-90	Matthew W. Foster	1927-28	Roscoe H. Volland	1965-66	Maynard K. Hine	2003-04	Eugene Sekiguchi
1890-91	Alison W. Harlan	1928-29	Percy R. Howe	1966-67	William A. Garrett	2004-05	W. Richard Haught
1891-92	William W. Walker	1929-30	Robert B. Bogle	1967-68	F. Darl Ostrander	2005-06	Robert M. Brandjord
1892-93	John D. Patterson	1930-31	Robert T. Oliver	1968-69	Hubert A. McGuirl	2006-07	Kathleen S. Roth
1893-94[2]	John D. Patterson	1931-32	Martin Dewey	1969-70	Harry M. Klenda	2007-08	Mark Feldman
1894-95	James Y. Crawford	1932-33	George W. Dittmar	1970-71	John M. Deines	2008-09	John S. Findley
1895-96[3]	James Y. Crawford	1933-34	Arthur C. Wherry	1971-72	Carl A. Laughlin	2009-10	Ronald L. Tankersley
1896-97	James Truman	1934-35	Frank M. Casto	1972-73	Louis A. Saporito		
1897-98	Thomas Fillebrown	1935-36	George B. W. Winter	1973-74	Carlton H. Williams		

[1] In 1861, the Annual Session was canceled due to the Civil War. Since there was no meeting, the president and officers presiding at the 1860 meeting continued to preside during 1861.

[2] In 1893, only a short, formal business meeting was held in conjunction with the World's Columbian Dental Congress, which the ADA helped organize as part of the World's Columbian Exposition. Since it was only a formal meeting held to satisfy the dictates of the bylaws, it was decided at the meeting that instead of electing a new president and officers those presiding in 1893 would also preside in 1894.

[3] James Y. Crawford fell seriously ill after the first day of the 1895 Annual Session. He eventually recovered although the illness was prolonged. Vice presidents S. C. G. Watkins and Thomas Fillebrown filled in for him and performed his presiding officer duties. Crawford was re-elected at the 1895 meeting and presided at the 1896 Annual Session.

[4] John F. Biddle of Pittsburgh, Pennsylvania, was elected president-elect at the 1925 Annual Session but died on January 17, 1926, before he was installed or could serve as president for the term 1926–27.

[5] In 1945, the Annual Session was canceled as the organization was unable to obtain government permission to hold a convention because of resource restraints that the country was under due to WWII (e.g. fuel and food rationing, transportation and housing shortages). Since there was no meeting of the HOD, elections could not take place so the BOT decided that the president and officers presiding at the 1944 meeting would continue to preside until the HOD could meet again.

Appendix C

Secretaries and Executive Directors

From 1860–1913, the ADA elected secretaries that oversaw the administration of the organization. The recording secretary was responsible for recording the annual meeting minutes and maintaining the proceedings of the organization. The corresponding secretary worked with the recording secretary and was responsible for maintaining the organization's correspondence. In 1913, the two functions were merged and became the responsibility of one general secretary. In 1917, the office was made a paid full-time, for-hire position. The secretary's position title was changed to executive director in 1968. The executive director serves as the secretary of the House of Delegates and of the Board of Trustees.

CORRESPONDING SECRETARY

1860–62	W. Muir Rogers
1862–63	John F. Johnston
1863–64	Charles R. Butler
1864–65	George W. Ellis
1865–66	Luther D. Shepard
1866–67	Asa Hill
1867–68	Charles R. Butler
1868–69	James McManus
1869–72	I. A. Salmon
1872–74	Jonathan Taft
1874–75	George L. Field
1875–77	John H. McQuillen
1877–78	M. H. Webb
1878–79	A. O. Rawls
1879–80	M. H. Webb
1880–82	Albion M. Dudley
1882–87	Alison W. Harlan
1887–94	Fred A. Levy
1894–96	Emma Eames Chase
1896–97	Fred A. Levy
1897–00	Emma Eames Chase
1900–01	Mary E. Gallup
1901–02	Josephine D. Pfeiffer
1902–03	W. D. Tracy
1903–06	Charles S. Butler
1906–08	Burton L. Thorpe
1908–10	Homer C. Brown
1910–13	Charles W. Rodgers

RECORDING SECRETARY

1860–68	Jonathan Taft
1868–69	Edgar Park
1869–74	Mason S. Dean
1874–77	C. Stoddard Smith
1877–78	Mason S. Dean
1878–00	George H. Cushing
1900–06	Adelbert H. Peck
1906–10	Charles S. Butler
1910–13	Homer C. Brown

SECRETARY

1913–27	Otto U. King
1927–46	Harry B. Pinney
1946–67	Harold Hillenbrand

EXECUTIVE DIRECTOR

1968–69	Harold Hillenbrand
1970–78	C. Gordon Watson
1979–85	John M. Coady
1986–92	Thomas J. Ginley
1992–93	William E. Allen
1993–01	John S. Zapp
2001–08	James B. Bramson
2009–	Kathleen T. O'Loughlin

Appendix D

Distinguished Service Award Recipients

Established in 1970 by the Board of Trustees, the Distinguished Service Award is the "highest award which the Association can confer on members of the dental profession or of allied health professions." Recipients have included ADA past presidents, researchers, educators, legislators, philanthropists, public health leaders, and ADA staff.

1971	Gerald D. Timmons	1992	Thomas J. Ginley
1972	J. Ben Robinson	1993	William E. Allen
1973	Philip E. Blackerby		Michael L. Perich
1974	Harold Hillenbrand	1994	James B. Edwards
1975	Maynard K. Hine	1995	Arthur A. Dugoni
1976	Percy T. Phillips	1996	Ken Austin
1977	Robert B. Shira		Joan Austin
1978	Ralph R. Lopez	1997	Clifford H. Miller
1979	Daniel F. Lynch	1998	Samuel P. Harris
1980	Harry Lyons	1999	Rafael L. Bowen
1981	Paul T. Lawson	2000	Charles W. Norwood
1982	George C. Paffenbarger	2001	Lawrence Meskin
1983	Carlton H. Williams	2002	Jack H. Harris
1984	John W. Tiede	2003	Anthony R. Volpe
1985	Alvin L. Morris	2004	David A. Whiston
1986	Leon Eisenbud	2005	Larry M. Coffee
1987	Charles M. Stebner	2006	Charles A. McCallum
1988	Lynden M. Kennedy	2007	Dushanka Kleinman
1989	F. Gene Dixon	2008	Leslie Seldin
1990	Frank P. Bowyer	2009	Kenneth L. Kalkwarf
1991	John L. Bomba		

Appendix E

Gold Medal for Excellence in Research Award Recipients

The ADA Gold Medal for Excellence in Research Award was first presented in 1985 and is awarded every three years. The award honors individuals who through basic or clinical research contribute to the advancement of the profession of dentistry or to major improvement in the oral health of the community.

1985	Irwin D. Mandel	1994	Harald Löe	2003	Robert J. Gorlin
1988	Basil G. Bibby	1997	Takao Fusayama	2006	Lorne Golub
1991	Robert J. Genco	2000	William Bowen	2009	Harold C. Slavkin

Appendix F

Norton M. Ross Award for Excellence in Clinical Research Recipients

The Norton M. Ross Award for Excellence in Clinical Research was first presented in 1991 and is awarded annually. The award recognizes individuals who have made significant contributions in clinical investigations that have advanced the diagnosis, treatment, and/or prevention of craniofacial-oral-dental diseases as well as outstanding research accomplishments in other areas. The award honors the memory of Dr. Norton M. Ross who spent the majority of his professional career in academic and research positions and whose work elevated dental clinical research to a higher level of scientific standards that had a positive impact on the oral health of the public.

1991	Sigurd P. Ramfjord	1998	Roy C. Page	2005	Samuel F. Dworkin
1992	Richard Sture Nyman	1999	Sigmund S. Socransky	2006	Stephen Offenbacher
1993	Daniel M. Laskin	2000	Bruce J. Baum	2007	John Featherstone
1994	William R. Proffit	2001	Lorne Golub	2008	Jack Caton
1995	Robert J. Gorlin	2002	Thomas Van Dyke	2009	Jan Lindhe
1996	Sol Silverman, Jr.	2003	Robert J. Genco		
1997	Karl F. Leinfelder	2004	Deborah Greenspan		

Index

Staff Acknowledgments

The editors would like to acknowledge the support and contributions of the following ADA staff with this project:

Executive liaison:	**Michelle Kruse** (Administrative Services)
Editorial review:	**James Berry**, **Judy Jakush**, **Stacie Crozier**, **Liz Maxwell** (Publishing)
Legal review:	**Wendy Wils**, **Michael Kendall**, **Jackie Edler** (Legal Affairs)
Design and marketing services:	**Abbe Wright**, **Lisa Sall** (Membership)
Supplemental photography:	**Steve Horne** (Membership)
Planning:	**Barkley Payne** (ADA Foundation), **Wendy-Jo Toyama** (Membership)
Administrative support:	**Kathy Barbush** (Education)

Staff of other departments who provided support, information, and resources include the **ADA Library**, **Conference and Meeting Services, Dental Practice**, **Human Resources**, **Science, and Product Development and Sales**.

Thanks are also due to author **Bill Beck** of Lakeside Writers' Group, who wrote the text for chapters one through nine, and Donning Company Publishers staff **Anne Cordray**, **Tonya Hannink**, and **Steve Mull**.

Special thanks goes to ADA **President John S. Findley**, DDS, and ADA **Executive Director Kathleen T. O'Loughlin**, DMD.

The Editors *(research, editing, photo selection, caption writing, and permissions)*:
Mary Kreinbring (ADA Library), Project manager and editor
Andrea Matlak (ADA Library), Research manager and editor

▶ ADA Archivist Andrea Matlak (third from right) shows historical photographs from the ADA Archives to other ADA staff who contributed to the book project (from left): Michael Kendall, Judy Jakush, Wendy Wils, Stacie Crozier, James Berry, Steve Horne, and Michelle Kruse.

Resources

ADA Corporate Seals

1897–1922

▶ First official corporate seal during a period when the organization was known as the National Dental Association. The winged torch is a symbol of knowledge providing light and guidance.

1922–1959

◀ The corporate seal was redesigned to include organization and incorporation dates when the Association was incorporated under the name American Dental Association in 1922.

1959

▶ Special commemorative seal adopted for use during 1959, the one-hundredth anniversary year of the ADA.

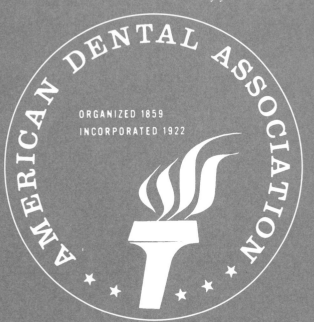

1960–1987

◀ The corporate seal was given a more modern look in 1960.

1988–

▶ The corporate seal was revised slightly in 1988 to coordinate the style of the organization and incorporation dates to that of the rest of the seal.